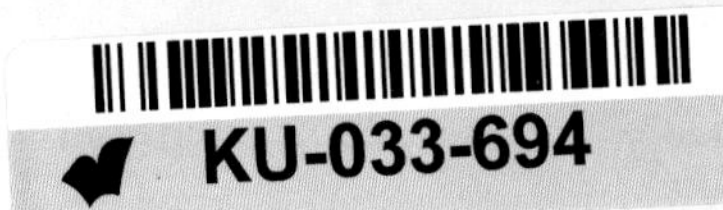

TRUSTING GOD

day by day

365 DAILY DEVOTIONS

TRUSTING GOD
day by day

365 DAILY DEVOTIONS

JOYCE MEYER

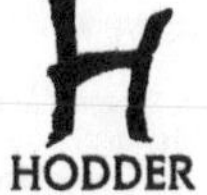

HODDER

First published in Great Britain in 2012 by Hodder & Stoughton
An Hachette UK company

This paperback edition first published in 2015
1

A CIP catalogue record for this title is available from the British Library

ISBN 978 1 473 61963 0
eBook ISBN 978 1 444 74596 2

Printed and bound in the UK by Clays Ltd, St Ives plc

Hodder & Stoughton policy is to use papers that are natural, renewable and recyclable products and made from wood grown in sustainable forests. The logging and manufacturing processes are expected to conform to the environmental regulations of the country of origin.

Hodder & Stoughton Ltd
Carmelite House
50 Victoria Embankment
London
EC4Y 0DZ

www.hodderfaith.com

TRUSTING GOD
day by day
365 DAILY DEVOTIONS

January 1

Do Your Best with What You Have

You shall not covet your neighbor's house, your neighbor's wife, or his manservant, or his maidservant, or his ox, or his donkey, or anything that is your neighbor's. EXODUS 20:17

How do you feel about your life? Do you like it, love it, and enjoy it, or do you hate it and wish you had a different one than you have? Do you look at other people and their lives and wish you were them and had their lives? Do you want to look the way they look, own what they own, have their career or their family? Or are you happy with the life God has given you?

In the Bible, wanting what others have is called coveting, and it is forbidden by God. He even included it in the Ten Commandments. You are never going to have anyone else's life, so wanting it is a waste of time. You won't look like them, either, so learn to do the best you can with what you have to work with.

I have adopted a new phrase lately, and it is helping me to deal with reality and not waste my time being upset about things I cannot do anything about. I have been saying, "It is what it is!" Somehow, that is a reality check for me, and I quickly realize I need to deal with things the way they are, not the way I wish they were.

Nobody has a perfect life, and it is entirely possible that if you want someone else's life, they are busy wanting someone else's, too; perhaps they even want your life. Unknown people want to be movie stars, and movie stars want privacy. The regular employee wants to be the boss, and the boss wishes he did not have so much responsibility. A single woman wants to be married, and sometimes a married woman wishes she were single. Contentment with life is not a feeling, but it is a decision we must make. Contentment does not mean that we never want to see change or improvement, but it does mean we can be happy where we are and will do the best we can with what we have. It also means we will maintain an attitude that allows us to enjoy the gift of life.

Trust in Him If God wants you to have what someone else has, you can trust Him to bring it to you, but first you must be happy with what you have and do the best you can with it.

January 2

Talk About the Good Stuff

But I tell you, on the day of judgment men will have to give account for every idle (inoperative, nonworking) word they speak.

MATTHEW 12:36

It seems to me that we talk about how we feel more than practically anything else. We feel good or bad, happy or sad, excited or discouraged, and a thousand other things. The inventory of the various ways we feel is almost endless. Feelings are ever-changing, usually without notification. These feelings don't need our permission to fluctuate; they merely seem to do as they please for no specific reason we can identify. We have all experienced going to bed feeling just fine physically and emotionally, only to wake up the next morning feeling tired and irritable. "*Why? Why do I feel this way?*" we ask ourselves, and then we usually begin to tell anyone who will listen how we feel. It is interesting to note that we tend to talk a lot more about our negative feelings than we do our positive ones.

If I wake up feeling energetic and excited about the day, I rarely announce it to everyone I come in contact with; however, if I feel tired and discouraged, I want to tell everyone. It has taken me years to learn that talking about how I feel increases the intensity of those feelings. So it seems to me that we should keep quiet about the negative feelings and talk about the positive ones.

You can always tell God how you feel and ask for His help and strength, but talking about negative feelings just to be talking does no good at all. If negative feelings persist, asking for prayer or seeking advice based on biblical truth is a good thing, but once again I want to stress that talking just to be talking is useless.

If we have to wait to see how we feel before we know if we can enjoy the day, then we are giving feelings control over us. But if we are willing to make right choices regardless of how we feel, God will always be faithful to give us the strength to do so.

Trust in Him How are you feeling? If your feelings are positive, tell someone. If they are negative, tell God, and trust Him to work things out. Regardless of how you feel, choose to enjoy your day!

January 3

Success Starts with Your Thoughts

We destroy every proud obstacle that keeps people from knowing God. We capture their rebellious thoughts and teach them to obey Christ. 2 CORINTHIANS 10:5 NLT

Nobody is successful in any venture just by wishing they would be. Successful people make a plan and talk to themselves about that plan constantly. You can think things on purpose, and if you make what you think about match what you actually want to do, your feelings may not like it, but they will go along.

I slept great last night, and when I woke up at 5:00 a.m., I didn't feel like getting up. It was so cozy under the fluffy cover, and I felt like staying right there. But I had a plan. I had decided how many hours I would write today, and in order to do that I had to get up. I thought, *I am going to get up now*, and I got up!

Do you make an effort to choose your thoughts, or do you just meditate on whatever falls into your head, even if it is in total disagreement with what you have said you want out of life? When your thoughts are going in a wrong direction, do you capture them and submit them to Christ as the Bible instructs (see 2 Cor. 10:5)?

I want to encourage you today—the good news is you can change. As I have said for years, we are in a war and the mind is the battlefield. We either win or lose our battles based on winning or losing the war in our minds. Learn to think according to the Word of God, and your emotions will start lining up with your thoughts.

If you have had years of experiencing wrong thinking and letting your emotions lead you as I did, making the change may not be easy, and it will definitely require a commitment of study, time, and effort. But the results will be worth it. Don't say, *"I am just an emotional person, and I can't help the way I feel."* Take control. You can do it!

> Trust in Him Keep your thoughts in line with the plan God has for your life—a plan to prosper you, and not to harm you (see Jer. 29:11). Take control of your thoughts by trusting them to Him.

January 4

You're Not Built for Guilt

> *Not that I have now attained [this ideal], or have already been made perfect, but I press on to lay hold of (grasp) and make my own, that for which Christ Jesus (the Messiah) has laid hold of me and made me His own.* PHILIPPIANS 3:12

Making people feel guilty about anything is not God's mode of operation. The source of guilt is the devil. He is the accuser of the brethren, according to the Bible (see Rev. 12:10). God will convict us of wrong choices and actions, but He never tries to make us feel guilty. Guilt presses us down, but godly conviction brings an opportunity to change and progress.

We are not built for guilt. God never intended His children to be loaded down with guilt, so our systems don't handle it well at all. Had God wanted us to feel guilty, He would not have sent Jesus to redeem us from guilt. He bore, or paid for, our iniquities and the guilt they cause (see Isa. 53:6 and 1 Pet. 2:24–25). As believers in Jesus Christ and as sons and daughters of God, we have been set free from the power of sin (see Rom. 6:6–10). That doesn't mean we'll never sin, but it does mean that when we do, we can admit it, receive forgiveness, and be free from guilt. Our journey with God toward right behavior and holiness is progressive, and if we have to drag the guilt from past mistakes along with us, we'll never make progress toward true freedom and joy. Perhaps this is the main reason why so few people actually enter into and enjoy the inheritance promised through relationship with Jesus Christ.

Your future has no room for your past. How much time do you waste feeling guilty? It is important that you think about this, because spending time dwelling on past mistakes is something God has told us not to do. No one is perfect. The good news is Jesus came for those who were sick (imperfect), not those who were well (perfect).

Trust in Him What triggers your struggle with guilt (when you make a mistake, or when you're thinking about your past, when you see someone who was a part of your life during that period, etc.)? Pray specifically about that incident, and trust God to set you free.

January 5

Torn Between Right and Wrong

I do not understand my own actions [I am baffled, bewildered]. I do not practice or accomplish what I wish, but I do the very thing that I loathe [which my moral instinct condemns]. ROMANS 7:15

We often feel like a war is going on within us. One part of us (the inner person) wants to do what we know to be right, and another part (the outer person) wants to do what is wrong. The wrong thing can feel right, while the right thing feels wrong. Remember, we cannot judge the moral value of any action by how we feel. Our feelings are unreliable and cannot be trusted to convey truth.

Frequently we find that we want to do right and wrong at the same time. Our renewed spirit craves holiness and righteousness, but the carnal (fleshly) soul still craves worldly things. Even the apostle Paul describes feeling the same way in Romans, chapter 7. Paul says that he has the intention and urge to do what is right, but he fails to carry it out. He fails to practice the good that he desires to do and instead does evil. Thankfully, by the end of the chapter, Paul has realized that only Christ can deliver him from the fleshly action, and as we continue to study his life, we learn that he developed an ability to say no to himself if what he wanted did not agree with God's Word. He learned to lean on God for strength and then use his will to choose what was right no matter how he felt. Paul said he died daily, which meant that he died to his own fleshly desires in order to glorify God (see 1 Cor. 15:31).

The truth is that we must die to ourselves if we want to genuinely and truly live the lives God has provided for us through Jesus Christ. When we are willing to live by biblical principles rather than emotion, we are dying to selfishness and will enjoy the abundant life of God. I am sure you've heard the saying, "No pain... no gain!" Every good thing in life requires an initial investment before we see the reward.

Trust in Him Pray and ask God to show you a specific area where you need to let go of selfishness. Once He shows you, don't get discouraged or be afraid—trust God to change you!

January 6

There's Great Value in Variety

Behold, what I have seen to be good and fitting is for one to eat and drink, and to find enjoyment in all the labor in which he labors under the sun all the days which God gives him—for this is his [allotted] part. ECCLESIASTES 5:18

If we do the same thing over and over, sooner or later we're going to get bored. We don't have to wait for something nice to happen to us, we can be aggressive and do something nice for ourselves. For many of you, I know this is a new thought that may seem foreign and even unspiritual. But I can assure you that it is part of God's plan. You can create variety, and it will keep your life more exciting.

I sat with my computer on my lap for about four hours this morning and then stopped for a while to do some other things I needed to do. When I went back to my writing, I decided to sit in a different part of the house just for variety. I chose a place that had plenty of light where I could look out the window. Simple little things like this cost nothing, but they are very valuable.

No day needs to be ordinary if we realize the gift God is giving us when He gives us another day to live and enjoy. An extraordinary attitude can quickly turn an ordinary day into an amazing adventure. Jesus said He came so that we might have and enjoy life (see John 10:10). If we refuse to enjoy it, then it's no one's fault but our own.

I would like to suggest that you take responsibility for your joy and never again give anyone else the job of keeping you happy. Add a little variety to your life—break up your routine, do something different, and so on. When you do, expect God to meet you and help make your ordinary...extraordinary!

Trust in Him What are two specific things you're going to do differently today? Add some variety to your ordinary, daily routine, and trust that God is going to bless it.

January 7

Form New Habits

Therefore if any person is [ingrafted] in Christ (the Messiah) he is a new creation (a new creature altogether); the old [previous moral and spiritual condition] has passed away. Behold, the fresh and new has come! 2 CORINTHIANS 5:17

God's Word teaches us that when we receive Christ as our Savior and Lord, He gives us a new nature. He gives us *His* nature. He also gives us a spirit of discipline and self-control, which is vital in allowing us to choose the ways of our new nature. He gives us a sound mind (see 2 Tim. 1:7), and that means we can think about things properly without being controlled by emotion. The way we once were passes away, and we have all the equipment we need for a brand-new way of behaving. God gives us the ability and offers to help us, but we are not puppets and God will not manipulate us. We must choose spirit over flesh and right over wrong. Our renewed spirits will then control our souls and bodies or, to say it another way, the inner person will control the outer erson.

Without God's help we have difficulty doing things in moderation. e frequently eat too much, spend too much money, have too much ertainment, and talk too much. We are excessive in our actions ause we behave emotionally. And after the thing is done and cannot ndone, we regret doing it. But we can choose to form new habits, loing something just because we feel like it but instead doing what roduce the best result in the end.

do not have to live in regret. God gives us His Spirit to enable nake right and wise choices. He urges us, guides and leads us, but we still have to cast the deciding vote. If you have been casting the wrong vote, all you need to do is change your vote. Forming new habits will require making a decision to not do what you feel like doing unless it agrees with God's will.

Trust in Him God wants you to live out of your new nature, not your old one. Every time you put your trust in Him and cast the deciding vote to obey, His Spirit transforms you and makes you more like Him.

January 8

Take Care of What God Has Given You

Do you not know that your body is the temple (the very sanctuary) of the Holy Spirit Who lives within you, Whom you have received [as a Gift] from God? You are not your own... 1 CORINTHIANS 6:19

What if you went to a church and it was run-down? Peeling paint, broken doors, and smudged windows that didn't let the light in? You'd wonder about the pastor, wouldn't you? The church is his instrument for celebrating the glory of God, yet if he doesn't respect the church enough to take the time to keep it in good condition, what does this say about his relationship with God?

The same question applies to your own body—taking care of the body God has given you is the most important kind of "home maintenance" you can do! Your body is the home of your spirit where God dwells. To do the work you were meant to do, you need to keep it in shape.

I still have to remind myself of this. Once I hurt my voice by speaking in a seminar with an extremely sore throat. That morning when I woke up, I knew I shouldn't speak, but I thought about the disappointment of the audience if I didn't. So I forced myself to speak, but the next day I could not make a sound. I couldn't the next day, either, or the day after that. The condition continued, and I began to worry. I finally went to the doctor, who told me I had damaged my vocal cords. He said each time we push ourselves beyond reasonable limits, we do some damage, and if we do it too often, we get to a point where we can't recover. He said it might reach a point where I could not teach at all if I did not respect my voice and take care of it.

I nearly jeopardized my entire public ministry! If I had permanently damaged my voice, I would have wound up helping far fewer people and derailing my life's calling. Now I'm more careful about protecting the tools I need to do God's work—my voice, my mind, my heart, my emotions, and my body. Please take care of yourself so you can glorify God and do all that He has intended for you to do.

Trust in Him **How can you take better care of your body—the place where God dwells? Show God you love Him and trust Him by taking good care of your temple.**

January 9

Making Right Choices Makes Life So Much Better

Strive to enter by the narrow door [force yourselves through it], for many, I tell you, will try to enter and will not be able.

LUKE 13:24

Like most of us, you are probably tempted to take all the easy paths, but God's path is rarely easy. The Bible describes those other paths—the ones that lead to destruction—as "broad" because not a lot of effort is required to remain on them. We are encouraged by God to take the narrow path, the more difficult one, which is also the one that leads to life.

We have to make a strong effort to push through the negativity in the world, but if we will do our part, God will always do His. Not everyone is willing to make the effort. They are addicted to ease and simply flow with their feelings. Jesus died for us so we could have a wonderful, abundant life that is filled with peace, joy, power, success, and every good thing. He was willing to go to the cross and pay for our sins even though physically, mentally, and emotionally it was very difficult. We, too, must be willing to do what is right, and our reward will surely come. God's grace will always enable us to do the right thing if we are willing to do so.

Study the Word of God regularly, and then when trouble comes, you will already have your spiritual tank full of fuel that will enable you to make right choices. Don't be the kind of person who prays or has time for God only when you feel like it or have a disaster. Seek God because you know you cannot navigate safely in this world without Him.

You and I can let our minds drift aimlessly day after day, and we can be controlled by our emotions, or we can strive to gird up our minds, choose our thoughts carefully, and manage our emotions. God has set before us life and death, good and evil, and has given us the responsibility of making the choice (see Deut. 30:19). Choose life!

Trust in Him What choice are you currently facing? What path will you choose? Remember, the right choice won't always be easy, but you can trust God, Who gives you strength and rewards you, to help you do it.

January 10

Looking Nice Is Not a Sin

Let not yours be the [merely] external adorning with [elaborate] interweaving and knotting of the hair, the wearing of jewelry, or changes of clothes; but let it be the inward adorning and beauty of the hidden person of the heart, with the incorruptible and unfading charm of a gentle and peaceful spirit, which . . . is very precious in the sight of God. 1 PETER 3:3–4

Many Christians misunderstand the challenge to value inner beauty over outer appearance, as stated in the above passage. They take the concept to an extreme, believing that any effort to look nice is a sin. What Peter is encouraging us to do, however, is to resist the temptation to confuse outer beauty for what is most important, which is a gentle and peaceful spirit. In other words, don't be vain or put all your confidence in how you look, because God focuses on what is inside.

But Peter doesn't say the only way to be virtuous is to wear a brown sack, stop bathing, and give away all your possessions! True, a few people have found God by renouncing all material possessions, but I think in general it is much harder to find *anything* if you suffer from the constant distractions of discomfort, or if you go out of your way to be as unattractive as possible and get mistreated by others because they think you are a religious fanatic. God cares most that you go forth clothed in righteousness. But righteousness *plus* a nice outfit never hurt anyone! If people see that you respect yourself, they'll respect you, too.

Like everything else in life, it is a question of balance. Keep the big picture in mind. Ask yourself, *"What is the work that God has put me on earth to do?"* Then decide what amount of attention you should pay to how you look and feel to get the maximum energy, health, and charisma you need to do that work as successfully as possible.

Trust in Him Do you spend an appropriate amount of time taking care of the body and spirit God has given you? He wants you to look your best, inside and out. Do your part to be a good steward of what He gave you, and trust Him to let you know if you are out of balance.

January 11

Nevertheless

Nevertheless, that time of darkness and despair will not go on forever. ISAIAH 9:1 NLT

I once read a book that was based entirely on the word *nevertheless*. It taught the reader to take every problem in his or her life, look at it honestly, and then say, "nevertheless," and find some offsetting positive thing in the individual's life that brought the problem into perspective.

It might sound something like this: "*I have a lot of hard work to get accomplished in the next two weeks;* **nevertheless,** *after that my schedule is much more open, and I will be able to have some fun and get some extra rest.*" All mothers get weary from time to time and might say, "*My kids are driving me crazy;* **nevertheless,** *I'm so blessed to have these children in my life, and I know there are families who can't have children at all.*" A father who has to work two jobs to make ends meet might say, "*I am so tired of working all the time;* **nevertheless,** *I am thankful that God has provided me with jobs.*"

No matter who we are or what our challenge in life is, there is always a "nevertheless"—some positive thing we can look at or talk about that brings the rest of life into perspective. Why don't you try it? The next time you are tempted to complain about your life in any way, go ahead and state your complaint, and then say, "nevertheless," and find something positive about your life to offset the complaint.

Trust in Him No matter what you are going through in life, you can trust God to be with you. Think about your current situation and find your "nevertheless." Say it out loud to encourage yourself by finding the positive in every situation.

January 12

When to Start and When to Stop

TO EVERYTHING there is a season, and a time for every matter or purpose under heaven... ECCLESIASTES 3:1

We often study the *steps* of Jesus, but fail to study the *stops* of Jesus. We all need to learn when to stop. Jesus stopped what He was doing in order to listen to people and help them. He stopped to rest, to have dinner with friends, to make wine for a wedding, and to do lots of other simple but important things. One of my biggest problems for many years was that I simply did not know when to stop.

My chiropractor has told me to stop every forty-five minutes when I am writing, to get up and stretch out the muscles in my back so I don't end up in pain. But when I am in a flow, it is so hard to stop! If we don't know when to stop, we will end up with regrets later.

When Jesus visited Mary and Martha, Mary knew when to stop, but Martha didn't. Mary sat at Jesus' feet so she would not miss the moment, but Martha just kept working (see Luke 10:38–41). I wonder how many times in my life I missed the moment because I would not stop working. I know I missed moments with my children when they were small because I valued work over playing with them.

Ecclesiastes tells us there is a time for everything, and that everything is beautiful in its time. Work is beautiful, but if we work when it is time to play, then work is no longer beautiful. It can create a stress that has the ability to destroy our health. Play is beautiful, but if we play when we should be working, then play becomes a lack of discipline that can destroy us. A good life is all about balance. We have to know when to start and when to stop.

Trust in Him Psalm 62:8 tells us we can trust God at all times because He is our refuge. A refuge is a safe place where we can rest from busyness and worry. Take time to stop and let Him be your refuge.

January 13

Look for a Reason to Laugh

A time to weep and a time to laugh, a time to mourn and a time to dance... ECCLESIASTES 3:4

I believe we need to look for reasons to laugh every day. My daughters often call me to share funny things their kids did or things they are noticing about the children's personalities as they are growing up. I am glad they take the time to share those things with me. We laugh, and then I tell Dave and he laughs, too. We could have missed the laughter if they would have been too busy to call or felt it was unimportant.

I just spent five days with my youngest grandson, and I laughed more in those five days than I normally do in two months. He has learned to laugh out loud, and so he does it for no reason at all. He just suddenly laughs out loud and then, when we laugh at him laughing, he laughs again and again. He does it as long as we will keep the game going. I can assure you that he is not worried, anxious, or thinking about all of his mistakes in life. No wonder Jesus told us to be like little children if we want to enter and enjoy His Kingdom.

Funny things probably happen to you every day; learn to look for them and realize how important it is to stop for laughter. I wasted too much of my life being mad and sad, and I have a lot of catching up to do. I am committed to taking every opportunity I can find to laugh; when I can't find one, I am going to try to make one. Some of us are naturally more serious than others. You don't have to feel bad if that is your personality. It is mine, too. But you don't have to live without laughter. You can begin to intentionally look for reasons to laugh!

I think Jesus was playful and He looked for reasons to laugh. I can imagine Him teasing His disciples and playing pranks on them. I know that He was serious and sober minded, but He was always in perfect balance, so He had to have humor, too.

Trust in Him **Have you laughed today? If not, come up with a reason and laugh right now! Trust that God wants you to enjoy life; lighten up and look for the humor in your circumstances today.**

January 14

God Will Give You All the Wisdom and Power You Need

Fear and trembling have come upon me; horror and fright have overwhelmed me. And I say, Oh, that I had wings like a dove! I would fly away and be at rest. PSALM 55:5–6

David prayed that he could fly away from trouble and be at rest, but running from trouble is not always the answer. There are times we must face the enemy and defeat him in God's power just as David defeated Goliath. God has given us "going through" power. It is not God's will for us to run or hide from challenges, but to confront them head-on, knowing we can fight a battle and remain at rest. After all, the battle is not ours, but God's!

God won't let you run away from your troubles *and* keep going forward in His purpose for your life. He won't force you to face them, but eventually you'll realize that these same problems will keep showing up if you don't face them. The good news is God gives us power and wisdom to deal with our situations.

Elijah tried to run and hide, but God made him go back to the place he ran from and continue the work he had been called to do. After God allowed him to rest, He confronted him about his attitude. He asked why he was hiding and what he thought he was doing. Elijah answered out of a bitter attitude and distorted thinking. He said he alone was left to serve God and people were seeking to kill him. He told God that all the Israelites had forsaken His covenant, destroyed His altars, and killed His prophets, and once again Elijah sounded as if he was filled with self-pity as He told God that he was the only one left who was faithful to God. (see 1 Kings 19:9–14). God told Elijah that, in actuality, He had seven thousand prophets left who had not bowed their knees to Baal, and He also told Elijah to get back to work.

When we are not well rested, our thinking gets distorted and we lose proper perspective. We want to run away from responsibility, but as we can see with Elijah, God will not allow us to do that because escape is never the answer to life's challenges.

Trust in Him If you are going through a difficult time right now, don't be discouraged and run away. Trust God to be with you, and He will give you the grace and the wisdom to get through it.

January 15

God's Rest for You

For he who has once entered [God's] rest also has ceased from [the weariness and pain] of human labors, just as God rested from those labors peculiarly His own. HEBREWS 4:10

Each day we have certain purposes we wish to accomplish, and at the end of the day it is proper to rest, not only physically, but our souls also need a rest. We need rest physically, mentally, emotionally, and spiritually.

Faith allows us to rest spiritually, mentally, and emotionally. Even our will gets a rest when we have trust in God. We don't worry or reason, we are not upset or downcast, and we are not trying to make something happen that is not God's will—we are at rest! Paul was singing in jail. Jesus was praying for others while being crucified. Joseph decided that if he was going to be a slave, he would be the best slave his owner ever had. And later Joseph decided that if he was going to be a prisoner (even though he did not commit a crime), he would be a prisoner with a good attitude.

We need to be honest about what the real cause of our stress is. Is it really our circumstances in life, or is it the way we respond to the circumstances? There is a rest available, and we must strive to enter it. Entering the rest of God should be our number one priority after receiving Jesus as our Savior. I ask you: Have you learned to sit and enter God's rest? We may say that we are trusting God, but there is no evidence of trust unless we stay seated in Christ.

Trust in Him Are you upset, worrying, or trying to make something happen? You don't have to be! God has a place of peace and rest for you, and all you have to do to enter His rest is put your trust in Him.

January 16

Give God Your All

Praise the LORD, my soul; all my inmost being, praise his holy name. Praise the LORD, my soul, and forget not all his benefits—who forgives all your sins and heals all your diseases...

PSALM 103:1–3 NIV

The tiny word "all" is used 5,675 times in the Bible, give or take a few depending on which translation you are reading. It is a small word that means a great deal, and yet we pay so little attention to it. If we read a Scripture that has the word *all* in it and ignore the "all," it changes the entire context of the Scripture. The word *all* takes us into infinity. Where does "all" stop? How far does it go and what does it include?

Jesus is the Lord of all. Our Al-mighty God, all-sufficient Savior, all blessings flow from Him, and He is all that we need. We frequently say that God is our all, but have we ever stopped to truly understand the impact of that one little word? "All" leaves nothing outside of God's control.

God knows *all* things (see John 21:17)! Don't miss the "all" in that statement. He knows the end from the beginning, so He must know everything in the middle. He also has all power, all authority; all things are under His feet, and He fills everything everywhere with Himself (see Matt. 28:18 and Eph. 1:21–23). He sees all, hears all, and is everywhere all the time. If these things are true, then why do we still worry and become anxious? Why do we get emotionally upset when we have a problem or things are not going our way? It must be because we truly don't believe He has all power, knows all things, and loves us with all of the love that exists in the universe.

How many of our sins does He forgive? Does He forgive some, most, or all? The Bible says that He forgives them all and continually cleanses us from all unrighteousness. It is one of those "all and forever-now" things. God did not put our sins off to the side so He could glance over at them occasionally; He has removed them completely (see Ps. 103:12).

Trust in Him "All" leaves nothing outside of God's control, so turn all your problems and worries over to Him. Give Him your all, and you can trust that He will be your all in all.

January 17

There Is Nothing God Can't Handle

. . . With men [it is] impossible, but not with God; for all things are possible with God. MARK 10:27

If there are no impossibilities, then we can live in constant victory and nothing can threaten us or make us feel afraid of the future. Everything that is in the will of God will be accomplished in His way and timing.

Is life too much for us? Is there anything that we just cannot handle? Not according to God, for He says through the apostle Paul that we can do *all* things through Christ Who is our Strength. We are ready for anything and equal to anything through Him Who infused inner strength into us (see Phil. 4:13).

Before we let go and let God be our all in all, we usually have to find out the hard way that we cannot do it all on our own. The hard way means we keep trying and failing over and over until we admit total dependence on God. It can be a long and painful journey and some never reach the end of themselves, but for those who do, it is the beginning of living with their soul at rest. They know they can't do it all—but they also know that God can, and they decide that watching Him do what needs to be done, as only He can do, will be entertaining. I love to watch God work. It is one of my greatest pleasures in life.

Since we know that God is keeping the universe running properly every second of every day, why would we doubt that He can take care of us? He has all power, all authority, all wisdom, and He loves us with a perfect love that is promised to us unconditionally and forever. Are you leaning on Him in every situation? Do you believe God is good, and that He wants to be good to you? Put your faith in Him and enter His rest.

Trust in Him Do you believe God has the power to help you, and that since He has all wisdom, He knows exactly what to do and when to do it? Lean on Him *completely* and trust Him to give you the strength to do what you need to do, while you wait on Him to do what only He can do.

January 18

You Have Nothing to Worry About

Casting the whole of your care [all your anxieties, all your worries, all your concerns, once and for all] on Him, for He cares for you affectionately and cares about you watchfully. 1 PETER 5:7

Worrying is totally useless. I was a worrier, so I know what a stronghold it can become in our lives. I also know that it is a bad habit that is not easily broken, but since all things are possible with God, then it is possible for us to live free from worry, anxiety, and fear. If you are willing to give up worrying, then you will be able to enter into an attitude of celebration. You can trust God and enjoy life while He solves your problems.

Nothing is outside of God's control, so in reality there is nothing to worry about. When we begin to look at worry in a realistic manner, we see how totally useless it is. Our minds revolve endlessly around and around a problem, searching for answers that only God has. We may ponder a thing and ask God for wisdom, but we do not have God's permission to worry. Pondering a thing in God is peaceful, but worrying can be torment. When we worry, we torment ourselves! We can pray and ask God to help us not to worry, but ultimately we must choose to put our thoughts on something other than our problems. A refusal to worry is proof that we trust God and it releases Him to go to work on our behalf.

I wonder how much of our mental time is spent worrying, reasoning, and fearing—possibly more than is spent on anything else. Instead of meditating on our problems, let's choose to meditate on the "alls" of God. He says you can cast "*. . . [all your anxieties, all your worries, all your concerns, once and for all] on Him, for He cares for you . . .*" (1 Pet. 5:7). Let us realize how unlimited His power is and trust Him to do what we cannot do.

Trust in Him What are you worried about? Do you believe God will take care of you, do what you can't do, and work every situation out for good? Then give yourself permission to stop worrying. Make your trust in Him more powerful than your worries!

January 19

How to Find Rest in Your Soul

He is before all things, and in him all things hold together. And he is the head of the body, the church; he is the beginning and the firstborn from among the dead, so that in everything he might have the supremacy. COLOSSIANS 1:17–18 NIV

When we give God our all, we are actually saying to Him, *"God, Your will be done and not mine."* It is the only way we can live with our soul at rest. Otherwise, we are always wrestling with something that is not working out the way we want.

The apostle Paul begged those he taught to dedicate *all* of their members and faculties to God for His will and use (see Rom. 12:1). If we refuse to do that, God will find a submitted vessel (someone else) to work through, and we will miss out on God's best for us.

Think about Noah. Why did God choose Noah and his family to be saved in the ark during the flood? What was so special about this one man? The Bible says that Noah did according to *all* God commanded him. Maybe Noah wasn't the first person God asked to build the ark, but he was the one willing to give God his *all*. And Noah was richly blessed because of his trust in God. I doubt that Noah understood what God was asking him to do when He required him to build an ark for an upcoming flood. Noah must have been the laughingstock of his region. I am sure that his obedience hurt his reputation with men. Are you willing to obey God if your obedience is likely to hurt your reputation?

God is not necessarily looking for people with amazing abilities, but He searches for availability and a person who is willing to simply do whatever He asks them to do. If we will lift our hands to God and say, *"I am available to do whatever You want me to do,"* we will have peace and joy as we journey through life.

Trust in Him Has God asked you to do something but you are hesitating to give Him your all? Don't worry about what others think, and don't worry if it seems beyond your ability. Do all you can do and trust God to do the rest.

January 20

Let Joy into Your Life

Weeping may endure for a night, but joy comes in the morning.
PSALM 30:5

Part of disciplining ourselves to celebrate life is refusing to live in mourning. There is a time to mourn, but we dare not let it become a way of life. The Bible says that weeping (mourning) endures for a night, but joy comes in the morning. There are things that happen in life that rightfully need to be mourned over, but joy always returns to balance things out. We must let the joy back into our lives after times of sadness and not feel guilty about enjoying life after disappointment or even tragedy has struck. There is a time to mourn and a time to rejoice, but we must not live in the state of mourning.

Part of life is dealing properly with sadness and disappointment. We cannot avoid them—and we should not deny the emotions that go with loss of any kind—but we can recover! I was saddened when I learned that a trusted employee had been stealing from our ministry, but I rejoiced that God brought the wrongdoing to light and it was discovered. I have a time of mourning when people I love die, but I can also rejoice that they knew Jesus and are spending eternity with Him. I am sad when I realize I have let an area of my life get out of balance through lack of discipline, but I can rejoice that I now see the truth and am back on track. For all mourning there is an offsetting reason to celebrate. And although mourning is proper and is even part of our healing, it cannot last forever.

We cannot live in a state of mourning over things that have happened that we cannot change. In Christ there is always a place of new beginnings, and that is good news worth celebrating.

Trust in Him If you are in a time of mourning, allow yourself to feel those feelings. But don't get stuck there. Trust that God has a plan for you and wants you to have joy in the morning.

January 21

Enjoy Your Everyday Life

Behold, what I have seen to be good and fitting is for one to eat and drink, and to find enjoyment in all the labor in which he labors under the sun all the days which God gives him—for this is his [allotted] part. Also, every man to whom God has given riches and possessions, and the power to enjoy them and to accept his appointed lot and to rejoice in his toil—this is the gift of God [to him].

ECCLESIASTES 5:18–19

I want you to notice the words *allotted part* and *appointed lot* in the above passage. What King Solomon is basically communicating here is this message: enjoy your life. Take your "appointed lot" in life and enjoy it. In other words, embrace the life—the personality, the strengths and weaknesses, the family, the resources, the opportunities, the physical qualities, the abilities, the gifts, and the uniqueness—God has given *you*.

The only life you can enjoy is your own. That statement may seem so obvious that it's unnecessary, but think about it. One of the primary reasons many people do not enjoy their lives is because they are not happy with the lives they have. When I speak to them about enjoying their lives, the first thought they often have is, *I would enjoy my life if I had your life, Joyce!* Instead of embracing the realities of their lives, these people spend their time thinking, *I wish I looked like So-and-So. I wish I had So-and-So's job. I wish I were married. I wish my marriage weren't so difficult. I wish I had children. I wish my children would grow up. I wish I had a new house. I wish I didn't have such a big house to clean. I wish I had a big ministry*...

The truth of the matter is, the first step to enjoying our everyday lives is to be grateful for the lives we've been given. We must not allow jealousy to cause us to be absent from our own lives because we want what someone else has. You have to take what you have and decide you are going to do the best you can with it. What are you doing with what you have been given?

Trust in Him God is asking you to be faithful with your life, not with someone else's. Trust that God knew what He was doing when He gave *your* life to *you*.

January 22

The Best Advice I Can Give You

Hear instruction and be wise, and do not refuse or neglect it.

PROVERBS 8:33

The best advice I could ever give you is to live your life according to the truth of God's Word, which is found in the Bible. I believe we should honor God's Word in our lives and give it a place of priority every day. We do this by reading and studying God's Word and following it to the best of our ability. From a personal perspective, I can honestly say I love God's Word. Nothing on earth has changed me the way it has—not just as a teacher or a minister, but as a follower of Christ.

The Bible has the wisdom you need for every issue you will ever face. It will not tell you specifically where to go on vacation next year or what color to paint your house, but it will impart to you principles of right living, right thinking, wisdom, and faith. It will instruct you through stories of men and women who lived long ago but faced many of the same human challenges and relational struggles you and I face today. The Scriptures will encourage you to persevere, inspire you to overcome, help you make good decisions, and teach you to hear and obey God's voice.

I am always saddened when I encounter people who view the Bible as an outdated, irrelevant religious book. Yes, its words are centuries old, but instead of being old-fashioned or obsolete, they are ancient truths that have stood the test of time and been proven over and over and over again. The words of Scripture are alive; they are saturated with the power of God. They are as real and applicable today as they have ever been—and in our world today, we desperately need to be grounded in this kind of godly truth. The Bible is not only meant for preachers and "church people"; it is a book for everyone in every walk of life. It is spiritual, but it is also extremely practical.

Trust in Him Are you trusting God to change you by spending time in His Word? Name one specific thought/habit/attitude that has changed in the past thirty days because of what God has shown you in His Word.

January 23

Pray Your Way Through the Day

Pray at all times (on every occasion, in every season) in the Spirit, with all [manner of] prayer and entreaty. EPHESIANS 6:18

Talking with God about everything gives us a sense of belonging, of being cared for by Someone Who is on our side and Who is powerful. One of the phrases I like to use when teaching about prayer is: "Pray your way through the day." This is certainly good advice to follow if we want to enjoy our lives each day. We need to remember we can pray anytime, anywhere. First Thessalonians 5:17 tells us to "be *unceasing in prayer.*" In other words, we need to keep the lines of communication with God open. We need to stay in constant fellowship with Him through prayer, all day, every day.

While there are times when we need to be very diligent, focused, and set apart as we pray, we do not have to wait until we are in church or some other designated place, or until we have a specific amount of time, before we pray. The best way I know to be *"unceasing in prayer"* is to live as though God is constantly paying attention to us, because He is. For example, we can pray quick, simple, effective prayers aloud or silently. We can say silently while sitting in a business meeting: *"Oh, God, help me make a good decision here. Give me Your wisdom to speak wisely and be a blessing to my company."* We can whisper a prayer as we drop off our children at school: *"God, protect them today. Help them learn everything they need to know. Give them favor with their teachers and their friends."*

We can also pray prayers of praise and thanksgiving as we go about our daily lives, saying things like: *"Thank You, Lord, for helping me through this day"* or, *"I worship You, God, for Your goodness this afternoon."* These types of prayers take only a few seconds, but they keep us focused on God, aware of His presence, and in continual communication with Him.

Trust in Him Starting today, form a habit of talking to God as your constant companion and helper. If you aren't used to this it will take practice, but before you know it, you won't have to remind yourself—you'll just do it!

January 24

Who You Are Is More Than What You Do

There is [now no distinction] neither Jew nor Greek, there is neither slave nor free, there is not male and female; for you are all one in Christ Jesus. GALATIANS 3:28

How would you respond if I asked, "Who are you?" Would your first inclination be to list the things you do and the roles you play in life? Would you say, *"I am a flight attendant," "I am a brain surgeon," "I am a banker," "I am a minister," "I am a wife and a mother,"* or *"I am a high school student"*? These answers would describe *what you do*, but none of them would tell me *who you are*.

As a believer, one of the most important realities for you to understand is who you are in Christ, your identity in Him. When I first heard the phrase "who you are in Christ," I did not know what it meant. But understanding these powerful words is vitally important. When people receive Jesus Christ by faith as their personal Savior, God sees them as made right with Him and as being "in" Jesus. Being in Christ provides you with certain rights and privileges, the rights and privileges that belong to the children of God.

If the daughter of the queen of England visited the United States, I doubt anyone would ask for a list of what she could do. She would have immediate access and favor because of who she is. If this dynamic works with a human being, just imagine how much more valuable it is to be a child of God. However, if the princess did not know who she was, she would not use her identity to her advantage.

The same principle applies to anyone who does not know who they are in Christ.

The difference between who we are in Christ and what we do is huge. We are so much more than our jobs, our accomplishments, or our failures. Our identity comes from Jesus. In and of ourselves, we are nothing, we have nothing, and we can do nothing of eternal value. But in Christ, we can be, do, and have everything God promises us in His Word.

Trust in Him Who are you? Trust the Truth in God's Word to know who you are in Christ. The next time someone asks who you are, answer, *"I am a child of God. I am in Christ."*

January 25

From Faith to Faith

For in the Gospel a righteousness which God ascribes is revealed, both springing from faith and leading to faith [disclosed through the way of faith that arouses to more faith]. As it is written, The man who through faith is just and upright shall live and shall live by faith.

ROMANS 1:17

This verse reminds us that we need to learn how to live from faith to faith. It means we approach everything we face, every challenge we meet, every decision we make, and everything we do with faith.

I certainly need faith in my everyday life and in my ministry. When I travel to conferences, I go in faith that I will arrive safely at my destination. When I begin teaching, I do so in faith that God has given me the right message for the audience. I have faith that I am anointed to teach God's Word, to help people, and to speak the right words. When I walk off the platform, I have faith that God has used my ministry to change lives. When I leave to go home, I have faith that I will arrive safely.

After many years of being doubtful and fearful, I have definitely decided faith is much better. Faith enables us to enjoy our lives and to do amazing things. Living by faith is not a *feeling* we have; it is a conscious decision we must make.

Faith is simply the conscious, deliberate choice to put our trust in God. It's at the heart of everything great we'll ever do. It becomes more natural and we get better at it the more we do it.

If you will begin by exercising faith for simple things, eventually you will have no difficulty trusting God for great things. I remember going to a garage sale and trusting God to help me find a pair of tennis shoes for one of my children for two dollars because that was all I had. I saw God's faithfulness, and eventually I was able to trust God to cover the needs we have for an international ministry.

Trust in Him Where is God asking you to trust Him today? Start there and continue to go from faith to faith, step by step with God, as you pursue the great things He has prepared for you.

January 26

Faith Is Trusting God

For it is by free grace (God's unmerited favor) that you are saved (delivered from judgment and made partakers of Christ's salvation) through [your] faith. And this [salvation] is not of yourselves [of your own doing, it came not through your own striving], but it is the gift of God; not because of works [not the fulfillment of the Law's demands], lest any man should boast. EPHESIANS 2:8–9

I like to define faith in a very basic, easy-to-understand way: living with a positive attitude that comes from a deep trust in God. Living by faith is looking at everything in a positive way and trusting in the power of God, Who loves us and wants the best for us. When we have faith, we can say with confidence in our hearts:

- *"I don't know what to do, but God does."*
- *"I don't understand what's going on in my life, but God will make a way for me."*
- *"I don't know how I can pay my bills this month, but God will provide."*
- *"This trial I have doesn't feel good; I don't like it, but I believe God works all things out for good to those who love Him and are called according to His purpose"* (see Rom. 8:28).
- *"I don't like the situation I'm going through, but what Satan means for my harm, God intends for my good"* (see Gen. 50:20).

These statements and the attitudes they represent demonstrate faith. Having faith means always trusting in God's love and looking beyond where you are to see the end result. Having faith means always being hopeful and refusing to accept defeat. People who live by faith can enjoy every day of their lives.

Trust in Him What are you currently facing that is uncomfortable or that you don't understand? Choose to have a positive attitude about your situation and trust God to work it out for good.

January 27

Invite God into Every Area of Your Life

I am the Vine; you are the branches. Whoever lives in Me and I in him bears much (abundant) fruit. However, apart from Me [cut off from vital union with Me] you can do nothing. JOHN 15:5

God wants to help us with the things that seem big to us and with the things that seem less significant. He wants to help us when we feel desperate and when we don't. I figured out years ago that everything in life is over my head; it's all too much for me to handle alone. I used to run to God only when I thought I was desperate, but then one day I finally realized I was desperate all the time; I just didn't know it.

The same is true for you. You are desperate for God all the time, whether you realize it or not. In John 15:5 Jesus says, "Whoever *abides* in me and I in him, he it is that bears much fruit, for *apart from me you can do nothing*" (ESV, emphasis added). As we abide in Him through faith, we can do everything, but apart from Him, we can do nothing that will have any real lasting value.

Our desperate need for God and His desire for us to abide in Him do not mean we have to sit around being "super spiritual" all the time. We do not need to feel obligated to read our Bibles or confine ourselves to a prayer closet for hours each day. It should be part of our lives, but we don't need to feel as if we are being "spiritual" when we do it and "unspiritual" when we do other things. When we really love God and He is first in our lives, everything we do becomes spiritual in a way because we are doing it with Him, in Him, through Him, by Him, for Him, and to His glory.

Let me encourage you to invite God into every area of your life through faith. Jesus died so we could enjoy our lives—every part of them.

Trust in Him Are there "other" things in your life that don't feel particularly "spiritual"? Trust God with every area of your life so that you can enjoy *all* things—the "big" and the "insignificant"—because you are doing them with Him.

January 28

Trust God Through the Hard Times

Yes, though I walk through the [deep, sunless] valley of the shadow of death, I will fear or dread no evil, for You are with me...

PSALM 23:4

Often when we think of trusting God, we think of trusting Him *for* things we need or want—financial provision, physical healing, the restoration of a relationship, or a promotion at work. A true relationship of trust in God extends beyond trusting Him *for* something and includes trusting Him *through* a situation. We need to learn to not simply look to Him for the results we desire; we need to learn to trust Him through the process of attaining them.

There was a time in my life when I focused intensely on trusting God *for* things, saying, *"I want this, God," "I want that, God,"* and *"I need such-and-such, God."* In the midst of my requests, He began to show me that getting all those *things* was not what was most important. Those things would come later, but back then He needed to teach me first how to trust Him while I was going *through* situations. He wanted me to learn that He may not always rescue us when we want out of circumstances, but He is always with us as we walk through them. Because He is with us, we can go through trials in our lives with stable, positive attitudes, trusting God completely, even against seemingly impossible odds.

Remember, your attitude in every situation is yours to command. No one can force you to have a bad attitude or a good one; it is entirely up to you. Maintain an attitude of faith, praise, thanksgiving, and positive expectation, and you will definitely come out of your situation victoriously at just the right time.

Trust in Him Is it easier for you to trust God *for* or *through*? Whatever situation you are in, maintain a positive attitude and trust God to be with you *through* it. He will reward you on the other side.

January 29

Trusting When We Don't Understand

[...though He slay me, yet will I wait for and trust Him...]

JOB 13:15

One of the great mysteries and facts about our walk with God is that we rarely understand everything He is doing in our lives. If we always understood, we would have no need to trust Him. As believers we often find ourselves in places of not knowing, and we catch ourselves questioning God: *"What does my future hold?" "Will I ever get married?" "What will my children be when they grow up?" "Will I have the provision I need in my old age?"*

We have to learn to trust God when we do not understand what is happening in our lives, and we need to become comfortable with unanswered questions. You and I may never have every answer we want when we want it, so we need to relax and get comfortable knowing and trusting God, the One Who does know. Without trust, it is impossible to enjoy today and be ready to face tomorrow with expectancy.

Job, who had many reasons to question God as he faced a staggering series of crises and losses, did not understand what was going on in his life, but he made the decision to trust God anyway. I believe that was the only way he could find peace in the midst of his terrible circumstances. Similarly, you and I will never have peace in our lives until we learn how to stop trying to figure everything out and how to start trusting God more.

If you are the kind of person who has to have everything figured out in order to settle down, let me encourage you today to accept the fact you are not likely to receive all the answers you want in this lifetime. Choose to stop demanding explanations and to begin practicing trust. Instead of asking God why, tell Him you trust Him. There have been many times in my life when I wanted with all my heart to know why something was or was not happening, but I knew God wanted my trust, not my questions.

Trust in Him Is there something in your life you don't understand, no matter how long and hard you think about it? Give it to God and put your trust in Him. Whether or not He ever explains it to you, *you* can trust Him to bless you and bring you through any crisis.

January 30

God Will Meet You in the Fire

We believe God is going to deliver us, but even if He does not, we are not conforming to your image of what you think we ought to be. We are going to do what God is telling us to do. You can do what you want to with your furnace. But whatever happens to us, we will have peace. DANIEL 3:17–18 (PARAPHRASED)

Shadrach, Meshach, and Abednego refused to worship the golden idol that King Nebuchadnezzar constructed and as a result were thrown into the fiery furnace (see Dan. 3). These three young men had no idea what would happen to them, but they were willing to put their lives on the line instead of disobeying God. We need people today who will take a stand for righteousness, for what is right according to God's Word. If this does not happen, our world will be in serious trouble.

Many times, people fail to stand up for righteousness because they are afraid of what will happen when they do. Will they lose their jobs? Will they lose their friends? Will God abandon them? In situations such as these, when we do not know what the outcome or result of a situation will be, we need to trust God and press forward to do what we believe is right. Even if we are persecuted for the sake of righteousness, God's Word says we are blessed (see Matt. 5:10). Those three Hebrew boys would've never experienced their incredible miracle if they weren't willing to trust God as they stood in that fire.

The world desperately needs men and women who will trust God even in the midst of the fires of persecution and outside pressure. God can put us in better places than people could ever put us if we trust in Him and if we are people of integrity and excellence. We need people who will put everything on the line and say, *"Even if I lose what I want, I will not compromise and do what I know in my heart to be wrong."* We need to fear the Lord above all else, and to trust Him at all times, in every situation, every day of our lives.

Trust in Him Trust God to meet you in the fire. Don't be afraid to stand up for righteousness because you know He'll never leave you or forsake you.

January 31

Give Your Brain a Break

For we who have believed (adhered to and trusted in and relied on God) do enter that rest, in accordance with His declaration that those [who did not believe] should not enter when He said, As I swore in My wrath, They shall not enter My rest; and this He said although [His] works had been completed and prepared [and waiting for all who would believe] from the foundation of the world. HEBREWS 4:3

How do we learn to "rest" in God? I can tell you to wait on the Lord and rest in Him all day long, but that does no good if you do not know *how* to enter His rest. To enter His rest you have to trust Him. I believe the simplest, easiest way to trust Him is to get your mind off your problems. You may think you could never do that, but you can. You do it by choosing to think about something else.

Sometimes, one of the best things you can do when you have a problem and seem to be unable to get it off your mind is to simply go do something. Call a friend; go to the grocery store; take a walk; change the oil in your car; watch a funny movie; read a book; or tackle a project you have been putting off doing.

Invest your mental energy in something other than your problem. You will find it difficult to trust God if you talk about your problems excessively, because the more you talk about them, the more upset you will be. Turn your thoughts elsewhere. Give your brain a break and you'll find yourself better able to rest in God.

Growing in the ability to trust God and to walk in faith is a lifetime journey; it does not happen quickly. As we grow spiritually, we have to remind ourselves over and over again to: cast our cares on God; be anxious for nothing; trust Him in every situation. As we are diligent to do these things, we find ourselves resting in the Lord more and more, and that is where we find peace, clarity, wisdom, and the strength to face each day.

Trust in Him If you are worrying about your problems, give your brain a break! Go do something and get yourself off your mind. Show God that you trust Him by turning your problems over to Him so that He can care for you and you can enter His rest.

February 1

One Good Choice After Another

Let your eyes look straight ahead; fix your gaze directly before you.

PROVERBS 4:25 NIV

Are you enjoying the life and blessings of God in your everyday life? Or have you made a series of choices resulting in disappointment, pain, or feeling that everything you do requires great effort and produces little reward? Don't spend your time and energy mourning all the bad decisions you have made; just start making good ones. There is hope for you!

The way to overcome the results of a series of bad choices is through a series of right choices. The only way to walk out of trouble is to do the opposite of whatever you did to get into trouble—one choice at a time. Maybe the circumstances of your life right now are the direct result of a series of bad choices you have made. You may be in debt because you have made a lot of bad choices with money. You may be lonely because of a series of bad choices in relationships or in the way you treat people. You may be sick because of a series of unhealthy choices: eating junk food, not getting enough rest, or abusing your body through working too much and not having enough balance in your life.

You cannot make a series of bad choices that result in significant problems and then make one good choice and expect all the results of all those bad choices to go away. You did not get into deep trouble through one bad choice; you got into trouble through a series of bad choices. If you really want your life to change for the better, you will need to make one good choice after another, over a period of time, just as consistently as you made the negative choices that produced negative results.

No matter what kind of trouble or difficulty you find yourself in, you can still have a blessed life. You cannot do anything about what is behind you, but you can do a great deal about what lies ahead of you. God is a redeemer, and He will always give you another chance.

Trust in Him If you have a situation that is too big for you to solve, then you are material for a miracle. Invite God to get involved, trust in and follow His directions, make one good choice after another, and you will see amazing results.

February 2

God Will Lead You into His Wisdom

Wisdom cries aloud in the street, she raises her voice in the markets... PROVERBS 1:20

God wants us to use wisdom to make right choices, and the Holy Spirit will lead us into wisdom if we will simply ask Him to do so.

Have you ever needed to make a decision and had your head (your intellectual abilities) try to lead you one way while your heart was leading you in another direction? Have you ever had a situation in which your flesh (your natural thoughts and feelings) seemed to be guiding you down one path, but something inside you kept nagging you to go another way? For example, have there been times when you stayed up late at night watching television, even though you knew you needed a good night's sleep to be strong and alert for an important meeting the next day—and you kept resisting the knowledge in your heart that you really should go to bed? Have you purchased something you were excited about on an emotional level, but knew in your heart you could not really afford and didn't even need it?

What is happening in the kinds of circumstances I have just described? Chances are, wisdom is crying out to you. Many times, it cries out in the form of the things you find yourself thinking you should or should not do—you should eat healthily; you should be kind to other people; you should not spend money you do not have. These are all practical examples of using wisdom in everyday life. When you sense such leadings, the Holy Spirit, Who speaks to your heart, is trying to help you make a wise decision, even though it may not be the choice you want to make or it may not seem to make much sense in your present circumstances.

When we know the wise choice to make and don't make it, the reason is often because we are allowing our flesh to lead us and to see if we can get away with unwise decisions—which is also known as "foolishness." The flesh leads us to foolishness, but God wants us to walk in wisdom and make choices now that we will be happy with later.

Trust in Him What decision are you wrestling with? Trust the Holy Spirit to lead you to the wise choice. It may take some time to learn to hear the Holy Spirit over your flesh, but God is patient and will continue to provide you with opportunities to listen for His leading.

February 3

Go to God First

Does not skillful and godly Wisdom cry out, and understanding raise her voice [in contrast to the loose woman]? On the top of the heights beside the way, where the paths meet, stands Wisdom [skillful and godly]; at the gates at the entrance of the town, at the coming in at the doors, she cries out... PROVERBS 8:1–3

Almost everywhere you travel, you are likely to come to a point where two roads intersect and you must choose whether to turn or to go straight. We all face intersections in our lives. They are our turning points, the places where we must make decisions.

If you are standing at a point of decision in your life right now, let me urge you to follow wisdom. Go to God and His Word first; don't automatically turn to the people and resources around you and ask them what you ought to do. God may answer your prayer by speaking through someone, but it is best to honor Him by seeking Him first.

Recently, I was with a friend who suffered from serious back problems. After an unsuccessful surgery, she continued to have terrible pain. Her doctor released her, saying there was nothing more anyone could do, and suggested she go to a pain-management clinic and learn to live with the pain. She began to seriously seek God about what she should do. I have an expert chiropractor who has helped me over the years. I told my distraught friend I really thought he could help her, too. After one visit, her pain diminished greatly. The chiropractor put her on a rehabilitation strength program, and after she returned to him a few more times she was soon completely pain free. Wow!

She did not run to me and ignore God; rather, in seeking God, He gave her advice through me. As I said, God may use a person to speak words of wisdom to us, but it is important that we seek Him because all true wisdom comes from Him. He deserves the credit, no matter what vessel He uses.

Trust in Him Are you at an intersection, faced with an important decision? Seek God first, obey His leading, and trust His wisdom. Be ready for Him to speak to you through His Word, prayer, or through a trusted friend.

February 4

Simplify Your Decisions, Simplify Your Life

But above all [things], my brethren, do not swear, either by heaven or by earth or by any other oath; but let your yes be [a simple] yes, and your no be [a simple] no, so that you may not sin and fall under condemnation.
JAMES 5:12

Life can become complicated when people do not know how to make decisions and stick with them. In the verse above, James is basically saying, *"Make a decision. Just say yes or no, and don't keep changing your mind."*

We often labor over the choices and options before us when, actually, we just need to make a decision and let it stand. For example, when you stand in front of your closet in the morning looking at all of your clothes, just choose something and put it on. Don't go back and forth until you make yourself late for work!

When you get ready to go out to eat, pick a restaurant and go. Don't become so confused that you feel there is no one place that will satisfy you. Sometimes I would like the coffee from restaurant A, the salad from restaurant B, my favorite chicken dish from restaurant C, and dessert from restaurant D. Obviously, I cannot have everything I want at the same time, so I need to pick one of those places and eat there. I can go to the others later.

Let me encourage you to start making decisions without second-guessing yourself or worrying about the choices you make. Don't be double-minded. Doubting your decisions after you make them will steal the enjoyment from everything you do. Make the best decisions you can, and trust God with the results. Don't be anxious or afraid of being wrong. If your heart is right and you make a decision not in accordance with God's will, He will forgive you and help you move on.

Trust in Him Be decisive. Whatever you need to do in life, just do it. Keep it simple and trust God with the results.

February 5

You Can Trust God's Timing

My times are in Your hands… PSALM 31:15

One of the biggest mistakes we make as believers is failing to remember that God's timing rarely matches our timing. We think and plan in temporal terms, and God thinks and plans in eternal terms. What this means is we want what feels good right now, what produces immediate results, but God is willing to be patient and deliberate as He invests in us over a period of time to produce results far better and longer lasting than we can imagine.

Just as our children try to talk us into giving them what they want right away, we often try to talk God into immediately giving us what we want. He loves us even more than we love our children, and He loves us too much to give in to our pleadings. He knows something born prematurely might struggle to survive, so He waits until He knows everything is properly prepared for the arrival of our dreams.

God sees and understands what we do not see and understand. He asks us to put aside our natural tendencies to want to figure out what should happen in our lives and when it should happen. He also desires us to stop being frustrated because things do not go according to our plan, and instead to relax, enjoy the ride, and trust He is working everything out according to His timing and the wisdom of His plan.

Without trusting God, we will never experience satisfaction and enjoyment in life; we will always be striving to "make things happen" within our timeline. We must remember God not only has plans for our lives, He also knows the perfect timing for each aspect of those plans. Fighting and resisting the timing of God is equivalent to fighting and resisting His will for our lives. God is working, often in ways we cannot see, to bring His plans to pass in our lives in the best possible ways. We simply need to trust Him as we wait for the arrival of our dreams.

Trust in Him You can trust that God is working on His plan for your life; He is preparing it for you and you for it. His plan may not come on your timetable, but the arrival of your dream *is* coming. Just have a seat (trust in Him, enter His rest), and when the time is precisely right, He'll call your name.

February 6

Love Covers Mistakes

...love covers all transgressions. PROVERBS 10:12

Sometimes, the best way to deal with an offense or with something that gets on our nerves is simply to overlook it. If we insist upon calling every little mistake to people's attention (this is called "nit-picking"), we are not being gracious and merciful.

Every member of every household on earth has some annoying habits. Nobody's perfect. In our home, I have habits Dave wishes I didn't have and he has habits I wish he didn't have. For instance, Dave does not always close his closet door. In our closets, the lights stay on if the doors are open. For years, I had a hard time simply closing the closet door for him; I always wanted to make sure Dave knew he left the door open and I had to close it again!

Our fleshly natures really enjoy telling people what they have done wrong and how we have fixed it. The best way for me to handle Dave's open closet door is to close it and go on about my day, not to say, "*You left your light on again*" every time he does it. There are similar things Dave needs to do for me. There are plenty of times when I am not perfect and I want him to cover my mistakes.

In adult relationships, both in marriage and in other relationships, we need to cover one another's mistakes. Although there are times when situations need to be confronted and resolved, there are other times when people are busy or rushed and they simply need us to step in and cover them without reminding them over and over of what we've done for them.

People do not want to hear about every little mistake they make. I really appreciate the times people cover my mistakes; I believe you do, too. I encourage you to apply Proverbs 10:12 to your everyday life. Before you point out what someone has done wrong, remember that love covers transgressions.

Trust in Him What is a habit that one of your family members has that annoys you? Have you tried covering it? Trusting God means obeying His Word, and His Word tells us to cover transgressions. Sow a little loving mercy into someone's life today by covering their mistakes.

February 7

Let Go and Let God Work

We are assured and know that [God being a partner in their labor] all things work together and are [fitting into a plan] for good to and for those who love God and are called according to [His] design and purpose. ROMANS 8:28

My husband is a very happy man; he is consistently joyful and peaceful. Over the years we have been married, he has enjoyed his life much more than I have enjoyed mine, and he has not spent (wasted) nearly as much time as I have being angry, upset, and frustrated.

When certain problems arise, Dave says, *"If you can do something about this, do it. If you can't, go on about your business, trust God, and let Him take care of it."* That always sounded good to me, but it used to take me longer to *"let go and let God work"* than it did him, but now I am catching up.

Recently, we were riding in the car together and Dave received a phone call about a change in one of our television air times. This happened to be on one of our best stations, and he did not like the change. He started getting upset, and I heard myself say, *"Don't let it bug you. God will make it work out for the best if we pray."* I didn't even have to try to be positive; it was my first response. I am continually amazed at how much God can change us if we continue praying and letting Him work in our lives. Here I was actually encouraging Mr. Positive, when most of my life it had been the other way around. That felt good!

If we really love God and want to do His will, then we must believe—no matter what happens in our lives—that God is in control and He will take everything that happens and make it work out for our good. Certain circumstances may not always feel good or appear to be good, but God will cause them to work together with other things in your life to bring about good. God is a good God, and He can take even the worst situations and bring something positive out of them.

Trust in Him Think about a situation in your life you can't do anything about. Say from your heart, *"I trust God and believe this will work out for my good."* Now let it go and let God work.

February 8

Learning to Deal with Criticism

And whoever will not receive and accept and welcome you nor listen to your message, as you leave that house or town, shake the dust [of it] from your feet. MATTHEW 10:14

Everyone who is truly successful in life has to deal with criticism. Sometimes criticism comes from people who do not understand what we are doing, cannot see the vision we see, or are jealous of our success. Sometimes criticism is legitimate but isn't delivered in a helpful way. Learning to deal with it in a godly way is always a great testimony to the people around us.

In Matthew 10:10–14, Jesus tells His disciples how to deal with criticism or with people who will not receive their message. His advice: *"Shake it off."* Jesus Himself was criticized frequently, and He usually ignored it (see Matt. 27:11–12). Often, the best way to respond to criticism is to say nothing at all. But when you must respond, here are a few suggestions for handling criticism in a godly way:

- Don't get defensive. Remember, God is your defense; He is your vindicator.
- Don't get angry or upset. Keep your peace, because peace brings power.
- Don't retaliate with criticism toward your critic.
- Don't assume your critic is wrong without being willing to examine yourself.

- Don't assume your critic is right and start feeling guilty without consulting God.
- Thank your critics, because they help you see things others wouldn't.

The Bible says only a fool hates correction (see Prov. 12:1), and although I believe that is true, I must say that in my life I have only known one person who I can honestly say appreciated it—and it wasn't me, although I wish I could say it was. Probably like most of you, I am somewhere between hating correction and loving it, but I am striving to have a positive attitude toward correction as well as everything else in life.

Trust in Him How have you handled criticism? God wants you to be successful, and a big step in the process is realizing you can trust Him with your reputation. You will be criticized—that is life—but God is with you, so you can handle it with a godly attitude.

February 9

Pay Attention to Your Heart

Let those who are wise understand these things. Let those with discernment listen carefully. The paths of the Lord *are true and right, and righteous people live by walking in them.*

HOSEA 14:9 NLT

There's more to life than meets the eye—especially the natural eye. Things are not always what they appear to be, so we must learn to be discerning. Simply defined, discernment is spiritual understanding, and developing it takes practice. As we grow in our understanding of God's Word and in our relationships with Him, we also grow in our ability to discern.

To live by discernment, we have to pay attention to our hearts. We have to know when we do not feel right about something. For example, let's say a businessman has been looking for a certain kind of business deal for quite some time and an opportunity for such a deal finally presents itself. As he reviews the paperwork, the deal appears to be sound. But when he begins to pray about entering into the deal, he senses he should not do it. Even though everything appears to be in order, he just does not have peace about the deal. The more he prays, the more he feels he should not do business with the people involved in the deal. This man is looking beyond the natural elements of the deal and using his discernment.

The best way for me to help you learn to live by discernment is to offer this simple advice: if you don't feel right about something in your heart, do not do it. You may discover later why you didn't feel good about it, but you may not. Either way, you can be at peace knowing you used your discernment instead of making decisions based on your mind, your emotions, or natural circumstances. Discernment is a precious gift from God that will help you avoid a lot of trouble in life if you pay attention to it.

Trust in Him When was the last time something didn't feel right to you? Pray and ask God to develop and increase your discernment as you study His Word. When something doesn't feel right in your heart, you can trust that it is God telling you it is not His will for your life.

February 10

Listen for God's Voice

And your ears will hear a word behind you, saying, This is the way; walk in it... ISAIAH 30:21

Most of the time, God does not speak to us in an audible voice. We hear Him in our hearts. Sometimes He speaks by reminding us of a truth or principle from His Word; sometimes He gives us thoughts or ideas we could not have had on our own; sometimes we simply have a strong sense of knowing what to do. We need to quiet all the noise in our lives and become sensitive to God's still, small voice. We need to choose to listen to God because He will speak to us.

God does not only speak in the urgent or important matters of life. He also guides us in the most seemingly insignificant situations. I was on my way home one day and intended to stop and get a cup of coffee, when I had a strong impression that I should call my secretary and see if she wanted a cup, too. When I called, she said, *"I was just standing here thinking, I would love a good cup of coffee right now."* You see, God wanted to give her the desire of her heart, and He wanted to work through me. I did not hear a loud voice or see an angel, nor did I have a vision; I simply had an inner sensing that I should offer her a cup of coffee. As a result, we both experienced great joy in knowing God cares about the smallest details of our lives.

Quite often we ignore little things like this. The more we do, the harder it is to develop sensitivity to the Holy Spirit. If someone is on your heart, I encourage you to pray for that person or call him or her and say, *"I was just thinking of you."* You never know how a seemingly small thing like a phone call can alter a person's day or maybe even change someone's life. Let me encourage you today to keep your heart sensitive to God's voice. He will speak to your heart and lead you in the way you should go.

Trust in Him Remember this: each time we disobey God, it becomes more difficult to hear Him the next time He speaks; but every time we trust Him, it gets easier to hear and be led by His Spirit. What is God saying to you today?

February 11

The Choice Is Yours

I [the Lord] will instruct you and teach you in the way you should go; I will counsel you with My eye upon you. Be not like the horse or the mule, which lack understanding, which must have their mouths held firm with bit and bridle, or else they will not come with you.

PSALM 32:8–9

In these verses, God makes plain His desire to lead and guide us, but He also tells us not to be stubborn. We need to follow Him willingly and joyfully.

I worked at a church in St. Louis for five years. I really liked my job there, but the time came when God wanted me to move on to something new. He said to me, "*Now I want you to take this ministry and go north, south, east, and west. I don't need you here anymore. I want you to leave this place.*"

That place was where my ministry started. I had a fulfilling job, a regular paycheck, and my name on my office door. But God said, "*I'm finished with you here.*"

"*How can that be?*" I wondered. "*After all, I'm a pillar of this church. How can the place run without me?*"

I continued to work at the church for a full year after God told me to leave, and that year was absolutely miserable. I did not understand why I was so unhappy, why there seemed to be no grace to do what I had great grace to do in previous years.

Finally, one morning, I cried out to God, "*God, what is wrong?*"

He spoke to my heart, "*Joyce, I told you a year ago to leave and you're still here.*" That was all He said.

God will not force us to follow Him. He gives us the gift of choice, so we can decide whether or not we will obey His leading. He will speak; He will lead; He will guide; He will make His plans and desires clear.

But He will not force His will on us; we must consciously and deliberately choose to follow Him.

Trust in Him Has God asked you to do something or quit something and you haven't obeyed Him? Are you stubbornly refusing to trust that He knows best? I recommend you choose to follow Christ.

February 12

Stop Getting and Start Receiving

And we receive from Him whatever we ask, because we [watchfully] obey His orders [observe His suggestions and injunctions, follow His plan for us] and [habitually] practice what is pleasing to Him.

1 JOHN 3:22

We often ask people if they "got" something, particularly when we speak of spiritual matters. *"Did you 'get' a breakthrough?"* we want to know, or *"Did you 'get' your blessing?"* Is the idea of "getting" from God biblical? The Bible teaches us about *receiving*, not about getting. The difference between getting and receiving is significant. To "get" means "to obtain by struggle and effort."

When everything in your life requires effort, life becomes frustrating and exhausting—and that's not the kind of abundant life Jesus came to give us. No, God wants us to live with a holy ease, a grace that keeps us from striving and struggling through life. That doesn't mean everything will be easy, but it means even difficult things can be done with a sense of God's presence and help.

"Getting" puts the burden on us to have to figure out things, to manipulate circumstances, and to try to force situations to work out a certain way. Receiving, on the other hand, means we simply take in what is being offered freely. We don't strive; we simply relax and enjoy what comes to us.

God wants to give us so much more than we can imagine. He is waiting to pour out blessings in our lives, and we need to know how to receive—both from Him and from others. Sometimes God works miraculously to meet our needs, but He frequently works through other people. If we pray for help, then we must let God choose how and through whom He will send it. We should not be embarrassed to be needy, because we are all needy in some way or another. God did not intend for us to be so independent we would never need help.

Trust in Him Are you struggling and striving to "get" something from God? Stop "getting" and start receiving. He *wants* to bless you! Trust God and receive by faith what you have asked for.

February 13

Do You Always Have to Be Right?

Pride goes before destruction, and a haughty spirit before a fall.
PROVERBS 16:18

Have you ever been absolutely sure you were right about something? Your mind appeared to have a store of facts and details to prove you were right—but you ended up being wrong. What did you do? Did you admit your error, or did you keep pushing and trying to find a way to defend your position?

In the past, when my husband and I were watching a movie or television show, we often argued over which actors and actresses were portraying the characters. It seemed to me that Dave thought Henry Fonda played half the characters in movies.

"Oh, look," he'd say as we watched a movie on television. *"Henry Fonda is in this movie."*

"That's not Henry Fonda," I'd answer back, and we'd start arguing and bickering. Both of us were so intent on being right that we would

insist on staying up much later than we should, just so we could see the credits roll at the end. Then one of us could say, *"I told you so!"*

Why do we want so desperately to be right about things? Why is it so difficult to be wrong? Why is it so important for us to "win" in a disagreement?

For years I felt bad about who I was, and in order to feel any confidence at all, I had to be right all the time. So I would argue and go to great extremes to prove I was right. I lived in frustration as I tried to convince everyone that I knew what I was talking about.

It wasn't until my identity became rooted and grounded in Christ that I began to experience freedom in this area. Now I know my worth and value do not come from appearing right to others. Trusting what Jesus says about me is enough.

Trust in Him Do you always have to be right? Pray and commit to trust that who God has made you to be and His love for you is more valuable than the confidence or pride that comes from being right.

February 14

Humility Produces Harmony

There are those who speak rashly, like the piercing of a sword, but the tongue of the wise brings healing. PROVERBS 12:18

For a long time I was an expert at trying to convince others that my way was the right way, but as the Holy Spirit has convicted me in this area, I have learned to be quiet when I find myself in the middle of a disagreement.

Both Dave and I have learned to listen to the Holy Spirit in this area. There are times when we just do not agree. My husband is very adaptable and accommodating. But there are certain issues that both of us feel very strongly about, and no one is going to convince either of us that we are wrong, except for God Himself.

Sometimes God convinces Dave, and sometimes He convinces me. If I press the issue trying to convince Dave, the harmony in our relationship is destroyed and strife enters our lives. But if I humble myself under the mighty hand of God and wait on Him, I have learned that He and He alone is able to convince my husband in certain situations.

Now whenever Dave and I are tempted to defend our pride by insisting that we are right, God has enabled us to say, *"I think I am right, but I may be wrong."* It is absolutely amazing how many arguments we have avoided over the years by using that simple act of humility. I have found that when I obey the Holy Spirit's prompting, a relationship can become harmonious once again.

Give your need to be right over to God, and watch your relationships improve. You'll discover that great spiritual power is released in unity and harmony.

Trust in Him Stop trying to convince your spouse or your friends of something in order to change them or because you want to be right. If you want to enjoy trouble-free, harmonious relationships, stop trying to control people and be quiet, and trust God to take care of any and all situations you find yourself in.

February 15

The Importance of Unity

Behold, how good and how pleasant it is for brethren to dwell together in unity! It is like the dew of [lofty] Mount Hermon and the dew that comes on the hills of Zion; for there the Lord has commanded the blessing, even life forevermore [upon the high and the lowly].

PSALM 133:1, 3

I love this psalm because this principle is so powerful: life is enjoyable when people live in unity and keep strife (conflict) out of their lives.

On the other hand, there is nothing worse than a home or relationship filled with an angry undercurrent of strife.

Perhaps that's why unity is one of the last things Jesus prayed about before He was arrested and crucified. During the Last Supper He prayed, "That they all may be one, [just] as You, Father, are in Me and I in You, that they also may be one in Us, so that the world may believe and be convinced that You have sent Me" (John 17:21).

You might be able to preach a sermon or memorize Bible verses. You might do many good works and share the message of salvation with others. However, if you do all this, yet you are living in strife rather than in unity, your life will lack peace, joy, and blessing.

If you are wondering why you aren't experiencing more of God's power and blessing in your life, look at your relationships. Do you have strife with your spouse, your children, your coworkers, or your fellow believers? Do you cause or participate in conflict in your church or on the job?

Do all you can to keep the strife out of your life and live in peace. Remember, where there is unity, there will also be anointing and blessing.

Trust in Him Think about your relationships. What do you see in them that might be hindering the flow of God's blessing in your life? God wants you to live in unity and be blessed. You can trust Him to help you get your life on track, but you have to be willing to do your part and stay in peace and unity.

February 16

Four Principles for Successful Daily Living

For let him who wants to enjoy life and see good days [good—whether apparent or not] keep his tongue free from evil and his lips from guile (treachery, deceit). Let him turn away from wickedness and shun it, and let him do right. Let him search for peace... and seek it eagerly....

1 PETER 3:10–11

I enjoy just reading over this passage and soaking up the power from its principles for successful daily living. It gives four specific principles for those who want to enjoy life:

1. **Keep your tongue free from evil.** God's Word states clearly, the power of life and death is in the mouth. We can bring blessing or misery into our lives with our words. When we speak rashly we often get into arguments, so choose your words carefully.

2. **Turn away from wickedness.** We must take action to remove ourselves from wickedness or from a wicked environment. The action we must take could mean altering our friendships; it could even mean loneliness for a period of time. But you can always trust God to be with you.

3. **Do right.** The decision to do right must follow the decision to stop doing wrong. Both are definite choices. Repentance is twofold; it requires turning *away* from sin and turning *to* righteousness.

4. **Search for peace.** Notice that we must search for it, pursue it, and go after it. We cannot merely *desire* peace without any accompanying action, but we must *desire* peace *with* action. We need to search for peace in our relationship with God and with others.

When I started living by these principles, not only did my relationships improve, but so did my health, my attitude, and all areas of my life. The same will be true for you.

Trust in Him Which of these four principles do you need to work on the most? Focus on one area at a time, and trust God to give you the power for a breakthrough so that you can enjoy your everyday life.

February 17

God Wants to Take Care of You

For we [Christians] are the true circumcision, who worship God in spirit and by the Spirit of God and exult and glory and pride ourselves in Jesus Christ, and put no confidence or dependence [on what we are] in the flesh and on outward privileges and physical advantages and external appearances. PHILIPPIANS 3:3

If we choose to put our faith (trust and confidence) in ourselves, we will quickly learn that self-care does not produce supernatural results. For years I wore myself out mentally, emotionally, and physically trying to take care of myself instead of casting my care on God and trusting Him to take care of me. Because of the sexual and emotional abuse I endured as a child at the hands of people who should have taken care of me, and again during my first marriage, I thought I was the only person I could trust. I did not understand that my efforts at self-care were only adding to the problems in my relationships and life.

The Book of James clearly shows us how strife comes in as we try to provide for ourselves instead of trusting God: "What leads to strife (discord and feuds) and how do conflicts (quarrels and fightings) originate among you? Do they not arise from your sensual desires that are ever warring in your bodily members? You are jealous and covet [what others have] and your desires go unfulfilled; [so] you become murderers. [To hate is to murder as far as your hearts are concerned.] You burn with envy and anger and are not able to obtain [the gratification, the contentment, and the happiness that you seek], so you fight and war. You do not have, because you do not ask" (James 4:1–2).

When you feel frustrated, it is usually because you are trying to do what only God can do. Retire from self-care and start trusting God more. Ask God for what you want and need and trust that He will give it to you in His own way and timing.

Trust in Him As long as we practice "self-care," we aren't letting God fully take care of us the way He wants to. In what areas of your life are you trusting yourself rather than trusting God? Thank Him for wanting to take care of you, and ask Him to help you put your trust in Him.

February 18

God Honors Our Trust in Him

He shall call upon Me, and I will answer him; I will be with him in trouble, I will deliver him and honor him. PSALM 91:15

Many people have difficulty trusting God because of past hurts. But God is not like the people who have hurt us. We can trust Him!

Although God wants to take care of us, His hands are tied by our unbelief and works of the flesh. He is a gentleman and will not just take over without being invited to do so. He waits until we give up the job of self-care and place our trust and confidence in Him. The law of faith, mentioned in 1 Peter 5:7, is this: *When you stop trying to take care of yourself, you release God to take care of you!* (Paraphrased.)

I have discovered that it is very hard to walk in obedience to God and in love with others if my primary interest is that "I" don't get hurt or taken advantage of. However, when I allow God to be God in my life, He honors three distinct promises He makes in Psalm 91:15: He'll be with me in trouble, He'll deliver me, and He will honor me.

Honor is a place of lifting up. When God honors a believer, He lifts up or exalts that person. When we let go and do not try to care for ourselves, we are admitting that we need God's help. It is an act of humility, and that act of faith places us in the direct line of God's exaltation. Peter wrote, "Therefore humble yourselves [demote, lower yourselves in your own estimation] under the mighty hand of God, that in due time He may exalt you..." (1 Pet. 5:6).

When we trust God, we are in line for a promotion. God will honor us and reward us as we place our faith in Him. In the world's system, you work hard and then get your reward. In God's economy, you trust Him deeply and then receive your reward.

Trust in Him When we trust in ourselves, it leads to strife and shows that we don't trust God to do what He says in His Word—be with us, deliver us, and honor us. When we trust God, however, it leads to the reward of peace—peace within ourselves, peace with God, and peace with others.

February 19

Make Friends with Yourself

...love your neighbor as yourself... MARK 12:33 NIV

Are you at peace with yourself? Since we spend more time with ourselves than we do with anyone else, not liking who we are is a major problem. After all, we cannot get away from ourselves. And if we don't enjoy ourselves, we usually don't enjoy anyone else, either.

This was true for me. I suffered from not liking myself for many years, but I didn't realize it. Nor did I understand that my self-rejection and self-hatred were why I didn't get along with most people and why most people could not get along with me.

The way we see ourselves is the way others will see us. We see this principle illustrated in Numbers 13, when the twelve spies Moses sent to investigate the Promised Land came back from their scouting expedition. Ten of the spies gave a very negative report: "There we saw the Nephilim [or giants], the sons of Anak, who come from the giants; *and we were in our own sight as grasshoppers, and so we were in their sight*" (Num. 13:33, emphasis added).

Because ten of the spies saw themselves as "grasshoppers," their enemy saw them as grasshoppers, too. How can we expect others to accept us if we reject ourselves? How can we expect to make peace with others if we haven't made peace with ourselves?

God's Word assures us that we have tremendous value because of who we are—God's beloved children. What I do is not always perfect. But I still know who I am—a child of God whom He loves very much.

You have tremendous worth and value. You are special to God, and He has a good plan for your life (see Jer. 29:11). You have been purchased with the blood of Christ (see Acts 20:28). The Bible refers to the "precious blood of Christ," indicating Christ paid a high price indeed to ransom you and me (1 Pet. 1:19). Believe you are God's beloved child. The truth will bring healing to your soul and freedom to your life.

Trust in Him Are you friends with yourself? Do you enjoy your company? Trust that your worth comes from who you are in Christ and begin to love yourself as you love Him!

February 20

Your Weakness Is His Strength

. . . God selected (deliberately chose) what in the world is foolish to put the wise to shame, and what the world calls weak to put the strong to shame. And God also selected (deliberately chose) what in the world is lowborn and insignificant and branded and treated with contempt, even the things that are nothing, that He might depose and bring to nothing the things that are, so that no mortal man should [have pretense for glorying and] boast in the presence of God.

1 CORINTHIANS 1:27–29

The Bible contains many examples of weak people through whom God chose to accomplish great things for His glory, including His disciples. They were ordinary men who possessed weaknesses, just like you and me.

The gospels clearly imply Peter was a rugged and volatile fisherman who displayed impatience, anger, and rage. In one crucial moment, he was so fearful that he would be discovered to be a disciple of Jesus that he succumbed to a cowardly act—he denied that he even knew Jesus. Andrew may have seemed too softhearted to be a leader; Thomas was a man riddled with doubt, afraid to place his trust in his Leader.

And then there was Matthew. The religious leaders of the day were outraged that Jesus would even consider socializing with this lowly tax collector. Imagine their horror when Jesus dined with Matthew and invited him to become one of His followers and close associates.

Probably the only man the religious leaders would have considered worthy of any admiration at all was Judas. To the world's eye, Judas had business strengths and personality qualities that spelled success. But his greatest natural strengths became his greatest weaknesses—and brought destruction into his life.

I find it interesting that those whom the world recommended, Jesus rejected. And those whom the world rejected, Jesus said, in essence, *"Give them to Me. I don't care how many faults they have. If they will trust Me, I can do great and mighty things through them."*

Trust in Him God sees your weaknesses as His opportunity, because when you lean on Him in weakness, He shows His strength through you. Trust Him to do great and mighty things through your weakness.

February 21

Always Remember: He Chose You!

Dwell in Me, and I will dwell in you. [Live in Me, and I will live in you.] Just as no branch can bear fruit of itself without abiding in (being vitally united to) the vine, neither can you bear fruit unless you abide in Me. I am the Vine; you are the branches. Whoever lives in Me and I in him bears much (abundant) fruit. However, apart from Me [cut off from vital union with Me] you can do nothing.

JOHN 15:4–5

For years I tried to fight my flaws and change myself, but I never made much progress. I had many traits that would not have been suitable for a minister. Yet I believed God had called me to minister on His behalf, and because He called me, He filled me with desire to do it. So, I tried to be everything I thought God wanted me to be. I would determine, resolve, and exercise all the self-control I could muster.

Although I did improve, there were still those awful moments when the real me emerged. I am sure during those times people looked at me and said, *"No way! God can't be calling you to do anything major for Him."*

I wanted to believe God and to believe what my heart was telling me, but I heard the voices of people, and I let their opinions affect me. I also listened to the devil, who gave me a running daily inventory of all my flaws and inabilities. He reminded me how often I had tried to change and failed.

Then, after I had spent years wondering, *"How can God ever use me?"* God finally showed me that my constant victory was dependent on my constant abiding in and leaning on Him. Knowing this truth forces me to lean on Him continually. My need drives me to seek Him and to lean on Him at all times. By God's grace, I finally came to believe He chose me on purpose. I was not pushed off on the Lord as a "last resort." He chose me!

Trust in Him **Are you trying to change yourself, by yourself? You cannot give God glory through your life unless you trust in Him, abide in Him, and lean on Him. Remember, He chose you, wants to use you, and is worthy of your praise!**

February 22

Quit Picking on Yourself

But [as for me personally] it matters very little to me that I should be put on trial by you [on this point], and that you or any other human tribunal should investigate and question and cross-question me. I do not even put myself on trial and judge myself.

1 CORINTHIANS 4:3

Are you struggling with other people's judgments and opinions of you? Look at Paul's comment above concerning the criticism of others. Some people were questioning Paul's faithfulness. He did not try to defend himself, nor did he become angry. He simply said, "*I do not care what you think. I do not even judge myself.*" Paul knew that if he was out of line, God would correct him, so he didn't have to worry about what people thought. Many times in the past I have opened to this passage and soaked it in, trusting the power of God's Word to deliver me from self-judgment and criticism. It's easy for me to focus on my flaws and to pick on the things I don't like about myself.

We are not to pass judgment on each other or ourselves. Paul wrote to the Romans, "Who are you to pass judgment on and censure another's household servant? It is before his own master that he stands or falls. And he shall stand and be upheld, for the Master (the Lord) is mighty to support him and make him stand" (Rom. 14:4).

We stand because Jesus holds us up. When children learn to walk, their parents are always close by, holding their hands and helping them keep their balance so they will not fall and hurt themselves. We stand because our Father supports us and holds us up! We are upheld by His power, not our own.

Encouraging someone and speaking truth into someone's life when God asks you to do so are healthy and wonderful things—but it's never right to make a quick, dismissive judgment. Our judgments based on external appearances don't have all the information and wisdom that God has—that's why we leave it to Him!

Trust in Him Trust the power of God's Word to help you quit picking on yourself. Take to heart Paul's words to the Corinthians: *"I do not care what you think. I do not even judge myself."*

February 23

You Can Remove "Spiritual Roadblocks"

It is good for me to draw near to God; I have put my trust in the Lord God and made Him my refuge, that I may tell of all Your works.
PSALM 73:28

There are many examples in God's Word of men and women who went through periods of questioning, doubting, blaming, and even criticizing God. But they realized they were being foolish. They repented and turned back to trusting God instead of being angry with Him.

This psalmist is one of those people. Here is my paraphrase of his progression from anger to trust in Psalm 73: *"God, it sure seems that the wicked prosper and do better than I do. I am trying to live a godly life, but it does not seem to be doing any good. It looks as if it's all in vain. I am having nothing but trouble, and when I try to understand it, the pain is too much for me. However, I have spent time with You, and I can understand that in the end the wicked come to ruin and destruction. My heart was grieved. I was bitter and in a state of upset. I was stupid, ignorant, and behaving like a beast. Now I see that You are continually with me. You hold my right hand. Who do I have in heaven, God, but You? Who will help me? If You don't, there is no one on earth who can help me. You are my strength and my portion forever. It is good for me to trust in You, O Lord, and make You my refuge"* (vv. 12–28).

If you are stuck in a place of bitterness toward God, I encourage you to go through the process of forgiveness. Anger toward God is a "spiritual roadblock"—perhaps stronger than any other. Why? Simply because anger closes the door to the only One Who can help, heal, comfort, or restore our emotions, relationships, and lives. While God doesn't need our forgiveness, we need to forgive Him and repent in order to be released from bitterness and resentment. If we have been harboring a grudge against God, we must forgive Him so we can experience His power and blessing in our lives and our relationships.

Trust in Him It isn't wrong to feel anger, but you must quickly realize you have no reason to hold on to anger against God, the One Who knows what is best for you. Don't let a "spiritual roadblock" keep you from trusting Him.

February 24

Live In Peace with One Another

And when they heard it, lifted their voices together with one united mind to God... ACTS 4:24

The church in Acts had great spiritual power because they had the same vision, the same goal, and they were all pressing toward the same mark. They prayed in agreement (see Acts 4:24), lived in harmony (see Acts 2:44), cared for one another (see Acts 2:46), met each other's needs (see Acts 4:34), and lived a life of faith (see Acts 4:31). The early church as described in Acts lived in unity and peace.

But when the church began to split into various factions with different opinions, the power of the church lessened. People who were unable to stay in agreement due to pride and other related problems caused the church to divide into many different groups.

The believers in the church of Corinth were people just like us, people in relationship with one another, arguing over trivial things that they should have left alone. We see in 1 Corinthians 1:12: "What I mean is this, that each one of you [either] says, I belong to Paul, or I belong to Apollos, or I belong to Cephas (Peter), or I belong to Christ." It sounds to me as though only the names have changed in today's arguments. Today we hear, *"I'm Catholic," "I'm Lutheran," "I'm Baptist,"* or *"I'm Pentecostal or Charismatic."*

Read on to verse 13: "Is Christ (the Messiah) divided into parts? Was Paul crucified on behalf of you? Or were you baptized into the name of Paul?"

Paul was telling the Corinthians to keep their minds on Christ—not each other. If we are to live in peace with one another and unleash God's power and blessing in our lives, we must do the same. Sometimes we get so worried and upset about what other believers are doing that we forget all about Jesus and that He has called us to live in unity with one another.

The Word of God instructs, encourages, and urges believers to live in harmony with each other because God wants us to have the blessed, powerful lives that come through His peace.

Trust in Him Do you have a problem with another believer, another church, or a different denomination? Either work it out with a humble attitude, or trust God and let go of your concerns. When you live in peace, you will have the blessed, powerful life God wants for you.

February 25

How to Win the Battle

Stand firm then, with the belt of truth buckled around your waist, with the breastplate of righteousness in place, and with your feet fitted with the readiness that comes from the gospel of peace.

EPHESIANS 6:14–15 NIV

The Bible says that if we meet our battles with peace and respond to the upsets in life with peace, we will experience victory. It's a paradox; it doesn't make any sense. How can we win if we stop fighting?

My husband used to make me mad because he would not fight with me. I was upset and angry, and I wanted him to say just one thing so I could rail on and on. But when Dave saw that I was just looking for an argument, he would be quiet and tell me, *"I am not going to fight with you."* Sometimes he would even get in the car and leave for a while, infuriating me even more, but I could not fight with someone who would not fight back.

Moses told the Israelites not to fight when they found the Red Sea facing them on one side and the Egyptian army chasing them on the other. They became frightened, and he told them, "Fear not; stand still (firm, confident, undismayed) and see the salvation of the Lord which He will work for you today. For the Egyptians you have seen today you shall never see again. The Lord will fight for you, and you shall hold your peace and remain at rest" (Exod. 14:13–14).

Notice that Moses told the Israelites to "hold [their] peace and remain at rest." Why? They were at war, and it was necessary for them to respond with peace in order to win the battle. God would fight for them if they would show their confidence in Him by being peaceful. If you hold on to your peace, He will do the same for you.

Trust in Him Are you fighting a battle when you should be holding your peace? Choose to stop fighting and trust God to fight for you. That is how to win a battle.

February 26

God's Anointing Helps You in Everything You Do

...Not by might, nor by power, but by My Spirit...
ZECHARIAH 4:6

The anointing of the Holy Spirit is one of the most important things in my life and ministry. It ushers me into the presence and the power of God. The anointing manifests in ability, enablement, and strength. The anointing ministers life to me. I feel alive and strong physically when the anointing is flowing, as well as mentally alert.

When we live in peace and harmony, we unleash God's anointing for more than just ministry. I believe there is an anointing for everything that we are called to do—not just for spiritual things. We can be anointed for cleaning the house, doing laundry, leading a home or business, or being a student. God's presence makes everything easy and enjoyable.

What other kinds of things may we expect to be anointed for? I believe a woman can go to the grocery store and be anointed by God to shop for her family's groceries if she will exercise her faith to release the anointing.

I believe there is an anointed sleep we can enjoy when we go to bed at night. However, if a person lies in bed and thinks of some situation that is full of strife, he or she is not likely to sleep well due to fretful dreams or tossing and turning all night.

I believe there is an anointing to go to your workplace and enjoy being there. The anointing will also help you do your job with ease. Again, if you have strife with your boss or with other employees, the anointing will be blocked. Whether the strife is open or hidden within your heart, the effect is the same.

So, keep strife out so that you can live by the anointing. God has given the anointing to you to help you in all you do. Stay peaceful and calm; be quick to forgive, slow to anger, patient, and kind. Protect the anointing in your life, and sow good seeds by helping others do the same. In so doing, you will reap a harvest in your own time of need.

Trust in Him Think of a time when you have felt God's Spirit on you—when time has flown by as you enjoyed what you were doing and did it with ease. Everything you do can feel just like that when you live in peace and harmony, trusting God's anointing to be unleashed in you for all things.

February 27

Protect the Peace in Your Life

Strive to live in peace with everybody and pursue that consecration and holiness without which no one will [ever] see the Lord. Exercise foresight and be on the watch to look [after one another], to see that no one falls back from and fails to secure God's grace.

HEBREWS 12:14–15

We can help our loved ones walk in peace by maintaining peace, especially when we know they are already under pressure. For instance, my family knows that just before one of my conferences, I am busy meditating on what God has given me to minister that day. I have asked them to help me by trying to keep the atmosphere peaceful.

We can help each other to avoid strife by being a little more sensitive to one another's needs. For example:

- When a husband comes home from an especially trying day at the office, his wife can minister peace to him by directing the children into an activity that creates a calmer atmosphere rather than a chaotic one.
- When a wife has been cleaning and cooking all day for a special holiday family get-together the next day, her husband can

minister peace to her by taking the children somewhere for the evening so that she can have a nice long block of quiet time.
- If a child has been taking final exams for a week and is already under stress, the parents might choose to withhold correction for a messy room or leaving a bike out on the driveway until the stress of the exams has ended.

It's important to know when you are most likely to succumb to conflict so that you can protect the peace and experience God's power in all of your life.

Trust in Him When are you most likely to feel stressed? What can you do to protect the peace in your life and keep strife out? Trust God to provide you with His divine strategy for being a peacemaker wherever you go.

February 28

The Incredible Promise of Peace

Everything that the Father has is Mine. That is what I meant when I said that He [the Spirit] will take the things that are Mine and will reveal (declare, disclose, transmit) it to you. JOHN 16:15

What an incredible promise Jesus makes to us in this Scripture. *Everything* the Father has is yours through Jesus. His Kingdom is one of righteousness, peace, and joy. Supernatural peace and joy, which are not based on positive or negative circumstances, belong to you as a believer.

Look at what John 14:27 says: "Peace I leave with you; My [own] peace I now give and bequeath to you. Not as the world gives do I give to you. Do not let your hearts be troubled, neither let them be afraid. [Stop allowing yourselves to be agitated and disturbed; and do not permit yourselves to be fearful and intimidated and cowardly and unsettled.]"

In essence, Jesus was saying, *"I am giving you My peace. I am going away, and the thing I desire to leave you is My peace."* His special peace is a wonderful possession. How valuable is peace? What is it worth?

Peace was worth the shedding of His blood. The prophet Isaiah said, "But He was wounded for our transgressions, He was bruised for our guilt and iniquities; the chastisement [needful to obtain] peace and well-being for us was upon Him, and with the stripes [that wounded] Him we are healed and made whole" (Isa. 53:5).

Jesus became the blood sacrifice that atoned for and completely removed your sin in order for you to live in peace. God's will for you is that you live in peace with Him, with yourself, and with others. Peace and enjoyment of life go hand in hand. You can enjoy life more with an abundance of peace.

Are you experiencing supernatural peace and joy? If not, remember the promise Jesus made to you and receive it. Reclaim the peace and joy that are rightfully yours.

Trust in Him Do you need to claim what is rightfully yours? God's will for you is that you live in peace with Him, with yourself, and with others. Trust that He wants you to have peace in the midst of your circumstances—whether they are good or bad.

March 1

Let Peace Decide

And let the peace (soul harmony which comes) from Christ rule (act as umpire continually) in your hearts [deciding and settling with finality all questions that arise in your minds, in that peaceful state] to which as [members of Christ's] one body you were also called [to live]. And be thankful (appreciative), [giving praise to God always].

COLOSSIANS 3:15

God wants you to live in peace; He wants to unleash His power and His blessings in your life. But the final choice is yours.

In baseball, an umpire makes the decision that settles the matter. Each team may believe the call should be in its own favor, but it is the umpire who makes the final decision. And once he does, that ends the matter.

Let peace be the umpire that has the deciding vote in the choices you make. If something does not bring you peace, cast it out. Don't live only for the moment. Use wisdom to make choices now that will satisfy you later on. When you are having a difficult time hearing from God or being able to decide what you should do in a certain situation, follow peace.

You have a unique call upon your life. You are an important part of the body of Christ. God has prearranged for you to have a powerful and productive life. Jesus paid for it. It is yours unless you allow the devil to steal it from you.

Make a decision today: *"I am finished with upset and turmoil; peace is mine, and I am going to enjoy it now,"* and begin to live in peace. Keep conflict out of your life; out of your thoughts, words, and attitudes; out of your relationships. Choose life! Choose peace!

Trust in Him Do you trust that God can speak to you through peace? God wants to unleash His power and blessings in you, so make peace the umpire of your life.

March 2

Be Purposeful in What You Say

Death and life are in the power of the tongue, and they who indulge in it shall eat the fruit of it [for death or life]. PROVERBS 18:21

If we truly believe our words are filled with life or death, why don't we choose what we say more carefully? There is a time to talk and a time to keep silent. Sometimes the best thing we can say is nothing. When we do say something, it is wise to be purposeful in what we say.

I firmly believe if we do what we can do, God will do what we cannot do. We can control what comes out of our mouths with the help of the Holy Spirit and by applying principles of discipline. Even when we talk about our problems or the things that are bothering us, we can talk about them in a positive and hopeful way.

One time I was having some back problems, and my daughter, Sandy, called to see how my back was. I told her it was still hurting, but I was thankful it wasn't as bad as it could have been. I said, "*I am sleeping well, and that is a positive thing.*" In other words, I didn't deny the problem, but I made an effort to have a positive outlook. I was determined to look at what I do have and not just at what I don't have. I believed in time the backache would be taken care of, and I believed that until then, God would give me the strength to do what I needed to do.

If you will make a decision that you are going to say as little as possible about your problems and disappointments in life, they won't dominate your thoughts and your mood. And if you talk as much as possible about your blessings and hopeful expectations, your frame of mind will match them. Be sure each day is filled with words that fuel joy, not anger, depression, bitterness, and fear. Talk yourself into a better mood! Find something positive to say in every situation.

Trust in Him Trust God to give you the strength to do what you need to do with a positive attitude no matter how you feel. Talk yourself into a better mood if you have to!

March 3

Self-Control Is a Fruit of the Spirit

But the fruit of the Spirit is love, joy, peace, patience, kindness, goodness, faithfulness, gentleness, and self-control.

GALATIANS 5:22–23 NIV

It's no wonder we humans want to control things... there's so much that's out of our control! But unfortunately, rather than trying to control ourselves, we usually try to control our circumstances or others around us.

I spent years trying to control the people in my life and my circumstances because I was afraid of being hurt or taken advantage of. But the only thing I achieved was constant frustration and anger. It took me a long time to realize that people respond very defensively when we try to control them. Everyone has a God-given right to freedom of choice, and they resent anyone who tries to take that from them. I finally realized that what I was doing was ungodly, and therefore it was never going to work. Not only would I never have peace because of my behavior, but I was also alienating most of the people I wanted to have relationships with.

God desires that we use the wonderful tools He has supplied us with to control ourselves instead of trying to control people and things. He has given us His Word, His Holy Spirit, and a wide variety of good fruit that we can develop. Self-control is actually a fruit of the Spirit-led life. If you have a tendency toward wanting to control the people and circumstances in your life, I want to strongly suggest that you give it up and turn your focus onto developing your self-control.

Although learning to control ourselves requires patience and endurance, it is well worth it in the end. Our circumstances can have much less control over us if our response to trouble is to use self-control.

Trust in Him When was the last time you tried to control someone else's behavior? Next time you're tempted to do so, turn your focus onto developing your own self-control, and put your trust in God to change the other person if He wants to.

March 4

You Can Control Your Anger Before It Controls You

He who is slow to anger is better than the mighty, he who rules his [own] spirit than he who takes a city. PROVERBS 16:32

Many Christians are confused about anger. They think that as godly individuals they should never get angry. Anger can be an involuntary response whether we want to feel it or not. A person with damaged emotions from past trauma or abuse may, and probably will, respond in a self-protective mode and display anger more easily than someone who was never mistreated. Thankfully, through God's help those damaged emotions can be healed, and we can learn to have more balanced and reasonable responses to people, things, and situations.

God's Word says, "When angry, do not sin" (Eph. 4:26). I recall one morning as I was preparing to go to preach, Dave and I got into an argument. I was studying and he said something to me that made me blaze up quickly with anger. We said some unkind words to each other, and then he left for work. I continued to think angry thoughts and have angry feelings. Then my anger turned into guilt, and I started thinking, *How can I possibly go to church and tell others how to conduct their lives according to Scripture if I cannot control my anger?* The feelings of guilt not only continued but they intensified. As the pressure mounted, I started to feel almost frantic when suddenly I heard God whisper in my heart, *"Feeling anger is not a sin; it is what you do with it that becomes sin."* That was one of the first lessons God gave me in understanding that emotions cannot be expected to merely go away because we have become Christians, but rather we are to learn how to manage them.

Controlling the passion of anger, especially if you have an aggressive and outspoken nature, can be one of the more challenging things you will face in life, but controlling it is certainly possible with God's help.

Trust in Him Will you make a decision not to let anger control you and your actions? Trust God with your emotions and He will teach you how to manage them.

March 5

Tell God How You Feel

Do not ever let your wrath (your exasperation, your fury or indignation) last until the sun goes down.

EPHESIANS 4:26

Anger expressed inappropriately is a problem, but so is repressed anger. Anger that is stuffed inside and not dealt with properly will eventually come out one way or another. It may show up in depression, anxiety, or any of a variety of other negative emotions—but it will come out. It can even manifest in sickness and disease. If we don't deal with our anger quickly, we will eventually either explode or implode.

The right way to express anger is to talk to God. Tell Him all about the way you feel and ask Him to help you manage the feelings properly. Talk to a professional or a mature friend if necessary, but do not pretend you're not angry when you are. That's not managing your emotions—that is ignoring them, and it is dangerous.

One thing that helps me deal properly with anger is to realize that sometimes God permits people to irritate me in order to help me grow in patience and unconditional love. None of the fruit of the Spirit develops without something to make us exercise them. Ouch! I wish I could magically have all these wonderful fruits working full force in my life without any effort on my part, but that is just not the way it works. The offending person's bad behavior is not right, but God often uses their behavior as sandpaper in our lives, to polish our rough edges. He is more concerned about changing our character than He is about changing our circumstances.

If I get angry when someone does something to me that's wrong, is my anger any less wrong than the wrong they committed? I think not. Sometimes their wrongdoing merely exposes my weakness and I am able to repent and ask God to help me overcome it. Be determined to get something good out of every trial you face in life, and don't let the sun go down on your anger.

Trust in Him **Are you angry about anything or at anyone? If your answer is yes, begin controlling that emotion right now, deal with it properly, and trust God to deliver you from your circumstances in His timing.**

March 6

One Presses You Down, the Other Lifts You Up

I acknowledged my sin to You, and my iniquity I did not hide. I said, I will confess my transgressions to the Lord [continually unfolding the past till all is told]—then You [instantly] forgave me the guilt and iniquity of my sin. **PSALM 32:5**

We must learn the difference between condemnation and conviction. Condemnation presses us down and manifests as a heavy burden that requires us to pay for our errors. Conviction is the work of the Holy Spirit, showing us that we have sinned and inviting us to confess our sins in order to receive forgiveness and God's help to improve our behavior in the future. Condemnation makes the problem worse; conviction is intended to lift us out of it.

When you feel guilty, the first thing to do is ask yourself if you are guilty according to God's Word. Perhaps you are. If so, confess your sin to God; turn away from that sin and don't repeat it. If you need to apologize to someone you have wronged, do it. Then... forgive yourself and let go of it! God already forgave you, and if you refuse to do the same, then you'll miss out on the joy of redemption that God wants us all to experience.

Sometimes you may well find that you are *not* guilty according to God's Word. For example, I can recall feeling guilty when I tried to rest. For years I drove myself incessantly to work, work, work because I felt good when I was accomplishing something and felt guilty if I was enjoying myself. That thinking is totally wrong according to God's Word. Even He rested from His work of creation, and He has invited us to enter His rest. The guilt I felt when I tried to rest was unscriptural, irrational, and downright ridiculous. When I stopped believing my feelings alone and started truly examining them in the light of God's Word, I stopped feeling guilty.

Trust God and His Word to reveal to you when your guilt is false and your thinking is wrong.

Trust in Him What makes you feel guilty? What does God's Word say about the situation? Stop believing your feelings that condemn you, and put your trust in His Word that convicts.

March 7

It's No Surprise to God

Fear not [there is nothing to fear], for I am with you...

ISAIAH 41:10

One of the strongest and most persistent fears that people experience is the fear that they won't have what they need. We want to feel safe in every area of life. But we're constantly attacked with the fear that we won't have what we need—whether it's finances, relationships, or the ability to do what God has called us to.

More than any other command in Scripture, God tells us not to fear. God never promises us a trouble-free life, but He does promise us His presence and the strength (mental, physical, and emotional) we require to get through our troubles.

Several years ago, a friend of mine went in for a routine checkup and learned days later that her doctor feared she might have non-Hodgkin's lymphoma, the most aggressive form of the disease. More tests were needed, and she was told it might take two or three weeks before a confirmed diagnosis could be reached.

I asked my friend how she got through those weeks of uncertainty and if she was afraid. *"Yes, I was afraid,"* she said. *"But I also knew that whatever the outcome was, it would be no surprise to God."* Then she said something else that might be of help to you. She told me that she realized if she worried for three weeks and then learned that she had lymphoma, she would have wasted three valuable weeks of her life. And if she worried for three weeks and learned that she did not have lymphoma, she would have still wasted three valuable weeks of her life. *"Believe it or not,"* she said, *"I didn't lose a minute's sleep for those twenty-one days."*

When the tests finally came back, my friend learned that she did indeed have non-Hodgkin's lymphoma. She had surgery and endured many months of chemo. I'm pleased to tell you that, ten years later, she's in terrific health. And she didn't waste three valuable weeks.

Trust in Him What are you afraid of? No matter what you are going through, it's no surprise to God. He's not unsure of what's around the corner or unprepared for whatever you're going through. Put your trust in Him and be confident in His plans for your life.

March 8

Are You Using Your Faith?

. . . Think of yourself with sober judgment, in accordance with the measure of faith God has given you. ROMANS 12:3 NIV

It may sound spiritual to say, *"I am full of faith,"* but are you *using* your faith? Faith is released by praying, saying, and doing whatever God asks us to do.

Praying. Most of us believe that prayer is powerful, so that should always be our first response. We invite God to get involved in our situations through our prayers. The Bible says tremendous power is made available through the prayers of a righteous man. Since we have been given the righteousness of God through our faith in Christ, we can come boldly to the throne of grace, and by faith, ask for help in plenty of time to meet our need (see Heb. 4:16). Don't merely pray for the problem to go away, or that you will get something you need or desire, but also pray that God will strengthen you during your waiting period. Pray that you will have the grace to wait with a good attitude. A good attitude glorifies God and is a good witness of our faith to others.

Saying. After we have prayed, it's important that we talk as if we truly believe God is working in our favor. We don't have to deny the existence of the problem, but we should talk about it as little as possible. It is also very important to include in our conversation that we believe God is involved and we are expecting a breakthrough. Hold fast your confession of faith in God!

Doing. The third ingredient in releasing your faith is to do whatever you believe God is asking you to do. Obedience is a key to our victory and shows that we have faith in God. Sometimes He even asks us to do nothing, and in that case, nothing is what we need to do.

If we are hearers of the Word and not doers, we are deceiving ourselves through reasoning that is contrary to the truth (see James 1:22).

Satan will use fear to steal our destiny if we allow him to, but our faith has more power than fear when it is released.

Trust in Him Are you using the faith God has given you? Release your faith by praying, saying, and doing, while you put your trust in Him.

March 9

God Wants You to Be You

And Moses said to God, Who am I, that I should go to Pharaoh and bring the Israelites out of Egypt? EXODUS 3:11

When God called Moses to lead the Israelites out of Egypt and into the Promised Land, Moses gave one excuse after another as to why he could not obey. All his excuses were rooted in fear. When Moses finally did take a step of faith, which manifested in obedience, he was used mightily by God.

What do you think of yourself? I encourage you to work with the Holy Spirit to see yourself the way God sees you—as a unique and powerful child of God. There is no power without confidence. Are you afraid God is not pleased with you? Do you regularly inventory all your faults, past failures, and weaknesses, and then feel weak like Moses did due to fear? If you do, then you are focusing on the wrong things. God gives us His power (grace) to enable us to do what is needed in spite of our weaknesses.

I experienced a lot of fear about myself, so if you are in that place right now, I can assure you that I know how you "feel." But, I am encouraging you to remember that your feelings don't convey truth; only God's Word does that. You may feel you are not what you are supposed to be, that you are strange or unusual, but the truth is we are all uniquely created by God for a special purpose and should learn how to enjoy ourselves.

I wasted some years trying to be like other people I knew, but I found that God won't help us be anyone other than ourselves. Relax, learn to love yourself, and don't be afraid that you won't be able to do what you need to do. The truth is that none of us can do what we need to do without God's help. If we look at only what we think we can do, we will all be frightened; but if we look at Jesus and focus on Him, He will give us the courage to go forward even in the presence of fear.

Trust in Him Are you focusing on the wrong thing? Start focusing instead on God's Word and learn to love yourself. He knew what He was doing when He made you. Be confident in His design. And trust Him to provide everything you need to be able to do what you need to do.

March 10

God Cares for You and Wants to Comfort You

When the righteous cry for help, the Lord hears, and delivers them out of all their distress and troubles. The Lord is close to those who are of a broken heart and saves such as are crushed with sorrow . . .

PSALM 34:17–18

I believe God mourns with us when we suffer a great loss. After all, when Jesus taught us to pray, He told us to call God "Abba," which is best translated as "Daddy." What daddy doesn't ache when his little boy comes home defeated after striking out at his Little League game? What mother doesn't feel her own heart break as her little girl comes home from school having been taunted on the playground? In the overall scheme of things, these are tiny losses and hurts, and the parent knows that. But the pain of seeing your child suffering is piercing nonetheless.

Immediately after teaching the disciples to pray what we know as the

Lord's Prayer, Jesus asked, "What man is there of you, if his son asks him for a loaf of bread, will hand him a stone? Or if he asks for a fish, will hand him a serpent?" (Matt. 7:9–10). In other words, because He is our Father, God suffers when we suffer. And while He could change our circumstances in an instant, more often than not, He doesn't. But when He sees His child suffer, He suffers, too.

When you are feeling loss and sorrow, ask God to hold you in the hollow of His hand, to whisper His comfort and to stroke your head, like a parent fussing over his fevered child. You may or may not *feel* that comfort, but God's Word is true, and so is He.

Trust in Him It may take a little time to get used to, but think of God as your "Daddy," the One you run to for comfort and the One Who cares. If you haven't had positive experiences with the father figures in your life, let God redeem that role for you as He has done for me. You can trust His Word that promises: "the Lord hears" (Ps. 34:17) and "He will never leave you nor forsake you" (Deut. 31:8 NIV).

March 11

The Righteous Shall Inherit the Land

For I was envious of the foolish and arrogant when I saw the prosperity of the wicked. PSALM 73:3

Sometimes we see the wicked succeeding and getting away with evil and it discourages us. As children of God, we expect to be blessed more than those who are not serving God. We might paraphrase a portion of Psalm 73 this way: *"It looked to me as if the wicked were better off than the righteous, until I realized God's patience does run out and He will deal with them."*

The Bible emphatically states that the wicked in the end will be cut off, but the righteous shall inherit the land. I don't think "the end" necessarily means the end of the world or the end of our lives. I think it means when all is said and done, in due time (God's time), the blessings of the child of God will surpass those of the wicked. The Word of God says in Galations 6:9 that if we refuse to become weary in well doing, in due time we shall reap if we don't faint.

It is a serious mistake to look at what other people have and compare it to what you have. God has an individual and unique plan for each of us, and comparison only tends to be a source of discouragement or pride. If we feel we are better off than others, we may become prideful (thinking more highly of ourselves than we should); if we feel they are better off than us, we may become discouraged and even depressed.

It is vital that you learn to accept and respect the person God made you to be. All of our behaviors may be far from what they need to be, but if we are willing to change, God will keep working with us, and every day we will get better and better in every way. Don't despise yourself because of your imperfections; instead, learn to celebrate your successes, even small ones.

Trust in Him Have you seen someone do something wrong and get away with it, or even be rewarded for it? Don't get discouraged or depressed when it seems like others are successfully getting away with evil. Continue to do what you know is right and trust God to work it out in the end.

March 12

Forgiveness Is Yours to Receive and to Give

Be gentle and forbearing with one another and, if one has a difference (a grievance or complaint) against another, readily pardoning each other; even as the Lord has [freely] forgiven you, so must you also [forgive]. COLOSSIANS 3:13

From Genesis to Revelation, we read of God's forgiveness toward us and of our need to forgive others. It is one of the main themes of the Bible. We're very eager to receive forgiveness, but we often find it extremely difficult to offer others the forgiveness that we have freely received from God. We may want to forgive, try to forgive, and pray to be able to forgive, and yet we remain bitter, resentful, and filled with angry and unforgiving thoughts. Why? If we want to forgive, why is it so difficult to do so?

The truth is, forgiveness hurts. It's painful. Fortunately, you can learn how to manage your emotions rather than allowing them to manage you. What can you expect from your emotions once you begin to operate in forgiveness toward yourself or others? God is ready and willing to forgive you, but are you equally ready and willing to receive His forgiveness? Your emotions can get in the way. You may not "feel" worthy of receiving such a wonderful and undeserved gift from God. You may "feel" you need to somehow pay for what you have done wrong. You may "feel" you must sacrifice in some way in order to pay for your sins. If you do feel that way, I totally understand and can even say it is quite normal, but I also must say it is not God's will for you.

I persecuted myself for many years trying to pay a debt that Jesus had already paid. Over time I've come not just to understand but to receive the truth that Jesus paid the price and took on Himself the ultimate hurt so I wouldn't have to. You and I can't pay a debt that has already been paid—the only thing we can do is receive it or reject it. When we do learn to freely receive God's forgiveness, then it is easier to let it flow through us to others.

Trust in Him Forgiveness hurts, but Jesus took that hurt so we could learn to forgive through Him. What's the hardest thing you've ever been challenged to forgive? No matter how much it hurts, trust God and forgive—you'll find His freedom and joy on the other side.

March 13

Three Things That Help Me Forgive

And whenever you stand praying, if you have anything against anyone, forgive him and let it drop (leave it, let it go), in order that your Father Who is in heaven may also forgive you your [own] failings and shortcomings and let them drop. MARK 11:25

The first thing that really helps me forgive is to remember this: *God forgives me for much more than I will ever have to forgive others for.* We may not do what others have done to us, but then again we may do things that are worse. In God's Kingdom sin does not come in sizes like small, medium, and large; sin is just sin! Do yourself a favor and forgive quickly and freely (without expectation or stipulation). The longer you hold a grudge, the more difficult it is to let it go.

The second thing that helps me forgive is to *think of God's mercy.* Mercy is the most beautiful gift we can give or receive. It cannot be earned and is not deserved—otherwise, it wouldn't be mercy. I like to think of mercy as looking beyond *what* was done wrong and on to *why* it was done. Many times people do a hurtful thing and don't know why they are doing it, or they may not even realize they are doing it. I was hurt so badly in my childhood that I in turn frequently hurt others with my harsh words and attitudes. But I did not realize I was being harsh; because life had been so hard and painful for me, that harshness had become part of me.

The third thing that helps me forgive others is to remember that *if I stay angry, I am giving Satan a foothold in my life* (see Eph. 4:26–27). When I forgive, I am keeping Satan from gaining an advantage over me (see 2 Cor. 2:10–11). If I don't forgive, I am poisoning my own soul with bitterness that will surely work its way out in some kind of bad behavior or attitude. One of the most valuable things I have learned is that I am doing myself a favor when I forgive.

Trust in Him Is there someone or something you need to forgive? Do yourself a favor and forgive quickly and freely. Trust God's forgiveness and mercy to be examples for how you should treat others.

March 14

First, Do What Is Right

Invoke blessings upon and pray for the happiness of those who curse you, implore God's blessing (favor) upon those who abuse you [who revile, reproach, disparage, and high-handedly misuse you].

LUKE 6:28

When we make a decision to forgive, we probably won't feel like forgiving. After all, we have been treated unjustly, and it hurts. But doing the right thing while we feel wronged is extremely important to our overall spiritual growth. It also glorifies God.

For many years I tried to forgive people when they hurt or offended me, but since I still had negative feelings toward them, I assumed I wasn't successful in the forgiveness journey. Now I realize that no matter how I feel, if I keep praying for the person who injured me and bless rather than curse him or her, I am on my way to freedom from destructive emotion. To curse means to speak evil of, and to bless means to speak well of. When someone has hurt us, we can refuse to speak evil of them, even if we're tempted to do so. We can also bless them by talking about their good qualities and the good things they have done. If we look only at the mistakes people make, we won't be able to like them. But looking at their whole lives gives us a more balanced picture of them.

You cannot wait to forgive someone who hurt you until you feel warm and loving toward that person. You'll probably have to do it while you are still hurting—when forgiving is the last thing you feel like doing—but doing it puts you in the "God league." It puts you squarely on the road that is "narrow (contracted by pressure)," but leads to the way of life (see Matt. 7:14). It puts you on the road that Jesus Himself traveled on. Don't forget that one of the last things He did was forgive someone who didn't deserve forgiveness, and He did it while hanging on a cross being crucified (see Luke 23:43). I think some of the last things that Jesus did were specially designed to help us remember how important those things are.

Trust in Him You may want to feel better first, but God wants you to do what is right first, which is to forgive. When you do, you are putting your trust in God.

March 15

Controlling Your Emotions During Crisis

Whatever happens, conduct yourselves in a manner worthy of the gospel of Christ. PHILIPPIANS 1:27 NIV

I know people who have been sick for an extended period of time and have the most beautiful attitudes. They never complain, are not grouchy, don't act as if the world owes them something, and they don't blame God or even feel sorry for themselves. But I also know people with the same circumstances who talk only about their illnesses, medical appointments, and how hard it all is for them. They are easily offended, bitter, and resentful. Every situation in life requires making a decision about how we are going to respond, and if we respond the way God would, then our trials will be much easier to handle.

Perhaps you have never thought about how important it is to manage your emotions during times of crisis. Most of us think, *I can't help how I act right now; I am having a hard time, and that is all there is to it*. That is a normal human reaction, but with God on our side helping us, we don't have to behave the way a "normal" person would. Satan is our enemy, and his goal is to get us so emotionally rattled that we say things that will provide him with an opening into our lives. Or he hopes we will make unwise decisions during painful times and create messes that we will have to deal with for a long, long time afterward.

I have believed for years that if I can hold my tongue and remain emotionally stable during times of difficulty, then I am honoring God and letting the devil know he is not going to control me. I'm not always successful, but I'm certainly a lot better than I once was. As I often say, *"I am not where I need to be, but thank God I am not where I used to be."* I am still growing, but at least I've learned the importance of managing my emotions. There is no doubt it is more difficult to manage your emotions when you're sick or going through a crisis, but hopefully you are learning it is possible.

Trust in Him Don't let circumstances defeat you before you even try to conquer them. Decide now that you will manage your emotions during times of crisis. Trust that God is on your side, and His grace is sufficient to meet your every need.

March 16

Eliminate Stress and Fill Your Life with God's Best

Peace I leave with you; My [own] peace I now give and bequeath to you. Not as the world gives do I give to you. Do not let your hearts be troubled, neither let them be afraid. JOHN 14:27

Nothing harms us emotionally the way stress does. We might say that anxiety is emotions out of control. When someone experiences anxiety, most of the time it's because their emotions have been stressed to the point that they are no longer functioning healthily. There are many situations that cause anxiety. The death of a spouse or child, divorce, and job loss are major events; however, not all the reasons are that serious. A lot of anxiety is caused simply by taking on more than we can handle.

I used to feel constantly overwhelmed due to stress, but it was because my schedule was unreasonable. And—even worse—I thought I was doing it for God. It is amazing to me now when I look back at how deceived I was. Always remember that if Satan cannot get you to *not* work for God, then he will try to get you to *overwork* for God. He really doesn't care which end of being out of balance we are on, because either one causes trouble.

The simple answer to living a life you can enjoy is to learn God's ways and follow them. Jesus said, "I am the Way" (John 14:6), and that means He will show us how to live properly. The answers we need are in God's Word, and we should make a decision that we will not only read the Bible, but we will obey it. If we refuse to make that decision and follow through, we will keep feeling stressed until we break.

Start asking God what you can eliminate from your life that is not producing good fruit. It may even be some good things that are just not the best things for you. Something can be right for us in one season of our lives and not right at all in another season. Follow your heart, and you will accomplish a lot of fruitful things and still have energy left over to enjoy the fruit of your labor.

Trust in Him What seemingly good things are crowding your life and keeping you from God's best? Decide that you will simplify your life and live with peace, not stress. Trust that God wants you to have the time to enjoy your life.

March 17

What Makes You Happy?

I delight to do Your will, O my God; yes, Your law is within my heart.
PSALM 40:8

What do you do that makes you really happy? People go on vacations, buy things, get married, get divorced, have kids, and change jobs searching for happiness. We even do things we don't like doing, just so we can be happy with the end result. A woman may not like to clean house, but she looks at her clean house and feels happy, so week after week she cleans it. Actually, I cannot think of anything we do that does not have happiness as a motivator.

There are many things that make me happy, but I have found obeying God is the number one thing that makes me happy—maybe not right away, but always in the end. When I am flowing with God I have a deep contentment that nothing else compares to. I may not always like what He asks me to do or not to do, but if I resist and rebel, I will not be happy deep down in my soul.

I think some people have a perception that Christianity is cold, impersonal, and joyless. That's because many who call themselves Christians have sour attitudes and sad faces. They are critical of others and quick to judge. Those of us who love and serve God and His Son, Jesus Christ, should be the happiest people on earth. We should be able to enjoy everything we do, simply because we know that God is present. It was a great day for me when I finally discovered through studying the Bible that God wants us to enjoy our lives (see John 10:10).

Be happy and enjoy all that you do through your relationship with Jesus. Since everyone simply wants to be happy, when they see you enjoying your life even in difficult circumstances, they will be open to learning about and receiving Jesus themselves.

Trust in Him What makes you happy? Does anything on your list offer the long-lasting happiness that obeying God does? God wants you to be happy and enjoy life. The secret to long-lasting happiness is to trust and obey!

March 18

Make a Decision to Be Excited Every Day

Never lag in zeal and in earnest endeavor; be aglow and burning with the Spirit, serving the Lord. ROMANS 12:11

I make a point of trying to be excited about each day that God gives me. The psalmist David said this: "This is the day which the Lord has brought about; we will rejoice and be glad in it" (Ps. 118:24). The "we will" says it all. David made a decision that produced the feelings he wanted rather than waiting to see how he felt. For years I got up each day and waited to see how I felt, then I let those feelings dictate the course of my day. Now, I set my mind in the right direction and make decisions that I know will produce emotions I can enjoy.

Most of our days are rather ordinary. We all have moments in life that are amazing, but a lot of life is Monday, Tuesday, Wednesday, Thursday, Friday, Saturday, Sunday, and back to Monday all over again. Recently I stood in front of 225,000 people in Zimbabwe preaching the Gospel of Jesus Christ and teaching the Word of God. It was my birthday, and 225,000 people sang "Happy Birthday" to me, and that was rather cool. Yesterday I went to Target to buy new kitchen rugs and then to the grocery store, but I can honestly say that I enjoyed Zimbabwe and the grocery store equally. Zimbabwe was a once-in-a-lifetime event that was exciting, and one I will never forget, but having another day to enjoy God is also exciting, even if the day is spent doing errands.

Everything we do is sacred if we do it unto the Lord and we believe

He is with us. Ask yourself right now if you truly believe God is with you. If your answer is yes, just think about how amazing that is, and my guess is that your enjoyment will increase immediately.

Trust in Him Have you decided to enjoy today? Trust that God is with you every day, in every moment—the big moments and the ordinary—and He wants you to enjoy them all.

March 19

Relax! God Is Working

Come to Me, all you who labor and are heavy-laden and overburdened, and I will cause you to rest. [I will ease and relieve and refresh your souls.] MATTHEW 11:28

Being relaxed feels wonderful. Being nervous, tense, and worried are not so wonderful. Why aren't more people relaxed? Jesus said if we are weary and overburdened, we should go to Him and He will give us rest, relaxation, and ease (see Matt. 11:28–29). Jesus wants to teach us the right way to live, which is different from the way most of the world lives.

It would be putting it mildly to say that I was an uptight woman for the first half of my life. I simply did not know how to relax, and it was due to me not being willing to completely trust God. I trusted God *for* things, but not *in* things. I kept trying to be the one in control. Even though God was in the driver's seat of my life, I kept one hand on the wheel just in case He took a wrong turn. Relaxation is impossible without trust!

If you know you can't fix the problem you have, then why not relax while God is working on it? It sounds easy, but it took many years for me to be able to do this. I know from experience that the ability to relax and go with the flow in life is dependent upon our willingness to trust God completely. If things don't go your way, instead of being upset, you can believe that getting your way was not what you needed. God knew that, so He gave you what was best for you, instead of what you wanted.

If you are waiting much longer than you had hoped to, you can get frustrated, angry, and upset, or you can say, "God's timing is perfect; He is never late. And my steps are ordered by the Lord." Now you can relax and simply go with the flow of what is happening in your life. When it comes to things that are out of our control, we can either ruin the day or relax and enjoy it while God is working on the situation. As long as we believe, God keeps working!

Trust in Him How relaxed are you? Your answer is directly related to how much you trust God. It may take you many years, like it did me, to fully trust Him, but each day will be better and better as you trust more and learn to relax.

March 20

Be Tender-Hearted

I will give them one heart [a new heart] and I will put a new spirit within them; and I will take the stony [unnaturally hardened] heart out of their flesh, and will give them a heart of flesh [sensitive and responsive to the touch of their God]... EZEKIEL 11:19

This Scripture means a lot to me because I was a hard-hearted person due to the abuse I had suffered in the earlier years of my life. This Bible verse gave me hope that I could change. God gives us things in seed form and we must work with the Holy Spirit to bring them to full maturity. This is much like the fruit of the Spirit, which is in us but needs to be watered with God's Word and developed through use.

As believers in Jesus, we have tender hearts, but we can become hard-hearted if we are not careful in this area. I find that taking the time to really think about what people are going through in their particular situations helps me to have compassion. Jesus was moved by compassion, and we should also be moved to pray, or help in some way.

Empathy is a beautiful emotion and thankfully one we don't have to resist! Let's learn to resist evil emotions that poison our lives and embrace emotions we can enjoy that will bring glory to God. Emotions are a gift from God; in fact, they're a large part of what makes us human. Without them, life would be dull and we'd be like robots. Because emotions are a vulnerable part of us, Satan seeks to take advantage and make what God intended to be good things into evil things.

We are blessed that Jesus has redeemed every part of us, including our emotions. God's desire is that you enjoy the life He has provided for you, but that is impossible to do unless you learn how to control your feelings instead of letting them control you. With God's help, you can do it!

Trust in Him Open your heart to a need you see in your family, community, or the world. Pray and ask God if you can help in some way. Embrace empathy—the emotion that longs to help when you see a need. God intended emotions to be good things, and they can be if you will trust them to Him and not let them control you.

March 21

Giving, Not Getting, Is the Way

Give, and [gifts] will be given to you; good measure, pressed down, shaken together, and running over, will they pour into [the pouch formed by] the bosom [of your robe and used as a bag]. For with the measure you deal out [with the measure you use when you confer benefits on others], it will be measured back to you. LUKE 6:38

Sin exists whenever a person goes against God and His ways. We tend to live "backward"—exactly opposite of the way we should live. We live for ourselves and yet we never seem to end up with what satisfies us. We should live for others and learn the wonderful secret that what we give away comes back to us multiplied many times over. I like the way a famous doctor named Luke put it: "Give away your life; you'll find life given back, but not merely given back—given back with bonus and blessing. Giving, not getting, is the way. Generosity begets generosity" (Luke 6:38 The Message).

We don't have to be taught how to be selfish—we all come by it honestly. It's programmed into our nature. Everyone wants to be "number one," which automatically indicates a lot of people will be disappointed, since only one can be number one at any time in any given area. Only one person can be the number one runner in the world; only one can be the president of the company or the best-known actor or actress on stage or screen. Only one can be the top author or the best painter in the world. Although I believe we should all be goal-oriented and do our best, I don't believe we should want everything for ourselves and care nothing about other people.

Selfishness does not make life work the way it was intended to work and is definitely not God's will for mankind; it's ruthless. You can't play games with it and hope to produce any lasting change. We need to declare war on selfishness.

Trust in Him In which of your relationships, attitudes, and habits are you being selfish? Declare war on those areas, die to yourself, and put your trust in God's pattern of generous giving that says, "Giving, not getting, is the way."

March 22

Love Is the Answer

But be doers of the Word [obey the message], and not merely listeners to it, betraying yourselves [into deception by reasoning contrary to the Truth]. JAMES 1:22

Love must be more than a theory or a word; it has to be action. It has to be demonstrated. God is love, and love has always been His idea. He came to love us to teach us how to love Him, and to teach us how to love ourselves and others.

When we do this, life is beautiful; when we don't, nothing works properly. Love is the answer to selfishness because love gives while selfishness takes. We must be delivered from ourselves, and Jesus came for that very purpose as we see in 2 Corinthians 5:15: "And He died for all, so that all those who live might live no longer to and for themselves, but to and for Him Who died and was raised again for their sake."

Recently, as I was pondering all the terrible problems in the world, such as millions of starving children, AIDS, war, oppression, human trafficking, incest, and much more, I asked God, *"How can You stand to see all that goes on in the world and do nothing?"* I heard God say in my spirit, *"I work through people. I am waiting for My people to rise up and do something."*

You may be thinking, as millions of others do, *I know the world has problems, but they are so massive—what can I do that will make a difference?* That is exactly the kind of thinking that has kept us paralyzed while evil continues to triumph. We must stop thinking about what we *cannot* do and begin to do what we *can* do.

Ask yourself: *"Will I continue being part of the problem or will I be part of the answer?"* I have decided to be part of the answer. Will you join me and let love be the central theme of your life?

Trust in Him What are you doing to make a difference in the world? God wants to use you. Trust Him to equip you to do what you can do, and He will do what you can't.

March 23

Show God's Love to His People

And you know that God anointed Jesus of Nazareth with the Holy Spirit and with power. Then Jesus went around doing good and healing all who were oppressed by the devil, for God was with him.

ACTS 10:38 NLT

I heard a story about a man who went to Russia with good intentions of telling people about the love of Jesus Christ. During his visit, many people were starving. When he found a line of people waiting hopefully to get bread for the day, he approached them with Gospel tracts in hand and began to walk the line telling them that Jesus loves them and handing each of them a tract with the salvation message on it. To be sure, he was trying to help, but one woman looked into his eyes and said bitterly, *"Your words are nice, but they don't fill my empty stomach."*

I have learned oftentimes people are hurting too badly to hear the good news that God loves them; they must experience it. And one of the best ways for those individuals to experience God's love is for us to meet their practical needs, in addition to telling them they are loved.

We must beware of thinking that words alone are enough. Jesus certainly preached the good news, but He also went about doing good and healing all who were oppressed (see Acts 10:38). Talking is not expensive, nor does it require much effort, but real love is costly. It cost God His only Son, and allowing real love to flow through us will also cost us. Perhaps we will have to invest some time, money, effort, or possessions—it will cost us something!

What can we do? We can care, we can be informed, we can pray, and we can take action. We can support ministries and organizations that are helping others, or if God asks us to, we can even choose to work in these arenas. If full-time work is not an option, we can consider doing something on a project basis or taking a short-term mission trip. God loves all people, and He is counting on us to do something about the hurt in the world.

Trust in Him Don't just tell people about God's love . . . show them. You can help feed the hungry, clothe the naked, care for the sick, and visit the prisoner (see Matt. 25:35–36). Trust God to show you how you can help meet the practical needs of His people so they can be open to receiving His love.

March 24

Whatever You Can Do Is Worth Doing

And the King will reply to them, Truly I tell you, in so far as you did it for one of the least [in the estimation of men] of these My brethren, you did it for Me. MATTHEW 25:40

When we look at the needs in the world today they are staggering. You may be thinking, *Joyce, what I can do won't even make a dent in the problems we have in the world.* I know how you feel, because I once felt the same way. But if we all think that way, nobody will do anything and nothing will change. Although our individual efforts may not solve the problems, together we can make a major difference. God won't hold us accountable for what we could not do, but He will hold us accountable for the things we could have done.

I had recently returned from a trip to India and was at the gym when a woman I often see there asked me if I really believed that all the effort required for these trips was solving anything since millions would still be starving, no matter how many we fed. I shared with her what God placed in my heart—something that forever settled the issue for me. If you or I were hungry because we hadn't eaten in three days and someone offered us one meal that would alleviate the pain in our stomachs for a day, would we take it and be glad to have it? Of course we would. And so are the people we help. We are able to set up ongoing programs for many of them, but there will always be those we can help only once or twice. Still, I know these outreaches are worth doing.

If we can give one hungry child one meal, it is worth doing. If we can help one person go without pain for one day, it is worth doing. I have resolved to always do what I can do and to remember what God said to me: *"If you can only relieve someone's pain one time for one hour, it is still worth doing."*

Trust in Him Has God planted an idea or a desire in your heart to help others in a specific way? Trust that whatever you can do is worth doing. Don't let the magnitude of the problem overwhelm you. God will show you what you can do—trust Him when He says it makes a difference.

March 25

Add Flavor Everywhere You Go

You are the salt of the earth, but if salt has lost its taste (its strength, its quality), how can its saltness be restored? It is not good for anything any longer but to be thrown out and trodden underfoot by men. MATTHEW 5:13

I think it's safe to say that most of what the world offers is tasteless—and I'm not talking about food. For example, most of the movies Hollywood produces and the way people treat each other in the world today are tasteless. Usually when we see any type of behavior that is in poor taste we are quick to blame "the world." We might say something like, *"What is the world coming to?"* Yet the phrase "the world" merely means the people who live in the world. If the world has lost its flavor, it is because people have become tasteless in their attitudes and actions.

Jesus said we are the salt of the earth (see Matt. 5:13). He also said we are the light of the world and should not hide our light (see Matt. 5:14).

Think of it this way: Each day as you leave your home, you can add God's light and flavor to any environment. You can bring joy to your workplace by being determined to consistently have a godly attitude, and through simple things like being thankful, patient, merciful, quick to forgive offenses, kind, and encouraging. Even simply smiling and being friendly is a way to bring flavor into a tasteless society.

Without love and all its magnificent qualities, life is tasteless and not worth living. I want you to try an experiment. Just think: *I am going to go out into the world today and spice things up.* Get your mind set before you ever walk out the door that you are going out as God's ambassador, and that your goal is to be a giver, to love people, and to add good flavor to their lives. The question each of us must answer is, "*What have I done today to make someone else's life better?*"

Trust in Him Determine to walk through life with a godly attitude, adding flavor everywhere you go. Trust God to take care of you while you sow good seed, making decisions that will be a blessing to others.

March 26

I Was Always on My Mind

He has sent me to bind up the brokenhearted, to proclaim freedom for the captives and release from darkness for the prisoners... ISAIAH 61:1 NIV

When I look back over the forty-five years Dave and I have been married, I am appalled at how selfish I have been, especially in the early years. I can honestly say I did not know any better. In the house where I grew up, all I ever saw was selfishness and I had nobody to teach me differently. Had I known how to be a giver instead of a taker, I am sure the early years of our marriage would have been much better than they were. Because of God in my life, I have seen things turn around and old wounds have been healed, but I wasted a lot of years that I can't get back.

In stark contrast to the way I was raised, Dave grew up in a Christian home. His mother was a godly woman who prayed and taught her children to give. As a result of his upbringing, Dave developed qualities I had never seen in my entire life until I met him. His example has been amazingly valuable to me. Had he not been very patient, which is an aspect of love, I am sure our marriage wouldn't have lasted, but I thank God it did. And after many years of marriage, I can honestly say it gets better all the time. I am happier now than I've ever been because I put more into the relationship than I ever have. I really enjoy seeing Dave do things he enjoys, and that's quite a contrast to all the years I was angry every time I didn't get "my way."

I was always on my mind, and nothing changed until I got fed up with my entire life being all about me, me, and more of me. Jesus came to open prison doors and set captives free (see Isa. 61:1). He set me free from many things, the greatest of which was myself. I have been set free from me! I continue to grow daily in this freedom, but I am thankful to realize that real joy is not found in getting my way all the time.

Trust in Him How do you respond when you don't get your way? Are you able to trust God to take care of you? Accept His invitation to set you free!

March 27

The Journey Toward Unselfishness

...I die daily [I face death every day and die to self].

1 CORINTHIANS 15:31

Selfishness is not learned behavior; we are born with it. The Bible refers to it as "sin nature." Adam and Eve sinned against God by doing what He told them not to do, and the sin principle they established was forever passed to every person who would ever be born. God sent His Son, Jesus, to die for our sins, and to deliver us from them. He came to undo what Adam did. When we accept Jesus as our Savior, He comes to live in our spirit, and if we allow that renewed part of us to rule our decisions, we can overcome the sin nature in our flesh. It doesn't go away, but the greater One Who lives in us helps us overcome it daily (see Gal. 5:16). That does not mean that we never sin, but we can improve and make progress throughout our lives.

I certainly cannot say I have overcome selfishness entirely—none of us can on this side of eternity. But that doesn't mean we don't do everything we can to grow closer to God and die to our selfishness. We can have hope of improving daily. I am on a journey and, although I may not arrive, I have determined that when Jesus comes to take me home He will find me pressing toward this goal (see Phil. 3:12–13).

The apostle Paul made the following statement: "...It is no longer I who live, but Christ (the Messiah) lives in me" (Gal. 2:20). Paul meant that he was no longer living for himself and his own will, but for God and His will. I was greatly encouraged when I discovered through study that Paul made this statement approximately twenty years *after* his conversion. Learning to live unselfishly was a journey for him, just as it is for everyone else. Paul also said, "...I die daily..." (1 Cor. 15:31). In other words, putting others first was a daily battle and required daily decisions. Each of us must decide how we will live and what we will live for; and there is no better time to do so than right now.

Trust in Him Are you pressing toward the goal of living for God rather than yourself? Dying to yourself is a process that you can improve daily. Trust God to give you the strength to die to yourself daily.

March 28

God Is Love

So we are Christ's ambassadors, God making His appeal as it were through us. We [as Christ's personal representatives] beg you for His sake to lay hold of the divine favor [now offered you] and be reconciled to God. 2 CORINTHIANS 5:20

I am sure you have heard John Donne's famous line, *"No man is an island."* These words are simply a way of expressing the fact that people need each other and affect each other. Our lives can and do affect other people, and we need to be sure we affect them in positive ways. Jesus told us to love one another because that is the only way the world will know He exists (see John 13:34–35).

God is love, and when we show love in our words and actions, we are showing people what God is like. Paul said we are God's ambassadors, His personal representatives, and He is making His appeal to the world through us (see 2 Cor. 5:20). Each time I think of that Scripture all I can say is, *"Wow! What a privilege and responsibility."*

One of the lessons I had to learn in life was that I could not have privilege without responsibility. That is one of the problems in our world today. People want what they are not willing to deserve. Selfishness says, *"Give it to me. I want it and I want it now."* Wisdom says, *"Do not give me anything I am not mature enough to handle properly."* The world is lacking in gratitude and, in large part, that's because we no longer want to wait or sacrifice for anything. I have found the things I am the most thankful for are the ones for which I had to work hardest and wait longest. God knows best when we are ready to receive His gifts and share them in a way that will make a positive impact on the world.

Trust in Him What effect is your life having on others? If you place your trust in God, and let His love shine through you, you can make a positive impact on the lives of many.

March 29

Be a Blessing Everywhere You Go

I APPEAL to you therefore, brethren, and beg of you in view of [all] the mercies of God, to make a decisive dedication of your bodies [presenting all your members and faculties] as a living sacrifice, holy (devoted, consecrated) and well pleasing to God, which is your reasonable (rational, intelligent) service and spiritual worship.

ROMANS 12:1

For most of my life, I woke up every day and lay in bed making plans for myself. I thought of what I wanted, what would be best for me, and how I could convince my family and friends to cooperate with my plans. I got up and went about the day with myself on my mind, and each time things did not go my way I became upset, impatient, frustrated, and even angry. I thought I was unhappy because I wasn't getting what I wanted, but I was actually unhappy because all I did was try to get what I wanted without any real concern for others. Do you ever behave this way?

Thankfully, I have discovered that the secret of joy is in giving my life away rather than trying to keep it, and now my mornings are quite different. This morning, before I began to work, I prayed and then took some time to think of all the people I knew I would come into contact with today. I then prayed through Romans 12:1, which speaks of dedicating ourselves to God as living sacrifices, offering up all our faculties to Him for His use.

As you think of the people you work with and will probably see today, ask the Lord to show you anything you might do for them. Set your mind to encourage them and be complimentary. Surely we can all find one nice thing to say to each person we meet. Simply trying to do so will help us keep our minds off ourselves. Trust the Lord to lead you as you go about your day.

Trust in Him If you want to dedicate yourself to God so He can use you to love and help others, say this prayer: "*Lord, I trust You with my eyes, ears, mouth, hands, feet, heart, finances, gifts, talents, abilities, time, and energy. Use me to be a blessing everywhere I go today.*" Now listen for God's leading to be a blessing throughout your day.

March 30

Seek to Do Good

See that none of you repays another with evil for evil, but always aim to show kindness and seek to do good to one another and to everybody. 1 THESSALONIANS 5:15

The Bible is filled with instructions for us to be active. The direction to be active instead of passive is rather simple, but millions of people totally ignore it. Maybe they think things will get better on their own. But nothing good happens accidentally. Once I learned that, my life changed for the better.

The Bible says we are to *seek* to be kind and good (see 1 Thess. 5:15). *Seek* is a strong word meaning "to crave, pursue, and go after." If we seek opportunities, we are sure to find them and that will protect us from being idle and unfruitful. We must ask ourselves if we are alert and active or passive and inactive? God is alert and active! I am glad He is; otherwise, things in our lives would deteriorate rapidly. God not only created the world and everything we see and enjoy in it, He also actively maintains it because He knows that good things do not simply occur; they happen as a result of right action (see Heb. 1:3).

God-inspired, balanced activity keeps us from being idle and unfruitful and thereby serves as a protection for us. Actively doing right things continuously will prevent us from doing wrong things.

Trust in Him **Are you pursuing goodness and kindness? Be alert and active, trusting God to inspire right action in your life while you *seek* to be kind and good.**

March 31

Remember the Source of All Truth

For we can do nothing against the Truth [not serve any party or personal interest], but only for the Truth [which is the Gospel].

2 CORINTHIANS 13:8

During the days when Jesus lived on earth, Pilate asked Him a question that has been raised through the centuries and is still being asked today: "What is Truth?" (John 18:38). Jesus had already answered this question plainly and simply: "I am the Way and the Truth and the Life" (John 14:6). When praying to God in John 17:17, Jesus also said, "Your Word is Truth." He not only knew the truth but when His own mind was being attacked by Satan, He spoke the truth of God's Word out loud (see Luke 4:1–13). This is one of the most effective ways to "cast down" wrong thoughts, reasons, theories, and imaginations. I look at it as interrupting the devil in the midst of his temptation.

We are partners with God. Our part is to trust Him, to know His Word and believe it, and His part is to do whatever needs to be done in every situation. We cannot know the Word of God unless we dedicate ourselves to diligent reading and studying. Nobody would expect to be a successful doctor without studying, so why should people expect to be strong in their faith without doing the same thing?

God's Word, the Bible, is truth. It teaches the truth; it teaches us a way to live that produces life. God's Word has stood the test of time and been proven in millions of people's lives over thousands of years. It works, if followed. I know this from years of personal experience and from the countless times I have seen other people's lives change in amazing ways simply because they believed and obeyed God's truth.

Trust in Him Are you doing your part to study God's Word, believe it, and trust Him? When you do, He will do the rest.

April 1

Worry or Trust? It's Your Choice

Lean on, trust in, and be confident in the Lord with all your heart and mind and do not rely on your own insight or understanding.
PROVERBS 3:5

Worry does no good and can impact your life in negative ways. I'm sure you have noticed how absolutely powerless you feel when you worry or you're anxious and troubled, because worry is indeed completely useless. It is a waste of time and energy because it never changes your circumstances.

I like to say worry is like sitting in a rocking chair, rocking back and forth; it's always in motion and it keeps you busy, but it never gets you anywhere. Worry keeps you and me from living in faith and steals our peace. When we worry, we are actually saying, "If I try hard enough I can find a solution to my problem," and that is the opposite of trusting God.

The cause of worry is simple: it's the failure to trust God to take care of the various situations in our lives. Most of us have spent our lives trying to take care of ourselves, and it takes time to learn how to trust God in every situation. You learn by doing it. You have to step out in faith, and as you do you will experience the faithfulness of God, and that makes it easier to trust Him the next time. Too often we trust our own abilities, believing we can figure out how to take care of our own problems. Yet most of the time, after all our worry and effort to go it alone, we come up short, unable to bring about suitable solutions. God, on the other hand, always has solutions for the things that make you anxious and worried.

Trusting Him allows you to enter His rest, and rest is a place of peace where you are able to enjoy life while waiting for Him to solve your problems. He cares for you; He will solve your problems and meet your needs, but you have to stop thinking and worrying about them.

Trust in Him There is no time like the present to begin learning a new way to live—less worrying, more trusting. This is the time to begin thinking and saying, *"I trust God completely; there is no need to worry!"*

April 2

Confidence: No More Pretending

...because of our faith in Him, we dare to have the boldness (courage and confidence) of free access (an unreserved approach to God with freedom and without fear). EPHESIANS 3:12

What is confidence? I believe confidence is all about being positive concerning what you can do and not worrying over what you can't do. Confident people do not concentrate on their weaknesses; they develop and maximize their strengths.

Let's say you are not a "numbers" kind of person. On a scale of 1 to 10, you might be a 3. You could obsess about your inability to "do the math." You could buy *Math for Dummies* and take a class at the community college. But your math obsession could eat up time that could be devoted to stuff you're an 8 or a 10 at—like teaching God's Word, creative writing, or rallying support for charity. In other words, you might rob time and effort from the 10s in your life just to bring a lowly

3 up to a mediocre 5. When you look at it this way, it's easy to see where you need to invest your efforts.

The world is not hungry for mediocrity. We really don't need a bunch of 4s and 5s running around, doing an average job in life. This world needs 10s. I believe everyone can be a 10 at something.

Confidence allows you and me to face life with boldness, openness, and honesty. It enables us to live without worry and to feel safe. It enables us to live authentically. We don't have to pretend to be somebody we're not, because we are secure in who we are—even if we're different from those around us. God has created every person in a unique way; yet, most people spend their lives trying to be like someone else and feeling miserable as a result. Trust me on this: God will never help you be some other person. He wants you to be you!

Trust in Him The world needs 10s, and God's designed you to be a 10 in something. Trust Him to develop your strengths. Think of a specific area of strength in your life—how can you move from 7 or 8 to 10?

April 3

Do It Deliberately

. . . If anyone intends to come after Me, let him deny himself [forget, ignore, disown, and lose sight of himself and his own interests] and take up his cross, and [joining Me as a disciple and siding with My party] follow with Me [continually, cleaving steadfastly to Me].

MARK 8:34

Jesus told us plainly what we need to do if we want to follow Him. The "cross" you and I are asked to carry in life is simply one of unselfishness. Most of us concentrate on what we can *get* in life, but we need to concentrate on what we can *give*. We think about what other people should do for us and often become angry because they do not give us what we want. Instead, we should think aggressively about what we can do for others and then trust God to meet our needs and fulfill our desires.

Please notice that I say we need to think *aggressively* about what we can do for others. Galatians 6:10 conveys the same meaning, encouraging us to "Be mindful to be a blessing." Simply put, to "be mindful" means to be intentional, to be purposeful and deliberate. God wants us to think on purpose and to make a point of being a blessing to others.

I do my best to be aggressive in thinking about who I can bless, and realizing I must give and help on purpose has been very beneficial to me. It did not come naturally. I had to learn to do it, but it has been one of the greatest, most rewarding lessons of my life. There are certainly times when I "feel" like being a blessing, but there are many times when I don't.

Sometimes I may also feel that people should be doing more for me, and in reality perhaps they should be, but that cannot be my concern. You cannot live by what you feel and ever have consistency and stability. Our ability to choose is greater than how we feel, and it is that ability we must activate. Be deliberate about loving others!

Trust in Him What specific thing can you do to bless someone in your life? Be deliberate—develop a plan to make this blessing a reality. When you live this way, you can trust that God will bless you, too.

April 4

Fear Is Not Going Away, So Do It Afraid!

God is with you in everything you do. GENESIS 21:22

Just because ordinary people take steps to accomplish extraordinary things does not mean that they do not feel fear. I believe the Old

Testament hero Esther felt fear when she was asked to leave her familiar, comfortable life and enter the king's harem so she could be used by God to save her nation. I believe Joshua felt fear when, after Moses died, he was given the job of taking the Israelites into the Promised Land.

I know I had fear when God called me to quit my job and prepare for ministry. I still remember the fear I felt then, but it frightens me more now to think of how my life would have turned out had I not faced the fear and pressed forward to do God's will. Fear does not mean you are a coward. It only means that you need to be willing to feel the fear and do what you need to do anyway. It's one of my favorite phrases: "Do it afraid!"

If I had let the fear I felt stop me, where would I be today? What would I be doing? Would I be happy and fulfilled? Or would I be sitting at home, depressed and wondering why my life has been such a disappointment? I believe a lot of unhappy people are individuals who have let fear rule their lives.

How about you, my friend? Are you doing what you really believe you should be doing at this stage in your life, or have you allowed fear and a lack of confidence to prevent you from stepping out into new things—or higher levels of old things? If you don't like your answer, then let me give you some good news: It is never too late to begin again! Don't spend one more day living a narrow life that has room for only you and your fears. Make a decision right now that you will learn to live boldly, aggressively, and confidently. Don't let fear rule you any longer.

Trust in Him Where has fear kept you from stepping out in faith? Don't wait for the fear to disappear; trust God and *do it afraid*!

April 5

Know That You Are Loved

Even as [in His love] He chose us [actually picked us out for Himself as His own] in Christ before the foundation of the world, that we should be holy (consecrated and set apart for Him) and blameless in His sight, even above reproach, before Him in love. For He foreordained us (destined us, planned in love for us) to be adopted (revealed) as His own children through Jesus Christ, in accordance with the purpose of His will [because it pleased Him and was His kind intent]... EPHESIANS 1:4–5

A confident person does not fear being unloved, because they know first and foremost that God loves them unconditionally. To be whole and complete, you and I need to know we are loved. Everyone desires and needs love and acceptance from God and others. Although not everyone will accept and love us, some will. I encourage you to concentrate on those who do love you and forget about those who don't. God certainly does love us, and He can provide others who do as well—if we'll look to Him and stop making bad choices about whom we bring into our circle of inclusion.

I believe we need to have what I call "divine connections." In other words, pray about your circle of friends. Don't just decide what social group you want to be part of and then try to get into it. Instead, follow the leading of the Holy Spirit in choosing who you want to be close to.

The first place to start if you need to be loved is with God. He is a Father who wants to shower love and blessings upon His children. If your natural father did not love you properly, you can now get from God what you missed in your childhood. Love is the healing balm that the world needs, and God offers it freely and continuously. His love is unconditional. He does not love us *if*; He simply and for all time loves us. He does not love us because we deserve it; He loves us because He is kind and wants to.

Trust in Him God chose you and loves you unconditionally. Thank Him for His love and ask Him to help you trust His Word and the people in your life who love and accept you for the gift that you are.

April 6

A Great Big Happy Life

It is more blessed (makes one happier and more to be envied) to give than to receive. ACTS 20:35

Since being good to people has been one of my personal goals, my "joy tank" never runs dry for very long. I have even discovered that when I do get sad or discouraged, I can begin to think on purpose about what I can do for someone else, and before long I am joyful again.

You may have heard many times that the Bible says, "It is more blessed to give than to receive" (Acts 20:35 NKJV). The Amplified Bible renders that verse this way: "It is more blessed (makes one happier and more to be envied) to give than to receive." You may know that verse, but do you really believe it? If you do, then you are probably doing your best to be a blessing everywhere you go. I must admit that, for many years, I could quote this verse, but I obviously didn't really believe it because I spent my time trying to be blessed rather than being a blessing.

I have now learned that we do not even know what "happy" is until we forget about ourselves, start focusing on others, and become generous givers. In order to be generous, we have to do more than simply plunk some change in a bucket during the holidays or give to the church once a week. Actually, I think learning to give in church should simply be practice for the way we should live our everyday lives. I do not just want to merely give offerings; I want to be a giver. I want to offer myself every day to be used for whatever God chooses. For this change to take place in my life I had to change my thinking. I had to think and say thousands of times, "I love people, and I enjoy helping them." This thought will be life-changing for you if you put it to work in your life.

As you become a generous giver, you will be amazed at how happy you will be and how much you will enjoy life. If you want to be like God, you need to always go the extra mile, always do more than you have to, always give more than enough, and always be generous.

Trust in Him God's called you to be a generous giver as you trust Him to supply all your needs. This includes your finances...but it doesn't end there. What other talents/resources can you give?

April 7

Imperfect, but Perfectly Loved

There is no fear in love [dread does not exist], but full-grown (complete, perfect) love turns fear out of doors and expels every trace of terror!

1 JOHN 4:18

We cannot love ourselves unless we realize how much God loves us, and if we don't love ourselves, we cannot love other people. We cannot maintain good, healthy relationships without this foundation of love in our lives.

By the time I met the man I have been married to since 1967, I was desperate for love but did not know how to receive it, even when it was available. My husband, Dave, really did love me, but I found myself constantly deflecting his love due to the way I felt about myself down deep inside. As I entered into a serious and committed relationship with God, through Jesus Christ, I began to learn about God's love. But it took a long time to fully accept it. When you feel unlovable, it is hard to get it through your head and down into your heart that God loves you perfectly—even though you are not perfect and never will be as long as you are on the earth.

There is only one thing you can do with a free gift: receive it and be grateful. I urge you to take a step of faith right now and say out loud, "God loves me unconditionally, and I receive His love!" You may have to say it a hundred times a day, like I did for months, before it finally sinks in, but when it does it will be the happiest day of your life. To know that you are loved by someone you can trust is the best and most comforting feeling in the world. God will not only love you that way, but He will also provide other people who will truly love you. When He does provide, be sure to remain thankful for those people. Having people who genuinely love you is one of the most precious gifts in the world.

Trust in Him You won't be able to receive God's love until you trust Him. Take a step of faith right now and say out loud, "God loves me unconditionally, and I receive His love!" Say it as many times as you need to until you believe it.

April 8

Faith Beats Fear

For God did not give us a spirit of timidity (of cowardice, of craven and cringing and fawning fear), but [He has given us a spirit] of power and of love and of calm and well-balanced mind and discipline and self-control. 2 TIMOTHY 1:7

I will not fear" is the only acceptable attitude we can have toward fear. That does not mean that you and I will never feel fear, but it does mean that we will not allow it to rule our decisions and actions.

The Bible says that God has not given us a spirit of fear. Fear is not from God; it is the devil's tool to keep us from enjoying our lives and making progress. Fear causes us to run, retreat, or shrink back. The Bible says in Hebrews 10:38 that we are to live by faith and not draw back in fear—and if we do draw back in fear, God's soul has no delight in us. That does not mean God does not love us; it simply means He is disappointed because He wants us to experience all of the good things He has in His plan for us. We can receive from God only by faith.

We should strive to do everything with a spirit of faith. Faith is confidence in God and a belief that His promises are true. Faith will cause you to go forward, to try new things, and to be aggressive. Unless we make a firm decision to "fear not," we will never be free from the power of it. "Do it afraid" means to feel the fear and do what you believe you should do anyway.

I encourage you to be firm in your resolve to do whatever you need to do, even if you have to "do it afraid!"

Trust in Him Choose to walk in faith, trusting God's promises. Remember to "fear not," and when you do feel fear, "do it afraid."

April 9

Stop Waiting and Start Trying!

And I am convinced and sure of this very thing, that He Who began a good work in you will continue until the day of Jesus Christ [right up to the time of His return], developing [that good work] and perfecting and bringing it to full completion in you. PHILIPPIANS 1:6

Many people are confused about what they are to do with their lives. They don't know what God's will is for them; they are without direction. I felt the same way once, but I discovered my destiny by trying several things. I tried working in the nursery at church and quickly discovered that I was not called to work with children. I tried being my pastor's secretary, and after one day I was fired with no explanation except, "This just isn't right." I was devastated at first, until a short while later I was asked to start a weekly meeting on Thursday mornings at church and teach God's Word. I quickly found where I fit. I could have spent my life being confused, but I thank God that I was confident enough to step out and discover what was right for me. I did it through the process of elimination, and I experienced some disappointments—but it all worked out well in the end.

If you are doing nothing with your life because you are not sure what to do, then I recommend that you pray and begin trying some things. It won't take long before you will feel comfortable with something. It will be a perfect fit for you. Think of it this way: when you go out to buy a new outfit, you probably try on several things until you find what fits right, is comfortable, and looks good on you. Why not try the same thing with discovering your destiny? A confident person is not afraid to make mistakes, and if they do, they recover and press on.

Trust in Him You cannot drive a parked car—it's time to put your car in drive! Choose a desire God's put on your heart and take a first step. Try it on. Even if it's not the right fit, your destiny will unfold as you continue to put your trust in God and try something new.

April 10

Avoid Comparisons

I praise you because I am fearfully and wonderfully made; your works are wonderful, I know that full well. PSALM 139:14 NIV

Confidence is not possible as long as we compare ourselves with other people. No matter how good we look, how talented or smart we are, or how successful we are, there is always someone who is better, and sooner or later we will run into them. I believe confidence is found in doing the best we can with what we have to work with and not in comparing ourselves with others and competing with them.

Like most people, I struggled for years trying to be like my neighbor, my husband, my pastor's wife, my friend, and so on. My neighbor was very creative at decorating, sewing, and many other things, whereas I could barely sew a button on and have confidence that it would not fall off. I took lessons and tried to sew, but I hated it. My husband is very calm and easygoing, and I was just the opposite. So I tried to be like him, and that didn't work, either. My pastor's wife was sweet, mercy-motivated, petite, cute, and a blonde. I, on the other hand, was aggressive, bold, loud, not-so-petite—and a brunette.

In general, I found myself always comparing myself with someone, and in the process, rejecting and disapproving of the person God created me to be. After years of misery, I finally understood that God does not make mistakes, He purposely makes all of us different, and different is not bad; it is God showing His creative variety. We should accept ourselves as God's creation and let Him help us be the unique, precious individual that He intended us to be. Confidence begins with self-acceptance—which is made possible through a strong faith in God's love and plan for our lives.

Trust in Him Make a decision that you will never again compare yourself with someone else. Trust God more than your ability to compare yourself. Then you can appreciate others for who they are and enjoy the wonderful person God created you to be.

April 11

Take Action

Be strong, courageous, and firm; fear not nor be in terror before them, for it is the Lord your God Who goes with you; He will not fail you or forsake you. DEUTERONOMY 31:6

I have heard that there are two types of people in the world: the ones who wait for something to happen and the ones who make something happen. One of the few mistakes we cannot recover from is the mistake of never being willing to make one in the first place! God works through our faith, not our fear. Don't sit on the sidelines of life wishing you were doing the things you see other people doing. Take action and enjoy life!

If a person is naturally introverted or extroverted, they will always have greater tendencies toward that natural trait—and that is not wrong. However, we can have the life we desire and still not deny who we are. So search your heart and ask yourself what you believe God wants you to do—and then do it. Where He guides, He always provides. If God is asking you to step out into something that is uncomfortable for you, I can assure you that when you take the step of faith, you will find Him walking right beside you.

When you want to do something, don't let yourself think about all the things that could go wrong. Be positive and think about the exciting things that can happen. Your attitude makes all the difference in your life. Have a positive, aggressive, take-action attitude, and you will enjoy your life more. It may be difficult at first, but it will be worth it in the end.

Trust in Him What sideline have you been sitting on, just wishing and waiting? What's keeping you from trusting God? Take action! You can do something today with the courage God gives you.

April 12

Choose Carefully

She considers a [new] field before she buys or accepts it [expanding prudently and not courting neglect of her present duties by assuming other duties]; with her savings [of time and strength] she plants fruitful vines in her vineyard. PROVERBS 31:16

This verse is very important to me. I am an aggressive person who wants to be involved in everything, but I have learned the hard way it isn't wise or even possible. When we try to do everything, we don't do anything well. Quality is much better than quantity. Our woman in Proverbs seems to be quite a good businesswoman. Verse 16 begins by saying she "considers" a new field before she buys it. She considers her present duties and is careful not to neglect them by taking on new ones. In other words, she seriously thinks about what she is about to do and does not act emotionally without forethought.

Oh, how much better life would be if we all took time to think about what we are about to do before we do it. It is amazing how many things I don't buy if I just go home and think about it for a while. It is amazing how one good night's sleep changes our minds. Not everything that looks good is good, and a wise person will take time to examine things thoroughly. If you think about it, what is good is sometimes the enemy of what is best. We should choose the more excellent things and not merely settle for another good thing.

I receive many good opportunities almost daily, and I have to decline to be involved in most of them. I know what I am called by God to do, and I stick with my call. Each of us has an allotted amount of time and energy, and we should manage it in such a way that we bear the most fruit we can. Don't court neglect of other duties by taking on new ones. A sure way to lose your confidence is to have so much to do that you are not doing any of it well.

Trust in Him When an opportunity arises, carefully consider how it will affect your present duties before you commit. Do you have the passion and resources for it? And most important, has God called you to it? Then you can trust God's hand will be on your decision.

April 13

Treat Yourself

She makes for herself coverlets, cushions, and rugs of tapestry. Her clothing is of linen, pure and fine, and of purple [such as that of which the clothing of the priests and the hallowed cloths of the temple were made]. PROVERBS 31:22

I am particularly fond of verse 22 because it tells me that our famous Proverbs woman had nice things herself. She lived a balanced life. She did a lot for others, but she also took time to minister to herself. Many people burn out because they don't take time to refresh themselves. We feel such a need to give and do for others that we ignore our own needs, or worse, we feel guilty for even thinking about ourselves. We need to be ministered to spiritually, mentally, emotionally, and physically. Each one of these areas is important to God; He made them, and He is interested in the well-being of all of them, including our physical and emotional needs. Our confident woman made herself cushions, rugs, and clothing. Her clothes were made of the same cloth that the priests wore. In other words, she had really nice stuff. The best!

Many people have the mistaken idea that Christianity means to do for everyone else but sacrifice everything in life you might personally enjoy. I don't believe this! We will certainly be called to times of sacrifice all throughout life, and whatever God asks us to give up we should give up gladly. But we don't have to make it a contest to see just how much we can do without in life in order to try to impress and please

God. Jesus said, "I came that they may have and enjoy life, and have it in abundance (to the full, till it overflows)" (John 10:10).

I believe we feel more confident when we look our best and take good care of ourselves. You are worth being cared for and don't ever forget it. You have value, and you should make an investment in yourself.

Trust in Him Do you believe God wants you to enjoy life? Then think of something you really enjoy and take the time to do it!

April 14

Don't Shrink

But the just shall live by faith [My righteous servant shall live by his conviction respecting man's relationship to God and divine things, and holy fervor born of faith and conjoined with it]; and if he draws back and shrinks in fear, My soul has no delight or pleasure in him. HEBREWS 10:38

Self-doubt causes a person to shrink back in fear. God's Word states in Hebrews that the just shall live by faith and if he shrinks back in fear, God's soul has no delight in him. That does not mean God is angry with us, but it does sadden Him that we are living so far below the confident life He provided through Jesus Christ.

Faith is being confident in God and His Word. Perhaps you have a good relationship with God and have no problem trusting Him, but when it comes to trusting yourself to do the right thing, you shrink—you allow fear to control you and pull you back.

God once told me that if I didn't trust myself, then I didn't trust Him. He said He was living in me and directing, guiding, and controlling me because I asked Him to do so. I needed to believe God's promises, not my feelings or thoughts. Of course, any one of us can miss

God and we can make mistakes. We can think we are going in the right direction and then discover we are wrong, but it's not the end of the world, nor is it anything to become excessively concerned about. If our hearts are sincere and we are honestly seeking God's will, even if we do make a mistake, He will intervene and get us back on track. Quite often, He does it without us even knowing.

Instead of always assuming you are wrong and living in the agony of self-doubt, I encourage you to believe you are being led by God unless He shows you otherwise. Just as God has promised in His Word, you can trust Him to lead you by His Holy Spirit into all truth (see John 16:13). If we are on the wrong track, God will help us get back on the right one.

Trust in Him What areas of your life fill you with the most doubt? Pray and ask God to give you new confidence to meet these challenges.

April 15

Your Change Begins with You

Fear not, for I have redeemed you [ransomed you by paying a price instead of leaving you captives]; I have called you by your name; you are Mine. ISAIAH 43:1

If you have made your mind up that you intend to enjoy the best life God has for you, then you must realize that the change you're waiting for begins in you. You must believe what God's Word says about you more than you believe what others say or what your feelings or own mind say. Your circumstances aren't your problem, because they won't last—but until you change your thinking, no matter what's going on in your life you'll still be stuck.

Maybe you have had negative messages fed to you since you were a child. It could have been parents who had troubles themselves and took their frustrations out on you. It could have been a teacher who delighted in belittling you in front of the class. Perhaps your parents excessively compared you to another sibling, giving you the impression that you were flawed. You may have experienced one or more broken relationships and become convinced it was your fault. But, whatever the reason for your self-doubt and negative attitude toward yourself, it has to change if you truly desire to enjoy God's best in your life.

See yourself as God sees you, not the way the world sees you or even the way you see yourself. Study God's Word and you will find out that you are precious, created in your mother's womb by God's own hand. You are not an accident. Even if your parents told you they never really wanted you, I can assure you that God wants you; otherwise you would not be here on earth. You are valuable, you have worth, you are gifted, you are talented, and you have a purpose on this earth. God says that He has called you by your name and that you are His.

Take a minute to look into your heart. What do you see there? How do you feel about yourself? If your answer does not agree with God's Word, I want to encourage you to begin today renewing your mind about yourself.

Trust in Him God says in His Word that you belong to Him, and that you're uniquely and carefully created by Him. Do you believe it?

April 16

Know Your Strengths

And God saw everything that He had made, and behold, it was very good (suitable, pleasant) and He approved it completely.

GENESIS 1:31

In order for you to enjoy life, you need to know where your strengths lie. Thinking about what you're good at is not conceited; it is merely preparation to do your job with confidence. I know anything I am good at is because God has gifted me in that area, and I thank Him all the time for the abilities He has equipped me with. Make a list of what you are good at and rehearse it daily until you gain confidence in your abilities.

Here's my list:
I am a good communicator
I am a hard worker
I am decisive
I am determined
I am disciplined
I am a loyal friend
I have a good short-term memory
I love to help people
I love to give

In Psalm 139 David describes how God creates us in our mother's womb with His very own hand, how He delicately and intricately forms us. Then he says, "Wonderful are Your works, and that my inner self knows right well." *Wow!* What a statement. David is basically saying, "I am wonderful, and I know that in my heart." He is not bragging on himself, but on God Who created him.

I also realize everything I need in life isn't on this list. I need God to bring people into my life who are strong in the areas where I'm weak—this keeps me humble and reminds me that it's not all about me.

What are you good at? Do you even know? Have you seriously thought about it, or have you been so busy thinking about what you are not good at that you have not even noticed your abilities?

Trust in Him Make a list of what you are good at and read it out loud to yourself every morning until you are convinced. Remember, God created you to be great—and you can trust His design.

April 17

Is Your GPS On?

Pray without ceasing. 1 THESSALONIANS 5:17 KJV

Praying is probably the most important part of preparing to do something, yet so many people today ignore or forget this vital part of the process. I suggest you don't do anything without first praying and asking God to get involved and make it work out right. Jesus said, "Apart from Me you can do nothing," and I believe Him (see John 15:5).

Prayer is like the GPS system in a car. When you turn it on and tell it where you're going, it shows you the path you need to take to get there. The Bible says that we should acknowledge God in all our ways and He will direct our steps and make them sure (see Prov. 3:6). Prayer gives us God's GPS—*guidance, provision, and strength*.

When Jesus ascended into heaven and sat down at the right hand of the Father, He sent the Holy Spirit to be our Helper in life. He is always ready to get involved, but we must ask for His help. If you don't turn on your GPS, it won't tell you when you're making wrong turns. It won't take the wheel away from you and keep you from getting lost. In the same way, the Holy Spirit offers world-renowned supernatural service, but you have to ask Him for it.

God will enable you to do things that will frequently surprise you if you take Him as your partner in life. But you must start with prayer.

Trust in Him Start your day by turning on your GPS through prayer. You'll find God's *guidance, protection, and strength*, which will help you trust Him and experience His presence all throughout the day!

April 18

Break Free from Other People's Expectations

Jesus Christ (the Messiah) is [always] the same, yesterday, today, [yes] and forever (to the ages). HEBREWS 13:8

Studies show that 10 percent of people will never like you. This means we won't have a perfect record with everyone and we should celebrate who we are. A person who knows how to do this does not allow the moods of other people to alter theirs.

A story is told of a Quaker man who knew how to live independently as the valued person God had created Him to be. One night as he was walking down the street with a friend he stopped at a newsstand to purchase an evening paper. The storekeeper was very sour, rude, and unfriendly. The Quaker man treated him with respect and was quite kind in his dealing with him. He paid for his paper, and he and his friend continued to walk down the street. The friend said to the Quaker, "How could you be so cordial to him with the terrible way he was treating you?" The Quaker man replied, "Oh, he is always that way; why should I let him determine how I am going to act?"

This is one of the amazing traits we see in Jesus. He was the same all the time. He changed people; they did not change Him.

When an unhappy person is unsuccessful in making you unhappy, they begin to respect and admire you. They see your Christianity is something real, and they may be interested in hearing what you have to say.

Even people who seek to control you will disrespect you if you allow them to do it. I encourage you to be your own person. Do what God expects you to do and don't live under the tyranny of other people's expectations.

Trust in Him Don't let others determine who you are or what you do. Don't put your trust in the opinions of people. Stay confident in who God's called you to be!

April 19

Listen to Love

Let each one [give] as he has made up his own mind and purposed in his heart, not reluctantly or sorrowfully or under compulsion, for God loves (He takes pleasure in, prizes above other things, and is unwilling to abandon or to do without) a cheerful (joyous, "prompt to do it") giver [whose heart is in his giving]. 2 CORINTHIANS 9:7

Because human nature is self-centered, generous giving does not come naturally to us. We have to build into our thinking the mind-set that we are generous. Begin to think and say, "I am a very generous person. I look for opportunities to give."

I have found that opportunities to give are all around me—and they are all around you, too. Finding out how you can bless another person is as easy as using your ears. If you simply listen to people, you'll soon know what they need or would like.

In casual conversation, a person who works for me once mentioned she liked things produced by a certain company. I asked someone to go for me and get a gift certificate to this company, and I gave it to her with a note telling her how much I appreciate all her hard work. She began to cry and said, "It's not the gift certificate that means so much to me. It's the fact that you actually heard me and remembered what I said."

I encourage you to begin listening to others and paying attention to what they say more than ever before. People want to know you're listening to them; they feel loved and valued when you listen to them. If you don't know what to do for someone, you're not listening to them because people tell you what they want, need, and like—and you'll know if you listen. You could start a list of things that you hear people say they want or need, and if you cannot provide it for them now, you can pray that God will give you the ability to do so. If you act on what you hear and bless people accordingly, you'll see that blessing others really is better than receiving anything for yourself. I assure you, the more you give, the happier you will be.

Trust in Him Think of three specific friends, neighbors, or coworkers you see regularly. Commit to listen intentionally the next time you're together, as you trust God to show you how to bless them.

April 20

You Can Cope with Criticism

It is the Lord [Himself] Who examines and judges me.
1 CORINTHIANS 4:4

No matter what you do in life you will occasionally be criticized by someone, so you must learn to cope with it and not let it bother you. Criticism is very difficult for most of us, and a person's self-image can be damaged by one critical remark. But it is possible to learn how not to be affected at all by criticism.

Like many other great people, the apostle Paul experienced criticism about many things. He experienced the same thing we do, which is that people are fickle. They love you when you are doing everything they want you to do and are quick to criticize when just one little thing goes wrong. Paul said he was not in the least bit concerned about the judgments of others. He said he did not even judge himself. He knew he was in God's hands and that in the end, he would stand before God and give an account of himself and his life. He would not stand before any man to be judged (see 1 Cor. 4:3–4).

Sometimes the people who are criticized the most are the ones who try to do something constructive with their life. It amazes me how people who do nothing want to criticize those who try to do something. I may not always do everything right, but at least I am attempting to do something to make the world a better place and to help hurting people. I believe that is very pleasing to God! After many years of suffering over the criticisms of people and trying to gain their approval, I finally decided that if God is happy with me, that is enough.

Each time someone criticizes you, try making a positive affirmation about yourself to yourself. Don't just stand by and take in everything anyone wants to dump on you. Establish independence! Be confident in God's love and approval, and don't be defeated by criticism.

Trust in Him The first step is not reacting to your critics, but it doesn't stop there. Jesus blessed those who persecuted Him because of His deep trust in the Father's plan. How can you bless people who are critical of you?

April 21

Do Something Outrageous!

And Peter answered Him, Lord, if it is You, command me to come to You on the water. He said, Come! So Peter got out of the boat and walked on the water... MATTHEW 14:28–29

I think it's good to occasionally (or perhaps frequently) do something that seems outrageous. Do something that people won't expect. It will keep your life interesting and keep other people from thinking they have you tucked away nicely in a little box of their own design. People become bored because their lives become predictable. One great woman who was seventy-six years of age said her goal was to do at least one outrageous thing every week. I just read this week that we should do one thing every day that scares us.

We are not created by God to merely do the same thing over and over until it has no meaning left at all. God is creative. If you don't think so, then just look around you. All the animals, bugs, plants, birds, trees, and other things are totally amazing. The sun, moon, and stars, planets, space, and gravity—all of which God has created—can boggle our minds. We could actually go on forever talking about the infinite variety of things God has created. In case you haven't noticed, God is quite outrageous and frequently changes things up in our lives. He is full of surprises and yet totally dependable. You know, we really can learn a lot from God!

I don't want people to think they have me all figured out, and although I want to be dependable and faithful, I don't always want to be predictable. Sometimes I get bored with myself and I have to pray and ask God for a creative idea to shake up my life a little and keep me on my toes.

Trust in Him Do something new and outrageous today. Ask God to help you be creative.

April 22

There's Peace in "No"

And let the peace (soul harmony which comes) from Christ rule (act as umpire continually) in your hearts [deciding and settling with finality all questions that arise in your minds, in that peaceful state] to which as [members of Christ's] one body you were also called [to live]. COLOSSIANS 3:15

A confident person can say "no" when they need to. They can endure people's displeasure and are able to reason that if the disappointed person truly wants a relationship with them, they will get over their disappointment and want them to be free to make their own decisions. They realize wanting to please others can be a trap that keeps them from the freedom of saying no.

Sometimes you have to say "no" to others in order to say "yes" to yourself, otherwise, you will end up bitter and resentful, feeling that somewhere in the process of trying to keep others happy, you lost yourself. You are valuable, and you need to do things that you want to do as well as doing things for others.

When you do feel you need to say no, you don't have to give a reason why. So often people want us to justify our decisions, and we really don't need to do that. I try to be led by God's Spirit—or another way of saying it is I try to be led by my heart—and sometimes I don't even fully understand why I feel something isn't right for me. But I have learned if I do feel that way, I am not going to go against my own conscience in order to have everyone be happy with me. I often say, "I just don't have peace about it," or "I don't feel right about it," or even a plain old "I don't want to" is sufficient.

There is nothing wrong with giving a reason if you have one, but I think we go overboard in trying to explain ourselves sometimes. If an offended person doesn't want to understand, they are never going to, no matter how many reasons you give. Follow your heart and keep your peace. Say "no" when you need to and "yes" when you should.

Trust in Him Sometimes it takes faith to say "No." God wants your heart to be at peace. Put your trust in Him and don't be afraid to say "no."

April 23

Like a Child

Truly I say to you, unless you repent (change, turn about) and become like little children [trusting, lowly, loving, forgiving], you can never enter the kingdom of heaven [at all]. MATTHEW 18:3

Jesus said we should become like little children if we expect to enter the kingdom of God. I believe that one of the things He was telling us is to study the freedom that children enjoy. They are unpretentious and straightforward; they laugh a lot; they're forgiving and trusting. Children are definitely confident, at least until the world teaches them to be insecure and fearful. I can remember our son Danny at the age of three walking through the shopping mall with Dave and me and saying to people, "I'm Danny Meyer, don't you want to talk to me?" He was so confident that he was sure everyone wanted to know him better.

Children seem to be able to make a game out of anything. They quickly adjust, don't have a problem letting other children be different than they are, and are always exploring something new. They are amazed by everything!

Oswald Chambers wrote in *My Utmost for His Highest*: "The freedom after sanctification is the freedom of a child; the things that used to keep the life pinned down are gone." We definitely need to watch and study children and obey the command of Jesus to be more like them. It is something we have to do on purpose as we get older. We all have to grow up and be responsible, but we don't have to stop enjoying ourselves and life.

Trust in Him Take time to watch children today and learn from them—play a game, adjust to your circumstances without complaint, let others be who they are—remember what it is like to be confident and bold and trust that God wants you to be just like that!

April 24

Fight Off Stagnation

And what this love consists in is this: that we live and walk in accordance with and guided by His commandments (His orders, ordinances, precepts, teaching). 2 JOHN 1:6

Have you ever seen a puddle of water that was stagnant? There's no circulation, no fresh water source, and the water just sits there. There's little life left. We can slide into stagnation. It happens a little bit at a time and often so slowly that it is almost imperceptible. I believe everyone will stagnate if they don't fight it. It is easy to just float along with everyone else, doing the same thing every day. We stop being daring, doing outrageous things, and being creative. We settle in, we slip into the world's mold, and we conform to what people expect. We become boringly predictable!

One of the most valuable things I have learned is to do things on purpose rather than waiting until I feel like doing them. I purposely take care of my responsibilities in life, because I know it is very important. I give on purpose. I actually look for people to be a blessing to because I have learned the vitally important lesson that Jesus taught about walking in love (see Eph. 5:2; 2 John 1:6). I purposely do something that is a little out of the ordinary for me every once in a while simply because I refuse to live in stagnation. I purposely spend time every day in prayer and fellowship with God because I want to honor Him and always give Him His rightful place in my life, which is first place.

If you take this aggressive action, living on purpose and refusing to stagnate, it will make a big difference in your quality of life. Don't just put in your time here on earth; enjoy your life and make the world glad that you are here.

Trust in Him Are you going through the motions of life, or are you living on purpose? Refuse to stagnate. Study Jesus' teachings and trust them enough to put them into practice. You'll see a big difference!

April 25

There's Only One You Really Need

I have strength for all things in Christ Who empowers me [I am ready for anything and equal to anything through Him Who infuses inner strength into me; I am self-sufficient in Christ's sufficiency].

PHILIPPIANS 4:13

Once I found myself worried about what I would do if my husband, Dave, died. How could I run the ministry on my own? After several days of this mental attack the Lord spoke to my heart and said, "If Dave died, you would keep doing exactly what you are doing because I am the One holding you up, not Dave."

I obviously need Dave and depend on him for many things, but God wanted to reestablish in my heart what was true from the beginning of our ministry: with or without Dave, or anyone else for that matter, I could do what God had asked me to do as long as I had Him.

When Peter, Judas, and others disappointed Jesus, He was not devastated, because His confidence was not misplaced. He was dependent and yet independent at the same time. I depend on many people in my ministry to help me accomplish what I am called to do. However, I see constant change. People leave who I thought would be with me forever, and God sends new people who have amazing gifts. I need people, but I know it is God working through people to help me. If He decides to change who He works through, that should be no concern of mine.

I appreciate all the wonderful people God has placed in my life. My husband and children are amazing. My ministry staff is top-notch, and the wonderful ministry partners God has given me are awesome. I need all of them, but if for any reason God ever decided to remove any of them from my life, I want to be a confident woman who knows that with God alone all things are possible. My confidence must be in Him more than it is in anything or anyone else.

Trust in Him **Are you overly dependent upon a family member, coworker, friend, job, or pet, to the point of worrying about what you would do without them? Put your trust in God. Remember, He's the only one you truly need.**

April 26

Don't Worry About Tomorrow

So do not worry or be anxious about tomorrow, for tomorrow will have worries and anxieties of its own. Sufficient for each day is its own trouble. MATTHEW 6:34

Trying to solve tomorrow's problems today only steals the energy God has prearranged for you in order to enjoy today. Don't waste your time worrying! It is vain and useless.

When Jesus instructed us not to worry about tomorrow, He was saying that we should deal with life one day at a time. He gives us the strength we need as we need it. When we take that strength He gives us and apply it to worry instead of living, we rob ourselves of the blessings God intended for us to have today. We miss out on good things because we worry about bad things that may not even come to be!

For several years a woman had trouble getting to sleep at night because she feared burglars. One night her husband heard a noise in the house, so he went downstairs to investigate. When he got there, he did find a burglar. "Good evening," said the man of the house. "I am pleased to see you. Come upstairs and meet my wife. She has been waiting ten years to meet you."

A confident person does not worry, because they see the future differently than those who are worriers. They confidently believe that with God's help, they can do whatever they need to do, no matter what it is. A positive attitude enables them to expect good things in the future, not bad ones. Confidence is the fruit of trusting God. When we trust

Him, we may not have all the answers, but we are confident that He does.

Trust in Him Are you worrying about tomorrow when you should be focusing on today? Trust God to equip you for whatever comes today, tomorrow, and in the future, so that you can receive the fullness of His gifts today.

April 27

Don't Make Big Decisions in the Storm

Be merciful and gracious to me, O God, be merciful and gracious to me, for my soul takes refuge and finds shelter and confidence in You; yes, in the shadow of Your wings will I take refuge and be confident until calamities and destructive storms are passed. PSALM 57:1

Life isn't one big, long sunny day. At some point, we all face storms—whether they come in the form of unexpected illness, job loss, financial crisis, marital difficulties, problems with children, or any number of other scenarios that are stressful, intense, and important. I have faced many storms in my life—some like the quick afternoon storms that are common in summertime and some that seemed like category four hurricanes. If I have learned anything about weathering the storms of life, I have learned that they don't last forever, and that if at all possible, I do not need to make major decisions in the midst of them.

When the storms of life arise, it's best to keep your mind and emotions as still as possible. Thoughts and feelings often run wild in the midst of crises, but those are exactly the times we need to be careful about making decisions. We must remain calm and discipline ourselves to focus on doing what we can do and trusting God to do what we cannot do.

Next time you face a storm or crisis in your life, I hope you'll remember these words, which I often say: "Let your emotions subside before you decide." Do your best to let things settle down before you make major decisions. You may not always have that choice, but as much as possible, put significant decisions on hold until your storm passes. Just as the wind blows about wildly during a storm, our thoughts can become quite wild and frantic, and that is not the best time to make major decisions.

Making this commitment will protect you from making quick, unwise decisions that could take you off the course God has for you.

Trust in Him Next time the wind blows and the waves crash, take the big life decisions off the table (where you're going to live, your job, your relationships, etc.) and wait. Once the storm passes, trust God to show you what He wants you to do.

April 28

Positively Possible

With men [it is] impossible, but not with God; for all things are possible with God. MARK 10:27

One of the best stories about how faith and confidence in God releases the power of potential took place centuries ago, when many parts of the ancient world were still unsettled. God promised the people of Israel they would possess a rich and fertile country, known as Canaan. He didn't promise them they could step across its borders without opposition, but He did promise them they would inhabit it—and when God makes a promise, He means it.

Taking God at His Word, the Israelites appointed twelve men to go into Canaan to "spy out the land" and bring back a report. Upon their return, ten spies admitted that the land flowed with milk and honey, and acknowledged that the fruit in Canaan was large and beautiful, but then remarked that the land was full of giants who would be impossible to overcome. They allowed the presence of the giants to detract from the promises of God.

In contrast, Joshua and Caleb brought back good reports, full of faith and confidence in God, and Caleb spoke up with confidence, saying, "Let us go up at once and possess it; we are well able to conquer it" (Num. 13:30). The ten spies thought the giants in the land were too big to kill, but Joshua and Caleb thought they were too big to miss. Joshua and Caleb were the only two men who were positive in the face of opposition from the giants. They didn't ignore the challenges, but they did not overemphasize them—and they were the only two who entered the Promised Land.

Being positive does not mean we deny the existence of difficulty; it means we believe God is greater than our difficulties. Believing in God can cause us to win any battle we face. When we are closed to "positive possibilities" we only see what is right in front of us, not what we could see if we would simply be positive and creative.

Trust in Him You can either be a "10-spy" or a "2-spy," but you can't be both. 10-spys trust what they see; 2-spys trust the God of the impossible even when they can't see Him. Choose to be a 2-spy today!

April 29

Fear Leads to Worry

And who of you by worrying and being anxious can add one unit of measure (cubit) to his stature or to the span of his life?

MATTHEW 6:27

Fear and worry are closely related. You might say fear is the parent of every kind of worry because every worry starts as a fear. The Bible clearly teaches that God's children are not to worry. When we worry, we rotate our minds around and around a problem and come up with no answers. The more we do it, the more anxious we feel. When we worry, we actually torment ourselves with a type of thinking that produces no good fruit. Worry starts with our thoughts, but it affects our moods and even our physical bodies.

A person can worry so much that it makes them feel depressed and sad. Worry places stress on your entire system and causes a lot of physical ailments like headaches, tension in muscles, stomach problems, and many other things. It never helps, and it does not solve our problems.

We can worry about hundreds of different things, from what people think of us to what will happen to us as we age. How long will we be able to work? Who will take care of us when we get old? What happens if the stock market crashes? What if gas prices go up? What if I lose my job? Quite often, worry does not even have a basis or a nugget of truth to it. There is no known reason to even think about the things that worry and then frighten us.

The only answer is to stop worrying by placing your trust in God. He has the future all planned, and He knows the answer to everything. What we worry about frequently never happens anyway, and if it is going to happen, worrying won't prevent it. God's Word promises us that He will take care of us if we trust in Him.

Trust in Him What are you worrying about? Cast your cares on Jesus. He wants you to trust Him with every thought, burden, and worry that you're carrying because He's fully capable of taking care of you (see 1 Pet. 5:7).

April 30

Encouragement Always Pays

[Remember] this: he who sows sparingly and grudgingly will also reap sparingly and grudgingly, and he who sows generously [that blessings may come to someone] will also reap generously and with blessings. 2 CORINTHIANS 9:6

All of us need encouragement. It is a tool that increases our confidence and inspires us to act with courage, spirit, or strength. That is what we need! We don't need anyone around to discourage us; instead, we need "encouragers" in our lives.

Because we all encounter difficulty while we are running our race and trying to reach our goals, we all need encouragement. The more we get, the easier it is to stay on track and avoid wasting days or weeks in discouragement, depression, and despair. One of the best ways I know to get something I want or need is to give some of it away. God's Word teaches us to sow and then we shall reap. If a farmer plants tomato seeds, he will get a harvest of tomatoes. If we plant encouragement in the lives of other people, we will reap a harvest of encouragement in our own.

What we make happen for someone else, God will make happen for us. Do you sometimes find yourself wishing you had more encouragement, maybe from your family or your friends or your boss? But how often do you encourage others? If you're not sure, then make an extra effort right away. You can be the channel that God uses to keep someone confidently pressing toward success rather than giving up.

Trust in Him Choose three people to encourage today. Trust that God will give you the perfect word they've been waiting to hear.

May 1

No More Negativity

We are assured and know that [God being a partner in their labor] all things work together and are [fitting into a plan] for good to and for those who love God and are called according to [His] design and purpose.

ROMANS 8:28

Confidence and negativity do not go together. They are like oil and water; they simply do not mix. I used to be a very negative woman, but, thank God, I finally learned that being positive is much more fun and fruitful. Being positive or negative is a choice—it is a way of thinking, speaking, and acting. Either one comes from a habit that has been formed in our lives through repetitious behavior.

You may be like me. I simply got off to a bad start in life. I grew up in a negative atmosphere around negative people. They were my role models, and I became like them. I really didn't even realize my negative attitude was a problem until I married Dave. He was very positive and began asking me why I was so negative. I had never really thought about it, but as I began to, I realized that I was always that way. I began to understand that I was expecting nothing good—and that is exactly what I got.

People don't enjoy being around an individual who is negative, so I often felt rejected—which added to my fears and lack of confidence. Being negative opened the door for a lot of problems and disappointments, which in turn fueled my negativity. It took time for me to change, but I am convinced that if I can change, anybody can.

You don't have to be negative. It's your choice. When encouraged to think positively, people often retort, "That is not reality." But the truth is that positive thinking can change your current reality. God is positive, and that is His reality. It is the way He is, the way He thinks, and the way He encourages us to be.

Thinking negatively makes you miserable, and why would you choose to be miserable when you can be happy?

Trust in Him What negative thought has been harassing your mind? Replace it with a promise from God's Word that you can trust.

May 2

A Well-Balanced Mind Stays Positive

For God did not give us a spirit of timidity (of cowardice, of craven and cringing and fawning fear), but [He has given us a spirit] of power and of love and of calm and well-balanced mind and discipline and self-control. 2 TIMOTHY 1:7

You can't control what happens to you, but you can determine to go through it with the right attitude.

In fact, you can choose *beforehand* that you will keep a positive attitude in the midst of every negative situation that presents itself to you. If you make this decision and meditate on it during a good time in your life, then when difficulty arises you will already be prepared to maintain a good attitude.

Throughout history, we have examples of people who have maintained good attitudes in the face of difficult times and thereby turned their problems into opportunities. Specifically, I think of various individuals who were imprisoned and composed some of the most influential writing the world has ever known, such as: "Letter from Birmingham Jail" by Martin Luther King Jr., *Pilgrim's Progress* by John Bunyan, and Sir Walter Raleigh's *The History of the World*. No doubt, these people could have had terrible attitudes as they faced terrible trouble, but they made a decision and maintained the best of attitudes through the worst of times and made contributions that are still read and heard today.

I don't think they were simply born positive people—I believe they had to make a choice. And their choice not only benefited themselves, but in the process, blessed the world.

One of the worst mistakes we can make in our thinking is to believe we are just not like *those positive people* and we can't help it. If you think you can't do anything about your thinking and attitude, then you're defeated before you even begin to try. Discipline yourself to stand strong with your positive attitude in every circumstance.

Trust in Him What was your attitude like the last time you faced a really difficult situation? Did your choices bless you and others? Did you put your trust in God? Looking back now, how could you have handled it differently?

May 3

Expect Favor

[What, what would have become of me] had I not believed that I would see the Lord's goodness in the land of the living! Wait and hope for and expect the Lord; be brave and of good courage and let your heart be stout and enduring. Yes, wait for and hope for and expect the Lord.

PSALM 27:13–14

God wants to give you favor—kindness that you don't deserve. We see mention of God's favor toward many in the Bible, and there's no reason to think He can't offer it to you as well. Learn to believe God for favor. Confess several times a day that you have favor with God and man. You will be amazed at the exciting things that happen to you if you speak God's Word instead of how you feel.

Supernatural favor can be expressed in different ways. You may get the job you want but are not naturally qualified for. People seem to like you for no special reason. You get the best seat in the restaurant with the best waiter. People give you things for no reason at all. Favor means that someone will stop and let you into a line of traffic while others are zooming by as if you are not even there.

Living in God's favor is very exciting. When Joseph was cruelly mistreated by his brothers and they sold him into slavery, God gave him favor everywhere he went. He had favor with Potiphar and was placed in charge of his household. He had favor with the jailer during his imprisonment for a crime he did not commit. He had so much favor with Pharaoh that Joseph became second only to Pharaoh in power. Yes, walking in God's favor is an exciting way to live. We see so many men and women whom we admire in the Bible being given favor: Ruth, Esther, Daniel, and Abraham, just to name a few. Resist and refuse to let doubt convince you that good things won't happen to you and your family; aggressively expect good things!

Trust in Him Ask God to give you divine, supernatural favor, and then trust He'll do it as you look for it in your life.

May 4

Your Trials Are Temporary

Consider it wholly joyful, my brethren, whenever you are enveloped in or encounter trials of any sort or fall into various temptations. Be assured and understand that the trial and proving of your faith bring out endurance and steadfastness and patience. JAMES 1:2–3

I have heard many people who live in parts of the world where there are four distinct seasons talk about how much they enjoy winter, spring, summer, and fall. They like the variety and the unique beauty, qualities, and opportunities of each season. The Bible tells us God Himself changes times and seasons (see Dan. 2:21).

Seasons change; this is true in the natural world, and it is true in regard to the seasons of our lives. It means that difficult times do not last forever. We may have "off" days, tough weeks, bad months, or even a year that seems to have more than its share of troubles, but every negative experience does come to an end.

Some of the trying situations we find ourselves in seem to go on far too long. When this happens, we are usually tempted to complain or become discouraged. Instead, we need to promptly adjust our attitudes and ask God to teach us something valuable as we press through the situation at hand. According to James 1:2–3, God uses trials and pressure to produce good results in our lives. He always wants to bless us. Sometimes His blessings come through unexpected circumstances we may view as negative, but if we will keep positive attitudes in the midst of those situations, we will experience the positive results God desires to give us.

If you are going through a difficult time right now, let me remind you that this probably isn't the first challenge you've ever faced. You survived the last one (and probably learned some valuable lessons through it), and you will survive this one, too. Your trials are temporary; they won't last forever. Better days are on their way. Just keep your attitude "up" instead of "down," and remember that this is just a season and it *will* pass.

Trust in Him This trial is temporary. Your season will change. You can trust this important truth. Take a deep breath and thank God for the season you're currently in, as well as the season He's bringing you into.

May 5

Let Go of the Past; Look to Your Future

If we [freely] admit that we have sinned and confess our sins, He is faithful and just (true to His own nature and promises) and will forgive our sins [dismiss our lawlessness] and [continuously] cleanse us from all unrighteousness [everything not in conformity to His will in purpose, thought, and action]. 1 JOHN 1:9

It is useless to worry about anything and doubly useless to worry about something that is over and done with and that nothing can be done about. If you made a mistake in the past that can be rectified, then go ahead and take action to correct it. But if you cannot do anything about it except be sorry, then ask for forgiveness from God and anyone you may have hurt and don't worry about it any longer.

Let me remind you that worry is useless...so why do it? God has given us wisdom, and a wise person will not spend their time doing something that produces nothing of any value.

There are many wonderful Scriptures in the Bible that teach us to let go of the past and look to the future. We're reminded to forget what is behind and keep our eyes facing forward, on God and His plan for us (see Phil. 3:13). We can find peace in the knowledge that God's compassion and kindness are new every morning and that His faithfulness is abundant (see Lam. 3:22–23). Also, we must never forget that He is able to overcome our mistakes and do far more than we could ever imagine that He could do for us (see Eph. 3:16, 20). God has provided a way for your past to have zero power over you, but it is up to you to receive His gracious gifts of forgiveness, mercy, and a new beginning.

Don't allow mistakes in your past to fester and threaten your future. When you ask God to forgive you for something that you have done wrong, He is faithful and just to do it. He continuously cleanses us from all unrighteousness (see 1 John 1:9). It's forgiven and forgotten—but you must do the same!

Trust in Him When you hear the word *past* what's the first memory or thought that comes to mind? If it is something that makes you feel guilty, then pray and ask God to help you let go and trust He has great things in your future.

May 6

You're Never Too Old to Grow in Your Thinking

...whatever is true, whatever is worthy of reverence and is honorable and seemly, whatever is just, whatever is pure, whatever is lovely and lovable, whatever is kind and winsome and gracious, if there is any virtue and excellence, if there is anything worthy of praise, think on and weigh and take account of these things [fix your minds on them]. PHILIPPIANS 4:8

Dr. Caroline Leaf, a leading brain scientist/learning specialist and committed Christian, notes in her teaching on the brain: "*The Word and science believe that the mind and the brain are one.*" The way you think is voluntary—you can control your thoughts. I want you to give your brain a new job and begin to teach your mind to work for you instead of against you.

One important way to do this is to make the intentional decision that you will begin to think positively. I realize your brain won't be able to fulfill the new role completely overnight. You may be asking it to undergo a radical transformation, and that will take time. So give it a little grace, but determine that with your diligence and God's help, your brain will go to work *for* you instead of against you and become a powerful, positive force in your life.

I like what Dr. Leaf says—that the human brain takes "*eighteen years to grow and a lifetime to mature.*" Don't miss this point. Although every other organ in the body is fully formed when a person is born, and simply gets bigger as the body gets bigger, the brain actually takes a full eighteen years to be fully formed. After that, it continues to mature until the day a person dies. This means, no matter how old you are, your brain is still maturing. This is great news because it means you do not have to be stuck in any old or wrong thought patterns. Your brain is still maturing, so you can still mature in your thinking.

Trust in Him What comes to mind immediately when I ask: *in what way(s) is your mind working against you?* Remember, it takes a *lifetime* for your brain to mature. Trust that it's never too late to change your mind!

May 7

Get over Guilt

As far as the east is from the west, so far has He removed our transgressions from us. PSALM 103:12

Millions of people destroy their lives by feeling guilty about something that is in the past and that they cannot do anything about. When God forgives our sin He also removes the guilt. But just as we must receive His forgiveness, we must also receive freedom from guilt and not let the emotion of guilt control us. If God says we are forgiven and pronounced not guilty, then we should believe His Word more than how we feel.

We frequently hear people say, "I will feel guilty about that the rest of my life." Or I have heard people say, "I will never get over what I have done." God's Word says that when He forgives us, He forgets the offense and there is no more penalty for sin where there is complete remission of it (see Heb. 10:17–18). Why decide that you will feel guilty the rest of your life when God has provided a way for you to live free from it?

Guilt is worry that is rooted in fear. We are afraid that God is angry, or that what we have done wrong is too big and too bad, even for God to forgive. We feel we don't deserve forgiveness, so we won't receive it. We worry about what people think of our past sins. We are afraid they will never forgive us or see us as good people again. Guilt has everything to do with the past, and it has the power to ruin your future. Get over it!

God holds nothing against you if you are sincerely sorry for what you have done and are trusting in the blood of Jesus to cleanse you from your former wickedness. The minute you repent, God forgives and forgets it, so why not follow His example and receive His forgiveness and forget it yourself?

Trust in Him What's the one thing that you feel the most guilty about? Have you asked God for forgiveness? Do you trust Him when He says He's forgiven you? Then let it go!

May 8

The Battle for Truth

...for in [your] faith (in your strong and welcome conviction or belief that Jesus is the Messiah, through Whom we obtain eternal salvation in the kingdom of God) you stand firm. 2 CORINTHIANS 1:24

One of the problems in the world today is that people want to "do their own thing" even if it makes them miserable. They don't want to take direction from anyone or be told what to do, and they certainly don't want to be accountable to God's Word.

This kind of arrogant independence and rebellion is responsible for many unpleasant results and even tragedies. I am sure, if you stop and consider it, you know of situations in which people (maybe you) have been determined to go their own way and ended up with terrible problems. This does not have to happen!

To be able to enjoy life and avoid unnecessary problems, you and I must live according to the truth in God's Word and not according to the lies we hear from other people, the world, or the enemy. We must know how to separate what is true from what is not. You can do this, but the battle for truth takes place in your mind, and you won't win it without a fight. You must examine *what* you believe and *why* you believe it. It is wise to be firmly convinced so when the devil challenges you concerning God's Word, you are prepared to stand firm.

We often find the children of Christian parents reaching an age where they begin to wonder if they really believe what their parents have taught them or not. Sometimes they go through a "crisis" period concerning their faith in God. They need to find their own faith because they can no longer live on the faith of their parents as they have done in the past. This can be a very healthy process. Most of them usually realize they do believe Jesus is their Savior, but it is a decision they need to make for themselves. You cannot stand through the storms of life based on someone else's faith. You must be fully assured in your own heart and mind.

Trust in Him Knowing what you believe only makes a difference if you trust it enough to act on it. What transforming truth from Scripture do you need to apply today?

May 9

Don't Let Dread Get a Hold on You

The Lord of hosts—regard Him as holy and honor His holy name [by regarding Him as your only hope of safety], and let Him be your fear and let Him be your dread [lest you offend Him by your fear of man and distrust of Him]. ISAIAH 8:13

Dread is a powerful, gripping fear. People dread many things, and most of them don't even realize what dread does to them. It sucks the joy right out of the present moment. But Jesus set you free from the power of dread. The life God has provided for us through Jesus Christ is a precious gift, and we should enjoy every moment of it.

Pray and ask God to show you every time you begin to dread any task or something lurking in your future that you're not quite sure of. Merely eliminating dread from your life will release more of your God-given confidence and help you experience more joy.

How often do you find yourself putting things off that you dread doing? Maybe it's that uncomfortable conversation you know you need to have, or those bills that need to be paid, or worse, maybe it's your annual taxes! Train yourself not to dread anything but to actually tackle it first. The sooner in the day you do the things you don't prefer doing, the more energy you have to do them. If you wait until the end of the day when most of your energy is gone and then try to do something you really don't like doing, it will be worse than doing it earlier. Dread causes us to procrastinate, but if you're ever going to do something, now is the best time!

Putting something off does not make it go away; it only allows more time to torment you. You can dread or you can confidently take action. As Christians with the power of the Holy Spirit inside us, surely we can manage to do an unpleasant task without dreading it and with a good attitude. God's power is not available just to make unpleasant things in our lives go away; it is frequently available to walk us through them courageously.

Trust in Him What are you dreading? Do it now and get it over with. Choose to do all things with joy and strength—don't trust your fear more than you trust God!

May 10

Putting Smiles on Faces

Therefore encourage (admonish, exhort) one another and edify (strengthen and build up) one another…

1 THESSALONIANS 5:11

When God created Adam and Eve, He blessed them, then told them to be fruitful and multiply and use all the vast resources of the earth that He gave them in the service of God and man.

Are you being fruitful? Is your life causing increase? When you get involved with people and things, do they increase and multiply? Some people only take in life, and they never add anything. I refuse to be that kind of person. I want to make people's lives better. I want to put smiles on faces.

We must all make sure that we are not like the rich man in the Bible who had so much that all of his barns were full with no room for more. Instead of giving any of it away, he decided that he would tear down the barns he had and just build bigger ones and collect more stuff for himself. He was a foolish man. He could have decided that he would use what he had to bless others, but he must have been a fearful, selfish man, who only had room in his life for himself (see Luke 12:16–20).

God called the man a fool, and said, "This very night they [the messengers of God] will demand your soul of you; and all the things that you have prepared, whose will they be?" The man was going to die that night, and all he would leave behind was "stuff." He had an opportunity to make the world a better place. He could have added to many lives and put smiles on thousands of faces. Instead, he fearfully and selfishly only cared about himself.

Forget about yourself and start doing all you can to help others.

Encourage, edify, lift up, comfort, help, give hope, relieve pain, and lift burdens. If that is your goal, you will be one of those rare individuals who actually make the world a better place and put a smile on every face.

Trust in Him What are you going to do today to put smiles on faces? It won't just happen—you have to be intentional about it. Listen for God to show you what to do and then trust that it will bless them . . . and you!

May 11

Don't Sweat the Small Stuff

Little children, you are of God [you belong to Him] and have [already] defeated and overcome them [the agents of the antichrist], because He Who lives in you is greater (mightier) than he who is in the world. 1 JOHN 4:4

It is highly probable that you dread more little things than you do major things. First of all, we have a lot of little things we deal with all the time, but the major things come fewer and farther in between. As I began to examine this area of dread in my own life, I realized it operated in little daily areas like going to the grocery store, doing laundry, running an errand, or looking for a parking place in a crowded shopping mall. I dreaded waiting because, historically, I have not been an extremely patient person. Waiting in lines or traffic, or for slow people to get a job done, were things I dreaded and allowed to frustrate me.

Like many of you, I have a lot to do, and I don't like wasting my time waiting. But, thank God, I have learned it does no good at all to dread something I have to do anyway. It steals my current joy, and I have lost enough of that in my life, so I am not willing to give up any more of it. I believe it glorifies God when we refuse to live in fear, worry, or dread.

When I find myself in a situation I would rather not be in, whether it is waiting or doing an unpleasant task, I make a decision that I will do it joyfully and not dread it, and then I exercise self-control. I use those faith muscles that God has given to me. You have them, too! If we allow fear and dread in our lives, they breed more fear, but if we practice walking in faith, it becomes easier to do it again and again.

Trust in Him Have you also wasted a lot of your life in fear, worry, or dread simply because you didn't trust that God would come through for you? If so, I believe those days are coming to an end for you! Refuse to give up your joy and instead practice walking in faith.

May 12

Follow God's Law, Not Murphy's

The thief comes only in order to steal and kill and destroy. I came that they may have and enjoy life, and have it in abundance (to the full, till it overflows). JOHN 10:10

Years ago, a man named Captain Edward A. Murphy was working on a project for the United States Air Force. He became angry and cursed a technician who made a mistake, noting that, "If anything can be done wrong, this man will do it." Over time, such thinking became known as "Murphy's Law," which basically states, "Nothing is as easy as it looks; everything takes longer than you expect; and if anything can go wrong, it will—at the worst possible moment."

Many people have never heard of Edward Murphy, but most of us know Murphy's Law. His negativity caught on and continues to impact the world. I believe God has laws that completely disagree with

Murphy's Law. The world may expect Murphy's Law to operate in their lives, but we need to resist that kind of negative thinking and embrace God's Law instead.

God's Law says that things may be difficult, there will be challenges, but we always have a reason to hope, we can always express ourselves through faith and love, and we can always trust that God is working on our behalf!

Negative thinking always produces a negative life. How much more could you enjoy your life if your thoughts agreed with God's Law, not Murphy's? God has a great life for you, one He wants you to enjoy thoroughly and live to the fullest. I challenge you to live by God's Law and consistently fill your mind with positive thoughts.

Trust in Him In what specific circumstance do you need to start believing God's Law instead of trusting Murphy's Law?

May 13

Your Mission from God

Be strong (confident) and of good courage, for you shall cause this people to inherit the land which I swore to their fathers to give them.

JOSHUA 1:6

A teacher has a powerful responsibility. Parents, coaches, teachers, and other role models have tremendous influence—for example, they can train children to fear failure or they can teach them to be hopeful as they overcome adversity.

A mother who struggles with fear will pass that along to her children. Even when she doesn't realize it, a phrase, an overly cautious attitude, or a reluctance to step out and try new things will be imparted to her little ones. But a mother with bold, courageous faith will inspire her children to chase the dreams God's placed in their hearts.

We should not teach our children to live recklessly, but we should teach them to be bold, to take action, and to never be so afraid of making mistakes that they won't try things. I believe we should teach our children and those under our authority to take chances in life. If we never take a chance, we will never make progress, and progress always requires stepping into the unknown. Experience gives us confidence, but we never get experience unless we step out and try things we have not tried before.

A child who is told over and over, "You better not try that, you might get hurt," will more than likely become reluctant to try new things. If children hear "Be careful" too frequently, they may learn to be so careful that they end up living a narrow life that has no room for adventure.

I want to encourage you to teach others by word and example how to be bold and courageous. Tell people to try things, reminding them that making a mistake is not the worst thing that can happen. And if someone, somewhere in your past trained you to fear failure or to focus on the worst thing that could happen, it's never too late to live by faith.

Trust in Him How are you influencing those around you—are you inspiring them to trust God with bold faith or cautioning them with what could go wrong?

May 14

What Does the Future Hold?

I will [earnestly] recall the deeds of the Lord; yes, I will [earnestly] remember the wonders [You performed for our fathers] of old. I will meditate also upon all Your works and consider all Your [mighty] deeds.

PSALM 77:11–12

None of us knows for sure what the future holds. This lack of knowledge often opens the door for fear. What if I become disabled? What if my spouse dies? What if my child dies? What if we have another world war? What about terrorism? What kind of world will I be living in twenty-five years from now?

Wondering about things we don't have answers to opens the door to fear. Instead of wondering, trust God that whatever your future holds, He will enable you to handle it when the time comes. Wherever you are going, God has already been there and paved the way for you. This isn't a one-time decision—it's a choice you make every day to trust Him.

I look at some of the things people go through, and I say to myself, *"I am afraid I could never go through that with the graciousness and courage I have seen them display."* Then I remind myself that when we must go through something negative, God gives us the strength to do so. When we merely fear going through something, we do it without any help from God at all. When I look back over my life and remember some of the things God has brought me through, I think, *How did I do that?* It was because of God's grace and power. He enabled me to do what I needed to do at the time, and He will always do the same thing for you if you ask Him to. We may not know the future, but if we know the One Who holds the future in His hands, we can look forward to it expectantly and without fear. If God brings you to it, He will bring you through it.

Trust in Him Next time you are tempted to look at a situation and think you could "never" go through something like that, remember a time when God has proven Himself trustworthy in your life. You trusted Him before—and you can do it again!

May 15

Get Up and Do Your Part

How long will you sleep, O sluggard? When will you arise out of your sleep? PROVERBS 6:9

Too much activity and no rest definitely is the culprit behind most stress, but no activity is also a problem. I am sure you have heard that exercise is a great stress reliever, and it is very true. I would rather be physically tired from exercise and movement than tired in my soul from doing nothing and being bored.

Work is good for all of us. As a matter of fact, God said we should work six days and rest one. That shows how important work and activity are in God's eyes. God has created us to work, not to sit idly by and do nothing. There are several good stories in the Bible about people who had serious problems and when they asked Jesus for help He told them to *"Get up!"*

In the fifth chapter of John we see one example. A man was crippled, and he lay by the pool of Bethesda for thirty-eight years waiting for his miracle. When Jesus came to the man and asked him how long he had been in that condition, the man gave the length of time and then continued to tell Jesus how he had nobody to put him into the pool at the right time and how others always got ahead of him. Jesus told the man to *"get up! pick up your bed... and walk!"* (John 5:8).

Get up and start doing whatever you can do to clean up the messes in your life. If they are marriage messes, then do your part. Don't worry about what your spouse is not doing; just do your part and God will reward you. If you have a financial mess, then stop spending and start paying off your debts. Get an extra job for a period of time if you need to. If you are not able to do that, then ask God to show you what you can do. Remember, "If you do what you can do, then God will do what you cannot do."

Trust in Him Don't wait thirty-eight years for your miracle while you do nothing. Whether it has been lack of knowledge, laziness, self-pity, or fear holding you back, choose now to *get up*! Do your part and trust God to do His.

May 16

See the Big Picture

For as he thinks in his heart, so is he. PROVERBS 23:7

When you focus excessively on the negative elements of a certain situation and overlook the good aspects, you are "filtering out" the positive and exaggerating the negative. Very few situations are 100 percent negative; most of the time, you can find something good in every circumstance, even if you have to be really diligent about it.

Let's say you are a mom with young children. Your four-year-old colors on the walls, cuts holes in his new pants, kicks his sister, and spills grape juice all over your freshly cleaned carpet. Let's also say he finally apologizes to his sister without being reminded, confesses to cutting his pants instead of saying, "The dog did it," makes an attempt to clean his room, and says you are the best mom in the whole world. To say he was absolutely horrible all day long and forget about his good moments would be filtering out the good, and it would leave your mind with nothing but negative thoughts. Though there certainly would have been some negatives about that day, it had its positive experiences, too.

I can't emphasize too strongly how important it is that you resist the temptation to characterize something as totally negative or to focus excessively on negative aspects of a situation. Look at the situation as a whole and find something positive about it.

When you're constantly focusing on the negative, you'll find it very difficult to trust that things will get better. But when you choose to find the positive things in even your worst challenges, you'll never run out of hope or the ability to put your trust in God.

Trust in Him What is the most negative situation in your life? Now, list three positive things about it or other aspects of your life. When you do, you'll find a fresh source of hope and a new ability to trust.

May 17

Embrace Change with Faith

I tell you the truth, unless you **change** *and become like little children, you will never enter the kingdom of heaven.*

MATTHEW 18:3 NIV 1984 (EMPHASIS MINE)

If you are stressed out all the time, something will have to change in order for the stress to be relieved. It will not just go away as long as you keep doing the same thing. We cannot expect to keep doing the same thing over and over and get a different result. If you want different results, you have to change what you are doing.

Take some bold steps of faith and change anything the Lord leads you to change. If what you are doing with your time is not bearing good fruit, then make a change. If you are not getting enough rest, make a change. If you are not disciplining your children and their behavior is causing you a lot of stress, then make a change. If you are not taking care of yourself, then make a change. If you are bored, make a change. If your friends are taking advantage of you, then make a change! Are you getting the point? Stress can be relieved if you're not afraid to make changes.

You may be afraid of change, but it is also possible that even if you find the courage to make the necessary changes, other people in your life won't like the changes you make. Don't be afraid of them, either.

You will get used to the changes, and so will they. If you don't take action now, you will still be complaining about the same things a year from now, and a year after that, and ten years after that, and there will be no end to your misery. The time is *now*! Boldness takes action, but fear breeds inactivity and procrastination. The choice is yours!

Trust in Him Don't waste time resisting change. God uses it to shape us, mold us, and make us new. Change keeps life fresh and adventurous—embrace change with faith and trust that God will pull you through.

May 18

Your Plans or God's Plans

A man's mind plans his way, but the Lord directs his steps and makes them sure. PROVERBS 16:9

We must learn to wait for God's plans to develop. He perfects everything that concerns us. True boldness moves in God's timing; it moves at the right time.

During the three years of Jesus' earthly ministry, people thought He was crazy. His own brothers were embarrassed by Him, and in an effort to save their reputation, they told Him He needed to go somewhere else and do His works. If He was unwilling to do that, they had another option for Him. They told Him to take action and stop doing His works in secret. They tried to convince Him it was time to show Himself and His works to the world. In other words, they wanted Jesus to impress the people with what He could do.

He responded to them by saying, "My time (opportunity) has not come yet..." (John 7:6).

How many of us could show that type of self-control? If you could do the miracles that He could do and were being made fun of and challenged to show your stuff, what would you do? Would you wait until you absolutely knew that it was the right time, or would you take action that was not sanctioned by God?

It is good to have plans, and I believe we should plan boldly and aggressively, but we must be wise enough to know that our plans will ultimately fail without God. God's Word says, "Except the Lord builds the house, they labor in vain who build it..." (Ps. 127:1). We can build without God as our foundation, but like any building without a strong foundation, we will eventually fall.

Trust in Him Are you operating in your own timing, or are you trusting God's timing? Trust God—His plans are always best!

May 19

You Can Overcome Opposition

So, since Christ suffered in the flesh for us, for you, arm yourselves with the same thought and purpose [patiently to suffer rather than fail to please God]. 1 PETER 4:1

God did not send the power of His Spirit into our lives so we could be weak-willed, wimpy, or the type of person who gives up when the going gets tough. God did not give us a spirit of fear, but of power, love, and a sound mind (see 2 Tim. 1:7).

In the beginning of my ministry, God gave me a dream. In the dream, I was driving down a highway and I noticed cars pulling off. Some were parking, and others were turning around to go back where they came from. I assumed there must be trouble up ahead but could not see what it was. As I boldly continued to drive forward, I saw a bridge with water from the river below starting to flow across it. I realized that the people in the cars were afraid they might get hurt or get somewhere and not be able to get back. My dream ended with me sitting in my car looking first at the water-covered bridge, back where I had been, and to the side of the road, trying to decide if I should park, retreat, or keep moving forward. Then I woke up.

God used that dream to show me that there will always be opposition when pressing toward a goal. There will always be opportunity to park and go no farther or turn around and give up. It was up to me to decide each time if I would give up or go on. That dream has helped me many times to press on when difficulties came and I was tempted to quit. I have decided that even though I sometimes make mistakes, and I may not always get the result that I hope for, I will never quit! Determination will get you a lot further than talent. So if you feel you lack in talent, take heart. All you need to win in life is a determination to never give up and keep pressing forward.

Trust in Him You can do whatever you need to do in life through Christ Who is your Strength. Trust Him completely and press toward victory.

May 20

Your Thoughts Are Powerful

I know and am convinced (persuaded) as one in the Lord Jesus, that nothing is [forbidden as] essentially unclean (defiled and unholy in itself). But [none the less] it is unclean (defiled and unholy) to anyone who **thinks** *it is unclean.* ROMANS 14:14 (EMPHASIS MINE)

Responding to a heated debate over whether or not Christians in the early Church should eat meat that had been offered to idols, Paul indicates in Romans 14:14 his strong belief that thoughts are very powerful. Paul did not believe meat offered to idols could be tainted, because he knew idols were nothing but wood or stone. However, many people did not see things as Paul did, and he understood that. So his advice to them was not to eat the meat if they *thought* it was unclean. He knew that once they believed the meat was unclean in their conscience, it didn't matter if it was unclean or not. Their thoughts would condemn them.

The more I ponder Romans 14:14, the more amazed I am by the depth of Paul's insight. The principle he understood was true when applied to meat offered to idols in ancient times, and it is still true today in any area of life. For example, if you think, "*I will never get a good job*," you aren't likely to get one. If your thoughts have convinced you that you can never do anything right, you'll tend to make more mistakes than normal and have a high rate of failure.

Also, for many people, whatever "they" say becomes truth—and "they" may be the news media, a celebrity, a group of friends, or others who enjoy sharing opinions but may or may not really have any idea what is true. When you and I believe lies, our minds can actually limit us and even keep us from doing what God created us to do.

But if we will contend for the truth, embrace the truth, and build our lives upon the truth, we will succeed in every endeavor.

Trust in Him What's the one thought holding you back from what God has for you? Trust God more than you trust that thought. Don't try to fight those thoughts with your willpower alone—challenge them with God's Word.

May 21

Disappointed? Get Reappointed

Man's steps are ordered by the Lord. How then can a man understand his way? PROVERBS 20:24

This Scripture has stabilized my emotions many times when I was in a hurry to get somewhere and found myself at a standstill in traffic on the highway. Initially, I get a sinking feeling, then I get aggravated, and then I say, "Well, since my steps are ordered by the Lord, I will calm down and thank God that I am right where He wants me." I also remind myself that God may be saving me from an accident farther down the road by keeping me where I am. Trusting God is absolutely wonderful because it soothes our wild thoughts and emotions when things don't go the way we had planned.

I learned long ago that with God on our side, even though we will experience disappointments in life, we can always get "reappointed." If you or I have a doctor's appointment and he has an emergency and has to cancel, we simply make another appointment. Life can be that way, too. Trusting that God has a good plan for us, and that our steps are ordered by Him, is the key to preventing disappointment from turning into despair.

How do you react when you get disappointed? How long does it take for you to make a transition and get reappointed? Are you acting on the Word of God or merely reacting emotionally to the circumstance? Are you controlled by what is around you, or by Jesus, Who lives inside you?

Trusting God completely and believing that His plan for you is right is infinitely better than trusting your own plan. It is impossible to be mad at someone you really believe has your best interest in mind. And God is always for us, never against us. He is the only One Who can help you and truly comfort you; therefore, it is much better to run to Him in your disappointment than away from Him.

Trust in Him Trust God to *reappoint* you—when you do, it will calm your thoughts and emotions.

May 22

The Good Kind of Hunger

Blessed are those who hunger and thirst for righteousness, for they will be filled. MATTHEW 5:6 NIV

Today more people are spiritually malnourished than ever before. Too many elements of society distract people from their eternal souls and encourage them to concentrate on material life instead.

Caught up in this lifestyle, many people mistake the void they feel inside for physical hunger. They were never taught to recognize spiritual hunger, or what to do about it if they do recognize it. Since they don't know what to do about the pain and loneliness, they reach for the quickest fix they know: food, drugs, alcohol, or other material pleasures.

If you have a rich spiritual life, you'll already be satisfied and fulfilled in the moment, and won't feel the need to "supplement" your moment with "*things.*"

We all have these moments at times. You wander through a summer field of fireflies and suddenly feel still and awed at the beauty of it all. You hold your new son or grandson on your lap and feel a great spiritual bond of love all around you. You're sitting in a pew Sunday morning and the light comes through the stained glass and fills your heart with joy. The moment is complete in itself. You don't think, *My heart is full of joy, and boy do I wish I had a slice of chocolate cake in my hand!* You can know the complete fulfillment of spiritual nourishment, and know that if you will experience it regularly, you'll have no problem craving earthly things.

In fact, we should all feel those transcendent moments more often than we do. I believe they are essential to physical, emotional, and spiritual health. And I think we spend too little time trying to achieve them and too much time meditating on our problems. Get your mind off the problems, and spend more time meditating on the one true source of nourishment—God's love.

Trust in Him **When was the last time you felt awed by God and filled to overflowing with joy? Trust God to meet with you this way on a regular basis.**

May 23

People Who Are Difficult to Get Along With

If you [merely] love those who love you, what quality of credit and thanks is that to you? For even the [very] sinners love their lovers (those who love them). LUKE 6:32

I am very thankful that I know the Word of God and have Him in my life to help and comfort me. But I try to remember that a lot of people in the world who are difficult to get along with don't have that. I always want my behavior to be a witness for Christ and not something that would make Him ashamed of me. That being the case, I have had to work very hard with the Holy Spirit to develop the ability to act on the Word of God when people are rude instead of merely reacting to them with behavior that matches or tops theirs.

This issue is actually very common, which means that we all will deal with difficult people on and off throughout our lives. People are everywhere, and not all of them are pleasant. So we must make a decision about how we are going to react toward them. Will you act on the Word of God and love them for His sake? Or will you merely react emotionally and end up perhaps acting worse than they act? Have you ever let a rude person ruin your day? Make a decision that you will not ever do that again because when you do, you are wasting some of the precious time that God has given you. When a day is gone, you can never get it back, so I urge you not to waste it being emotionally distraught over someone you may never even see again.

If you are in a situation that requires you to be with one of these hard-to-get-along-with people every day, I urge you to pray for them instead of reacting emotionally to them. Our prayers open a door for God to work through. Sometimes when we pray, God will lead us to confront a person like that. When He does, remember that confrontation should still be done in the spirit of love.

Trust in Him Is there a person in your life who's difficult to be around? Pray and ask God to teach you how to respond to them in every situation.

May 24

Change and Transition

Vindicate me, O Lord, for I have walked in my integrity; I have [expectantly] trusted in, leaned on, and relied on the Lord without wavering and I shall not slide. PSALM 26:1

Everything changes except God, and letting all the changes in our lives upset us won't keep them from occurring. People change, circumstances change, our bodies change, our desires and passions change. One certainty in life is change. We don't mind change if we invite it, but when it comes uninvited, our emotions can easily flare up.

John worked for an investment company for thirty-two years and was sure he would retire from that company. Without warning, the company decided to sell to a larger firm, whose management decided they didn't want to keep a lot of the employees, and John lost his job. He feels that he wasn't treated fairly when he was let go. Now what? John has a choice to make. He can either react emotionally by getting upset, stressed out, anxious, angry, and worried, feeling and saying lots of negative things. Or he can act on God's Word and trust God to be his vindicator and source of supply for every need. It is totally understandable that John has these emotions, but if he chooses to react based on his feelings, then he will be miserable and possibly make the other people in his life miserable. If he chooses to make decisions based on God's Word, however, he can make the transition with far less turmoil. Will his anger dissipate right away? Probably not. But if John truly gives his care over to God, his feelings will calm down and he can be confident that God will continue to work in his life, bringing justice for the injustice done to him.

Most changes take place without our permission. But we can choose to adapt. If we refuse to make the transition in our minds and attitudes, then we are making a huge mistake. Our refusal to adapt doesn't change the circumstances, but it does steal our peace and joy. But by acting on God's Word and not merely reacting to the situation, you will be able to manage your emotions instead of allowing them to manage you.

Trust in Him If it's not already here, your next change is on the way. Build your trust in God now by preparing your heart through spending time in His Word and coming to Him in prayer.

May 25

Celebrate Through Giving

May blessing (praise, laudation, and eulogy) be to the God and Father of our Lord Jesus Christ (the Messiah) Who has blessed us in Christ with every spiritual (given by the Holy Spirit) blessing in the heavenly realm! EPHESIANS 1:3

I have learned over the past few years through studying God's love that giving to others is one of the ways we can and should celebrate our own victories. It is a way of saying, "I sure am happy about what God has done for me, and I want to reach out and make someone else happy."

Giving is a central part of the Christian lifestyle, and we should do it aggressively and with joy. God has given us His Son Jesus as the best gift He could give, and in Jesus we have all other things. In Him we have been blessed with every spiritual blessing in the heavenly realm (see Eph. 1:3).

It is the will of God that we give thanks at all times and in everything (see 1 Thess. 5:18). Thanksgiving must have an expression in order to be complete. We can say that we are thankful, but do we show it? Are we expressing it? We say "thank you," but there are other ways of showing appreciation, and one of them is giving to people who have less than we do. Giving to the poor is commanded by God. It is one of the ways we can keep a continual cycle of blessing operating in our lives. God gives to us, and we show appreciation by giving to someone else; and then He blesses us some more so we can do it all over again.

The Bible puts it plainly. When God blesses you as He promised, find a poor man and give to him. Do not harden your heart, but open your hands wide to help him. If you give to him freely without begrudging it, then the Lord will bless you in all your work and all that you undertake (see Deut. 15:6–8, 10). What we give to others as a result of obedience to God is never lost. It leaves our hand temporarily, but it never leaves our life. We give it, God uses it to bless someone else, and then He returns it to us multiplied. I like the way God does things, don't you?

Trust in Him Do you believe God has blessed you? Then show your gratitude to God by being a blessing to someone today.

May 26

A Time to Remember

Having eyes, do you not see [with them], and having ears, do you not hear and perceive and understand the sense of what is said? And do you not remember? MARK 8:18

I have often said I think we forget what we should remember and remember what we should forget. Jesus chastised the disciples on one of their journeys because they had forgotten about a miracle He had done. They had started out on a trip and suddenly remembered that they had forgotten to bring enough bread. They had only one loaf, and that would not be nearly enough. In a short while Jesus began to teach the disciples to beware of, and on their guard concerning, the leaven of the Pharisees and Herod. Jesus of course was talking about being on their guard against deception, but the disciples reasoned among themselves that He was talking about the fact that they had forgotten to bring bread, as if that would have concerned Jesus at all. He then began to chastise them, asking if they had forgotten when He fed five thousand people with five loaves of bread. Had they forgotten another amazing miracle when He fed four thousand with seven loaves? Had they remembered, they would not be worried about going hungry because of not having brought enough bread with them.

If we would remember the miracles God has done in our past, we would not so easily fall into worry and fear when we face new challenges. When David was facing Goliath and nobody was encouraging him, he remembered the lion and the bear that he had already slain with God's help. Because of remembering the past, he had no fear of the current situation.

Are you facing something right now that looms before you like a giant in your life? Is it illness or financial lack? Is it relationship problems? Is it something you have never done before and you don't know where to begin? The truth is that it doesn't matter what it is because nothing is impossible for God. Take some time right now and recall some of the things He has helped you with and brought you through in the past. Think about and talk about those things, and you will find courage filling your heart.

Trust in Him Take time to remember a specific instance in which God provided for you. Celebrate it. This will increase your ability to trust Him.

May 27

Truly Know God

[For my determined purpose is] that I may know Him [that I may progressively become more deeply and intimately acquainted with Him, perceiving and recognizing and understanding the wonders of His Person more strongly and more clearly], and that I may in that same way come to know the power outflowing from His resurrection... PHILIPPIANS 3:10

There is a big difference in knowing God and knowing *about* God. When we truly know God, we also experience (know) His power. Many Christians live too much by feeling. If they feel joyful and happy, then they say God is blessing them, but if they feel blah, cold, or flat, then they might be heard asking, "Where is God today?" If their prayer is not answered to their satisfaction, they ask where God is. When we experienced the attacks on the Twin Towers in New York City on 9/11, a newscaster asked, "Where was God when all of this happened?" Had this newscaster known God, he would never have asked such a question.

If we have a true knowledge of God, we are not disturbed by any scientific view, or any theories of evolution, or so-called contradictions in Bible translations. We have a perfect assurance that God *is*, and knowing that, then we know that nothing else matters. We do not feel a need to explain things, because we know what cannot be explained in words. Paul said he saw things when he had visions of heaven that he could not explain. Men always want to explain God, but if we know Him truly, then the first thing we give up is trying to understand Him or explain Him. The person who knows spiritually has no need to understand everything mentally.

Pray daily for a spirit of wisdom and revelation that you might know God and His Christ, the Messiah, the Anointed One. Celebrate that you know God, that you are an eternal being, and that you are progressively coming to know Him better as each day passes by. What an amazing blessing it is to know God. It should make us want to shout for joy. Celebrate because you have joined Jesus' party!

Trust in Him Spend time with God today, getting to know Him a little more each day. You won't trust Him if you don't truly know Him!

May 28

Learn to Face Truth

And you will know the Truth, and the Truth will set you free.

JOHN 8:32

God's Word is truth, and learning to face truth in every situation is the road to victory. For many years I was extremely difficult to get along with, but I blamed my bad behavior on my circumstances and other people. I was totally unable to change until I faced the truth that I was the problem. I had a bad attitude, and I was selfish. It was emotionally painful for me to admit that I was the problem, but it was a pain that led me to freedom.

It is easy for us to see what is wrong with other people, but it is very difficult for us to see ourselves as we really are. Ask God to reveal you to you! Ask Him to show you anything about you that needs to change, then face it and let Him help you get free. God wants to set us free from the things that torment us, but it is not possible unless we face truth.

Satan is the father of deception and lies, and of course he wants us to be self-deceived so he can keep us in bondage. He is terrified of the truth because he knows that when we face truth, he will lose his control over us. Beware of blaming! Blaming others for existing problems started with Adam and Eve in the Garden of Eden and still exists today. Even if I am late for an appointment, I find myself wanting to blame someone for making me late, but the truth is that I should have managed my time better.

If you are willing to start seeking truth in every situation, you will grow spiritually and begin to experience more freedom and joy than ever before.

Trust in Him Jesus said, "I am the Way, the Truth, and the Life!" Ask Him to show you truth and trust that it will lead you to freedom!

May 29

Don't Just Be Open...Ask!

You do not have, because you do not ask. JAMES 4:2

God loves you very much and wants to help you, but you need to ask Him to. A man told me recently that when he feels overwhelmed, he lifts up one hand toward heaven and says, "Come get me, Jesus." God hears the faintest cry of your heart, so stop trying to do everything on your own, and ask Him for help.

For example, the next time you are tempted to eat because you're upset or sad, say "no" out loud. Then go sit quietly for a moment and ask God to help you in your situation. You'll be amazed at how much of a difference asking makes. More often than not, you'll find that you suddenly have the strength to resist the temptation. But you have to really ask; you can't just tell yourself that you're open to God's help.

You may not think that God cares about something as simple as your eating habits, but He does. He cares about everything that concerns you—the big as well as the small. He wants you healthy, and He is willing to help, if you'll just let Him. Don't pray to Him to simply break your addiction; instead, pray to Him to help you find the spiritual strength to make the lifestyle changes that will set you free from the problem. As we choose to do what is right and lean on Him to give us strength, His power enables us to follow through and experience victory.

Prayer and meditation on God's Word are excellent practices to nourish your spirit. It is spiritual food. Studying God's Word and prayer are traditional methods of making contact with God, but other activities can also make you receptive to His nourishing love. Read something that encourages you and gives you hope. Keep a gratitude journal where you list the good things that happened to you that day (and there are good things in *every* day). Feed your spirit regularly, and you will be healthy and strong inside and out.

Trust in Him What are you asking God for? It's never too big or too small to bring before Him in prayer—when you do, you can trust that He's heard you whether it feels like it or not.

May 30

Crowd Out the Bad Habits

Beloved, I pray that you may prosper in every way and [that your body] may keep well, even as [I know] your soul keeps well and prospers.
3 JOHN 1:2

Bad habits need room to operate. Not much—they're pretty clever—but there are situations where they can't get a foothold. One good strategy for keeping your bad habits at bay is to recognize what your temptations are and then set up your life in such a way that they have no room to operate. Fill your life with so many positive, spiritually reaffirming things that there's no room for anything else. If you are tempted to snack in the evening, then don't keep unhealthy snacks in the house. If you tend to overeat when bored, then be sure you have something fruitful to put your time into.

Choose activities that help to fill that space inside you, your "God-space," with the feelings of love and completeness you are looking for. Instead of sitting around doing nothing, visit a friend or relative you have not seen in a long time or go to a Christian conference. As God says, "Don't link up with those who will pollute you. I want you all for myself" (2 Cor. 6:17 The Message). Another good way to spend time is helping someone else in need. And exercise is a terrific way to fill time with healthy activity that leaves your spirit high and your body recharged.

What other activities can replace some of your current unfulfilling pastimes? What friends do you have who you know are good at encouraging your new health commitment? Call them up and plan some dates. For example, my youngest daughter is very interested in staying healthy. She reads about nutrition, exercise, and good health principles all the time. Anytime I need a little extra encouragement to stay on the right path, I simply ask her what she has learned lately. She always has plenty of things to share that challenge me to keep on keeping on!

Trust in Him Think of one positive, healthy activity that you can do today and do it! Trust God to make it a new, healthy habit in your life.

May 31

Secrets Can Make You Sick

Dear brothers and sisters, if another believer is overcome by some sin, you who are godly should gently and humbly help that person back onto the right path. And be careful not to fall into the same temptation yourself. Share each other's burdens, and in this way obey the law of Christ. GALATIANS 6:1–2 NLT

It would be amazing to know how many people in our society are mentally, physically, or emotionally sick from carrying around secrets buried inside that are eating away at them like a cancer. If you are one of those people, please start talking to God, and either He will completely relieve your burden or He will lead you in what to do next. It is dangerous to merely ignore things that need to be dealt with.

God's will for all of us is wholeness. It is not living with our souls full of holes and watching our lives leak out day after day. Bringing hidden things out into the open is admittedly difficult at times, but it is much more difficult to keep them hidden and live in the fear of being discovered. You might need to talk to a trusted spiritual leader, a loving family member, friend, or a counselor.

God will direct your steps if you will go to Him and tell Him you are fully willing. Having an intimate relationship with God means you can and should talk to Him openly and honestly about anything and everything. The more you talk to God, the better off you are.

One reason we find it so difficult to share our secrets is that it is often hard to find someone to talk to whom we can trust. We can't control what others do, but we can learn to be a faithful friend. If someone tells you something in confidence, never tell anyone else. If they tell you something that shocks or surprises you, do your best not to act surprised and don't judge them. The purpose for bringing things out into the open is for restoration, not for criticism and judging. We should always treat people who come to us to share their secrets as we would want to be treated.

Trust in Him Who do you trust with your secrets? Do you need to talk to someone? Don't put it off. Carrying those secrets around with you can make you sick.

June 1

You're an Everything/Nothing... and So Am I!

What is man that You are mindful of him, and the son of [earthborn] man that You care for him? Yet You have made him but a little lower than God [or heavenly beings], and You have crowned him with glory and honor. PSALM 8:4–5

Pride is a terrible sin, and we are instructed in God's Word not to think more highly of ourselves than we ought to (see Rom. 12:3). That doesn't mean that we need to have a bad opinion of or look down on ourselves. It does mean that we are to remember that we are no better than anyone else and that whatever God has enabled us to do is a gift from Him. We have no more right to claim credit for a special ability we have than we do for blue eyes or brown hair. Paul wrote to the Corinthians and asked them what they had that did not come as a gift from God (see 1 Cor. 4:7).

When we are warned not to think more highly of ourselves than we ought to, it means we are to realize that we are nothing apart from Jesus and without Him we can do nothing. The value we have is found in Him, and we can celebrate who we are only because of Him. Actually, when we celebrate who we are in Jesus, it is a way of celebrating Jesus Himself.

We make this a lot more difficult than it needs to be. It is simple—we are everything in Jesus and nothing in ourselves. I like to say, "I am an everything/nothing!" We celebrate because of the amazing work

God does in us, and not because of any worth we have in ourselves. As long as we continue giving God the glory for anything good that we manifest, we are on a safe and right track.

For some reason religion has taught people that to be godly they must have a low, or even bad, opinion of themselves, and I believe this kind of thinking has done incalculable damage to the plan of God. As long as we know we are lower than God and He is always our Chief and Head, then we are safe.

Trust in Him Say out loud daily, "I am nothing without Jesus, but in and through Him I am valuable and I can do great things."

June 2

Use Your Gifts Wisely

Having gifts (faculties, talents, qualities) that differ according to the grace given us, let us use them... ROMANS 12:6

My husband, Dave, once did one of the wisest things I've seen. Before we entered full-time ministry he worked as an engineer. He was offered a promotion that included a pay raise and a lot of prestige. But he turned it down. At first I was angry with him. I thought he was making a big mistake. Didn't he want to climb the corporate ladder? He explained that he had watched the other men in that position. They had to travel extensively, and they were constantly saddled with unreasonable deadlines that put them under tremendous stress. "That is not the way I want to live," Dave said. He chose the position that allowed him to stay within his abilities and stick to his core values—commitment to God and family, and comfort with self—rather than chasing corporate power so others would look up to him. Besides, why choose a higher paycheck if you just spend it on doctor bills to relieve your stress-induced illnesses?

The most important foundations to long-term happiness are being in right relationship with God, good health, a loving home life, work that is satisfying and not overly stressful, and enough money that you don't worry about finances.

I believe there could be much more happiness and less stress in the world if people would take the time to seek God about decisions. When you are offered a new position, ask yourself why you want it. If it's just for prestige, don't take it. Money is an important consideration and can make some things in life easier, but don't take any job purely for the money if it's going to make you less happy on a daily basis.

It is always wise to think about the long-term effect of every commitment. Don't merely think of the benefits, but also think of the way it will change your overall life. Every privilege comes with responsibility, so make sure you are ready for both before saying "yes."

Trust in Him Always follow peace and make decisions based on godly wisdom. Trust God to open doors for you that are right and close ones that are wrong.

June 3

Where Are You Going?

As he thinks in his heart, so is he. PROVERBS 23:7

To get somewhere, you have to know where you are going. You may not know the exact route, but you at least have a goal in mind. If you are driving from St. Louis to New Orleans, you have a goal. And you have lots of means to achieve that goal, from reading maps to stopping and asking directions. On the other hand, if you just get in your car in St. Louis and drive with no idea where you're going, you may get lost and you'll end up wasting a lot of time.

In your effort to enjoy life, you need to have a vision—a clear picture of what you would like to have in the future. For example, what would your life be like if you felt energetic and had excellent health? What would it take for you to reach that goal? Or, what would it be like to be debt free and how can you work toward that?

God has only one gear: forward! He has no park and no reverse. He wants you to start progressing toward your goals, but before you can do that you must get a clear image of those goals. Don't merely "wish" things were different in your life, but have a clear goal and work toward it.

If you are hung up on your past disappointments, you are never going to escape them. Think and talk about your future, not your past! Talk about the new you that you are becoming. Every successful person starts off by envisioning his or her success.

Create a vision of the ideal you. Writing down your goals helps bring them into the real world and makes them solid. Keep your vision and a list of your goals somewhere handy so you can consult it periodically and see how you're doing. Your list of goals can serve as stepping stones on your way to becoming your ideal self.

It's time to get out the road atlas of your life, pick your destination, and slide that transmission into gear: forward!

Trust in Him What is your vision from God and how are you pursuing it? In order to get there, you'll need to trust His voice and lean on His guidance.

June 4

Manage Your Emotions

In him lie hidden all the treasures of wisdom and knowledge.
COLOSSIANS 2:3 NLT

We all have emotions, but we must learn to manage them. Emotions can be positive or negative. They can make us feel wonderful or awful. They are a central part of being human, and that is fine. Unfortunately, most people do what they feel like doing, say what they feel like saying, buy what they feel like buying, and eat what they feel like eating. And that is not fine, because feelings are not wisdom.

Feelings are fickle; they change frequently and without notification. Since feelings are unreliable, we must not direct our lives according to how we feel. You can be aware of your feelings and acknowledge their legitimacy without necessarily acting on them. God has given us wisdom, and we should walk in it, not our emotions.

Healthy emotions are very important. They help us recognize how we truly feel and what we value. Good emotional health is vital for a good life. But a good life also means being able to manage our emotions and not be managed by them. Negative emotions such as anger, unforgiveness, worry, anxiety, fear, resentment, and bitterness cause many physical illnesses by raising our stress levels.

It seems to me that most people in our society today are mad, and the ones who aren't are sad. Thank God we no longer have to be like "*most people*." God doesn't want anyone to be a slave to their feelings. To manage your emotions and your life, you need to ask God for His wisdom instead of trusting your feelings.

The more stable our emotions are, the healthier we will be, and we all want to enjoy good health. I strongly encourage you to trust God to help you learn to manage your emotions so they don't manage you.

Trust in Him Trust God to lead you by wisdom, and don't merely follow your emotions. God will always lead you to a good place.

June 5

Believe the Best

A man reaps what he sows. The one who sows to please his sinful nature, from that nature will reap destruction; the one who sows to please the Spirit, from the Spirit will reap eternal life.

GALATIANS 6:7–8 NIV 1984

We can quickly ruin a day with wrong thinking. Friendships are destroyed because of wrong thinking. Business deals go wrong. Marriages fail. It's so easy to concentrate on everything that is wrong with your spouse instead of what is right, and soon you want to get away from the person you are married to, when what you really want to escape is your own negative mind.

Replace suspicion and fear with trust. Trust breeds trust. Trusting others, and especially trusting God, helps keep us healthy. When we trust, we are relaxed and at rest.

This is good-old common sense. Consider the following case: You are walking down an unfamiliar street and a man comes out of his house with his pit bull growling on a leash and mutters, "*What are you doing in my yard?*" You think, *Who is this nutcase?* and act angry and suspicious right back. His unfriendliness boomerangs back to him (and probably makes him unfriendlier still). On the other hand, if you are somehow able to look beyond his suspiciousness (maybe he was recently robbed?) and act extremely friendly and relaxed toward him, more often than not he will relax, too, and you'll have a friendly interaction that improves his day and yours.

Call this the "boomerang effect." Or follow the Bible and call it "reaping what you sow." Whatever you call it, the saying is true: you get what you give.

Trust in Him **Consider all the relationships in your life—where can you replace suspicion with trust?**

June 6

Learn to Live on the Resurrection Side of the Cross

Behold, it was for my peace that I had intense bitterness; but You have loved back my life from the pit of corruption and nothingness, for You have cast all my sins behind Your back.

ISAIAH 38:17

We must live on the resurrection side of the cross. Jesus was crucified and raised from the dead so that we might no longer be stuck in sin, living miserable lives. Many people wear a necklace called a crucifix, which is an emblem of Jesus hanging on the cross. Often we see a crucifix in a church with Jesus hanging on it. I know it is done to remember and honor Him and I am not against it, but the truth is that He is not on the cross any longer. The Romans crucified thousands of people, but only One rose again from the dead. Now He is seated in heavenly places with His Father and has also lifted us above the low level of thinking and living sinful, worldly.

The apostle Paul said he was determined to know Jesus and the power of His resurrection that lifted Him out from among the dead (see Phil. 3:10). Jesus came to lift us out of the ordinary, out of negative thinking, guilt, shame, and condemnation. He came to take our sins to the cross and defeat them. Sin has no power over us any longer because we are forgiven and the penalty has been paid.

Which side of the cross are you living on: the crucifixion side or the resurrection side? It is good and respectful to remember that Jesus suffered a terrible death for us on the cross, but we need to also realize that He rose from the dead and made a new life available to us. There is a popular song titled "Because He Lives," and it is about how Jesus' death and resurrection give us the power and privilege to live life in victory today. Because He lives, we can love ourselves in an unselfish way. A way that enables us to be all we can be for God's glory. The only way I know to say it is: get a new attitude about yourself! Stop thinking that your failures and mistakes are too much for God. He isn't looking at them, and you need to stop looking at them, too. Deal with them in Christ and go on!

Trust in Him Which side of the cross are you living on? Put your trust in the power of the resurrected life Jesus has given you.

June 7

Get the Small Things Right

Thus you will be enriched in all things and in every way, so that you can be generous, and [your generosity as it is] administered by us will bring forth thanksgiving to God. 2 CORINTHIANS 9:11

Have you ever gone out to breakfast with somebody whose meal cost them $8.00 and watched them torture themselves over the tip? They pay with a 10-dollar bill and have 2 one-dollar bills in change. The customary tip would be 20 percent, which would amount to $1.60. What will they do? Will they be generous and leave the whole $2.00 as the tip? Not on your life! That would be too much. Instead, they'll waste 10 minutes of their life getting change on that second dollar so they can leave $1.60 tip and save themselves $.40 rather than leave an "exceptionally generous" tip of $2.00.

But what would happen if they left the full $2.00? They'd save some valuable time—time undoubtedly worth more to them than $.40. And they'd bless the server. Not that the actual $.40 means much to her, either, but the message that goes along with that $.40 means the world! It says "*thanks*," and it says what she does has value. Maybe this message gets lost—she may just sweep up the tip without counting—but the generous person will always be blessed. He will know instinctively that he has done the better thing. What an opportunity…we can increase the happiness of others and ourselves for mere pocket change!

This is just one tiny example of the many ways in which the small things we do have surprisingly powerful repercussions. Small things set the tone for our days. Going the extra mile for people, whether it's a slightly larger tip, an unexpected compliment or gift, or even holding a door for them, costs you very little and gives you a lot. Make a decision to be the type of person who always goes the extra mile and does more than enough!

Trust in Him Go out of your way to do something nice today—open a door, leave a good tip, or share a beautiful smile with someone who crosses your path. Trust that God will speak to them through your kindness.

June 8

No Excuse to Stay Where You Are

You shall assign to them as their responsibility all they are to carry.

NUMBERS 4:27 NIV

One of the biggest problems in society today is that people don't want to take responsibility for their lives. They want quick fixes. Society has trained them to believe that if they have problems, somebody else is responsible. Their parents are responsible. Their spouses are responsible. Their schools or employers are responsible. Taking responsibility for our actions and choices is often hard to do, but it is vitally necessary if we want to enjoy the good life Jesus wants us to have.

I'm not saying you are responsible for the current state of your life. Lots of uncontrollable events occur in our lives. Sometimes we get poor training in childhood. Sometimes we have bad people in our lives who hurt us. The situation you find yourself in may or may not be your fault. But it is your fault if you take it lying down! You do not have to stay in that bad situation. You get to make a choice—and that choice is 100 percent yours.

No matter how you got to where you find yourself today, don't let it be an excuse to stay there. I had many excuses and reasons for my poor health, bad attitude, and unbalanced life. As long as I offered excuses, I never made progress. Taking responsibility for where we are is a must in making progress. Perhaps you did not get a good start in life, but you can have a good finish. If you have a bad habit of making excuses instead of taking responsibility, today is the best day to change!

Trust in Him Ask God to help you see an area of your life where you can take responsibility to make a positive change.

June 9

Celebrate You

Therefore if any person is [ingrafted] in Christ (the Messiah) he is a new creation (a new creature altogether); the old [previous moral and spiritual condition] has passed away. Behold, the fresh and new has come! 2 CORINTHIANS 5:17

I don't think it's dangerous to have a good opinion of yourself in Christ, but I do think it is dangerous not to. The truth is that you cannot rise above what you think. We are all limited by our own thinking. If we think small, we will live small. And if we think big, we will live big. God wants us to realize how big He is, and He wants us to be bold enough to think big thoughts. God did not chastise David because he thought he could kill Goliath—He was proud of him! David knew that his victory was in God and not in himself, but he was confident and courageous and refused to live small.

What your life amounts to is directly connected to what you think of yourself. We need to learn to think like God thinks. Some identify with the problems they have had in life and call themselves by that name. They say, "*I am divorced. I am bankrupt. I am an abuse victim. I am an alcoholic.*" They should say, "*I was divorced, but now I am a new creature in Christ. I was a victim of abuse, but now I have a new life and a new identity. I was an alcoholic, but now I am free and I have discipline and self-control.*" He has a good plan for each of us, but we must have our minds renewed (learn to think differently) if we ever hope to experience what Jesus purchased with His death and resurrection.

There is no doubt that we are way less than perfect, that we have faults and weaknesses. We make mistakes and bad choices, and often lack wisdom, but God is God and He views us the way He knows we can be. He doesn't love us more when we do well—but He knows we'll enjoy our lives more. God sees us as a finished project *while* we are making the journey. He sees the end from the beginning and is able to help us overcome whatever mistakes we make in between. God believes in you; you should, too!

Trust in Him Stop identifying with the problems in your life. Trust what God says about you—you are a new creature in Christ.

June 10

Don't Assume; Ask God

When I kept silence [before I confessed], my bones wasted away through my groaning all the day long. PSALM 32:3

We all have days when we feel more emotional than usual, and there may be many reasons why. Perhaps you didn't sleep well the night before, or you ate something that lowered your blood sugar or that you were allergic to. The occasional emotional day is something we don't have to be too concerned about. If my husband has a day like that, he never tries to figure it out. He simply says, "*This too shall pass.*"

There are also times we have emotional issues that need to be resolved and dealt with. We are often guilty of stuffing things down inside us rather than dealing with them. If you are a person who avoids confrontation, you can have a soul full of unresolved issues that need closure before emotional wholeness will come. I remember a night when I was unable to sleep, which is unusual for me. Finally, around five in the morning, I asked God what was wrong with me. Immediately I recalled a situation from the day before. I had been rude to someone and instead of apologizing to them and asking God to forgive me, I rushed through the situation and went on to the next thing I needed to do. Obviously, my wrong conduct was irritating my spirit, even though my conscious mind had buried it. As soon as I asked God to forgive me and made a decision to apologize to the person, I was able to go to sleep.

If you feel unusually sad or as if you are carrying a heavy burden you don't understand, ask God what is wrong before you start assuming things. It is amazing what we can learn by simply asking God for an answer and being willing to face any truth He might reveal about us or our behavior. Sometimes we feel emotional because of something someone has done to us or an unpleasant circumstance in our lives. But at other times we feel that way because of something we did wrong and ignored.

Trust in Him Ask God what is causing you to be emotional and be willing to face any truth He reveals.

June 11

Life's Not Fair...and That's Okay

Get rid of all bitterness, rage and anger, brawling and slander, along with every form of malice. EPHESIANS 4:31 NIV

Sadly, the world is filled with injustices. One of my uncles spent twenty years in prison for a crime he did not commit. His wife committed the crime and finally confessed right before she died. When he was finally released, his tuberculosis—contracted while he was in prison—had gotten so bad that he lived only a few more years. I remember my uncle was always a very kind man and seemed to have no bitterness at all about that great injustice.

Looking back, I believe his difficult life, lived with an attitude of forgiveness, gave God more glory than someone who has a great life but is never content. Our suffering does not please God, but when we have a good attitude in the midst of suffering it pleases and glorifies Him. Having a good attitude while we are waiting for God to bring justice into our lives makes the waiting time more bearable.

We live in a fallen, broken world. But in the midst of it all, Jesus is beautiful and He is a God who brings justice. Life isn't fair, but God is. He heals the brokenhearted and their wounds and bruises. We may not know why things happen the way they do, but we can trust that God knows and in the end He's going to sort all things out. It's so amazing that even in an unfair world we can know His love, forgiveness, and mercy. When we are sad and emotionally distraught, one of the very simple yet profound things that can help is this: to look at and be thankful for the good things we do have, rather than dwell on the injustices we've suffered. You might think, *I've heard that a thousand times!* But are you doing it?!

Many people are treated unjustly; they do not deserve the pain they experience, but I am so glad that even when I go through ugly, painful things, I do have Jesus in my life to help and strengthen me. Through His guidance we can be burned but not become bitter. We may feel angry, frustrated, discouraged, or depressed, but we do not have to let any of those feelings control us.

Trust in Him **How do you respond to injustice? Does it make you angry or does it prompt you to trust God more and thank Him for all His goodness even in this broken world? You'll find great peace when you choose to live this way.**

June 12

The Truth About Willpower

. . . "Not by might nor by power, but by My Spirit," says the Lord *of hosts.*
ZECHARIAH 4:6 NKJV

Willpower can be a powerful tool in the hands of a determined, disciplined individual. It can help you confront any problem you have and adjust your lifestyle. However, willpower only takes us so far and then we always run out of our own strength.

Now, what happens if, instead of turning first to willpower in your time of need, you turn to God? God releases His power into you and enables you to go all the way through to victory. Now you're energized for positive change, but willpower does not get the credit for our success, God does.

Jesus said in John 15:5, "Apart from Me you can do nothing." This is one of the most important and most difficult lessons we must learn if we want to enjoy the life Jesus died to give us. When we turn to anything or anyone before God, He is insulted and is obligated to let us fail so we will realize that "except the Lord builds the house, they labor in vain who build it" (Ps. 127:1).

We must learn to let God do the heavy lifting. Let Him supply the ability to energize our choices. We can choose to exercise or stop overeating, but our choice alone is not enough for complete victory. Willpower and determination will get us started, but they've been known to quit in the middle and leave us stranded. God never quits in the middle.

There are some people in the world who claim to be a self-made success, but if we follow their lives all the way through, they usually end up falling apart. God has not created us to function well without Him, and the sooner we learn that the better off we will be.

Start by asking God to get involved, to do the heavy lifting. Continue on with God and finish with God. What should we do when the burdens in life seem too heavy? Jesus said, "Come to me, all you who are weary and burdened, and I will give you rest" (Matt. 11:28 NIV).

Trust in Him Who/what is the first thing you turn to when you need to overcome a problem? Whatever "that" is, that's where you're placing your trust. Choose to put your trust in God in all things and at all times.

June 13

Five Ways to Trust God with Your Burdens

If any of you is deficient in wisdom, let him ask of the giving God [Who gives] to everyone liberally and ungrudgingly, without reproaching or faultfinding, and it will be given him.

JAMES 1:5

There are many practical ways that you can trust God with your burdens on a daily basis. Here are five I want to suggest you apply to your life because I've seen the difference they can make.

Ask. You will be amazed at what a huge difference it makes to directly invite God into your life to help solve your problems. It's astonishing how few people actually try this—even Christians! You need to take the time to quiet your mind and open it to God as you ask for His wisdom.

Attend Church. Some people manage to maintain very special relationships with the Lord for years without any support. They are few and far between. Most of us find that the weekly boost of prayer, Bible study, community, and sacred space we get at church gives us a far stronger bond. If you are struggling for ways to make contact with God, and you haven't tried church yet, don't put it off anymore.

Attend a Support Group. Support groups exist for a variety of problems, from alcohol to drug addiction to overeating. If you work best when you can share your struggle with others who are going through the same thing, then I encourage you to seek out one of these groups.

Begin Each Day with an Affirmation. First thing when you wake up in the morning, before all the busyness of the day comes flying at you, take a moment to renew your vows to God and refresh your spirit with His strength. This will give you the mental and emotional peace that is the foundation of success.

Pray in Moments of Doubt. No matter who you are, you will find moments when your determination weakens. When you get that feeling, don't quit, but don't blindly bull forward with the activity, either. Step back, take a moment, and call on God to come to you and carry you through.

Trust in Him Choose at least one action you can take to begin trusting God with your burdens and start that action today.

June 14

Tell God How You Feel

How long will You forget me, O Lord? PSALM 13:1

I find the Psalms written by David very interesting because he was not reticent about telling God exactly how he felt. But he also followed up by stating that he was trusting God to be faithful to keep His promises and would even remind God of something He had promised in His Word:

> How long will You forget me, O Lord? Forever? How long will You hide Your face from me? How long must I lay up cares within me and have sorrow in my heart day after day? How long shall my enemy exalt himself over me?
>
> Consider and answer me, O Lord my God; lighten the eyes [of my faith to behold Your face in the pitchlike darkness], lest I sleep the sleep of death, lest my enemy say, I have prevailed over him, and those that trouble me rejoice when I am shaken.
>
> But I have trusted, leaned on, and been confident in Your mercy and loving-kindness; my heart shall rejoice and be in high spirits in Your salvation. I will sing to the Lord, because He has dealt bountifully with me. (Ps. 13:1–6)

If I paraphrased the above in today's language, it might sound something like this: *"God, I am hurting so badly, I feel like I am going to die. How long will You wait before You do something for me? Do You want my enemies to say that they've won? God, I have trusted in You and will continue to do so. Let me see Your face even in the midst of my trouble so I can be encouraged. I feel lousy, God, but I will rejoice and have a good attitude because of Your salvation and Your promises of love and mercy. I will sing to You because You are good."*

I believe it was spiritually and even physically healthy for David to express to God how he really felt. It was a way of releasing his negative feelings so they could not harm his inner man while he was waiting for God's deliverance. He trusted God with his deepest, more intense feelings—and so can you. I've noticed that David frequently said how he felt or what his circumstances were and then he said, *"But I will trust God. I will praise God, who helps me."*

Trust in Him Tell God how you feel—the good, the bad, and the ugly. You can trust that He's not afraid of your deepest, most honest feelings. Then tell Him that you trust Him no matter how you feel!

June 15

We Want the Real Thing

I am speaking the truth in Christ. I am not lying; my conscience [enlightened and prompted] by the Holy Spirit bearing witness with me...
ROMANS 9:1

Nobody likes being tricked. We don't like false advertising, phony small-talk, or fake relationships. In our world, people often put on a plastic smile and tell everyone they're doing fine while inside they're falling apart. It's all an illusion.

As Christians we often believe we should feel better than we do, or that it is wrong to feel the way we do, so we hide our feelings from everyone. Sometimes we try to hide the way we really feel from ourselves. We pretend to have faith while we're full of doubt. We pretend to be happy while we are miserable; and we pretend to be in control and have it all together, but at home behind closed doors, we are totally different people. We don't want to admit that we are living phony lives, so we stay busy enough that we never have to deal with things as they really are. We may even bury ourselves in church work or spiritual activity as a way of hiding from God. He is trying to show us truth, but we would rather work for Him than listen to Him.

God just wants us to be honest and real. Don't fall into the trap of thinking all your feelings are wrong. Being a person of faith does not mean you will never have negative or ungodly feelings. We will experience feelings that need to be dealt with, but we can always exercise our faith in God and ask Him to help us to not allow our feelings to control us. The Bible says we live by faith and not by sight (see 2 Cor. 5:7). That means we don't make decisions based on what we see or feel, but according to our faith in God and His promises to us.

Trust in Him You need to trust that the real you, even on your worst day, is better than being fake or phony. Make the choice today to be honest, genuine, and authentic with God and with all the people in your life.

June 16

It Is Okay to Be Extravagant at Times!

And when the disciples saw it, they were indignant, saying, For what purpose is all this waste? MATTHEW 26:8

The Bible teaches us to be prudent, and that means being good managers of all our resources. Yet there are times when God gets rather extravagant with those whom He loves. Sometimes in an effort to not be wasteful we can become downright cheap and stingy. Some people are especially that way with themselves. I know people who are generous with others, but their general attitude toward themselves is that they can do without. They say, "I don't need that," or, "I can do without that."

But I believe they are depriving themselves because they don't feel worth the cost of the indulgence. In trying to avoid wasting anything they've been given, they've missed out on what God wanted to do for them.

Perhaps we can learn a lesson from Jesus. He was nearing the time of His suffering and death, and He went to Simon's house, where a woman named Mary came up to Him and poured expensive perfume on His head as He was reclining at the table. Since He was at the table I am assuming that He either was or had been eating. When the disciples saw what she did, they became indignant, saying, *"For what purpose is all this waste?"* They talked about how the perfume could have been sold and the money given to the poor.

Jesus replied by telling them not to bother the woman, because she had done a noble (praiseworthy and beautiful) thing for Him. Jesus said what she had done had helped prepare Him for the trials ahead (see Matt. 26:6–12). The perfume she poured out on Jesus was probably worth about one year's wages, but her extravagance certainly blessed Him. The love she showed to Him helped give Him the strength He needed to face the upcoming days of persecution, trial, suffering, crucifixion, and death.

In this particular instance, Jesus was saying that for this time and occasion He was worth the extravagance, or what the disciples saw as "waste." Don't live a reckless, wasteful life, but do remember that at times you are worth a little extravagance!

Trust in Him **Live with bold expectations and watch God do some very special things for you.**

June 17

A Guilty Conscience Is a Miserable Thing to Live With

Let us draw near to God with a sincere heart in full assurance of faith, having our hearts sprinkled to cleanse us from a guilty conscience and having our bodies washed with pure water.

HEBREWS 10:22 NIV

There are some things you should keep between you and God, but some things must be brought out into the open. I have an example from my own life that may be helpful. When I was twenty years old—and that was a long time ago—I stole money from a company I worked for. The man I was married to at the time was a petty thief, and he convinced me to write some payroll checks since I was the payroll clerk, and we would cash them and quickly get out of town. I am not blaming him because I should have said no, but there are times in life when we let people we love talk us into things that go against our consciences. When we do, it always ends up badly.

We did cash the checks and leave town, but eventually we came back, and sure enough there was an ongoing investigation about the stolen money. I was questioned, told more lies, and escaped being accused of the crime. My husband cheated on me with other women, stole property, and eventually was arrested and went to prison. We got a divorce, and many years later, married to someone else and about to enter the ministry, I knew that I had to go to the company I'd stolen from, admit my theft, and pay back the money. Wow! What if they had me arrested? I was so frightened, but I knew I had to obey God. I could not go forward until that thing from my past was confronted.

I went to the company and explained what I had done and that I was now a Christian and wanted to ask their forgiveness and pay back the money. They graciously let me do so, and I was set free from the nagging fear that someday I might get caught. I am convinced that if I had not obeyed God, I would not be in ministry today. God is willing to forgive us for anything, but we must confess it and make restitution wherever possible.

Trust in Him If God is telling you to bring something out into the open or confront a situation from your past, be obedient to Him. Don't let your fear of the consequences keep you from the freedom that's waiting for you on the other side.

June 18

"Let Me See Self-Control!"

And all your [spiritual] children shall be disciples [taught by the Lord and obedient to His will], and great shall be the peace and undisturbed composure of your children. ISAIAH 54:13

Our emotions tend to ebb and flow like ocean waves. It would be so nice if they would just ask permission to come or go, but they don't. They just do their own thing, and without any warning.

A rebellious child does a lot of things without a parent's permission, and just wishing that the child wouldn't do that won't change a thing. The parent must discipline the child to bring about change. The same principle holds true with emotions. They are often like rebellious children, and the longer they are allowed to do as they please, the more difficult it will be to control them.

My daughter, Sandy, and her husband, Steve, have twin girls. Steve and Sandy have studied parenting techniques, and one thing they work with their children on a lot is self-control. It's interesting to watch how it works for them. One or both of the girls may be behaving quite emotionally. They might be angry or acting selfish, and one of the parents will say, *"Girls, let's get some self-control. Come on, let me see self-control."* That's the girls' signal to fold their hands in their laps and sit quietly until they calm down and can behave correctly. It works beautifully! It will be easier for the twins to manage their emotions as adults because they are learning to do so early in life.

I spent the first eighteen years of my life in a house where emotions were volatile, and it seemed normal to me to let them rule. I learned that if you didn't get what you wanted, you yelled, argued, and stayed angry until you got your way. I learned how to manipulate people by making them feel guilty. I learned starting at an early age to be emotional, and it took lots of years to unlearn what I had learned. I encourage you to control yourself and teach your children at an early age how to do the same thing. If it is too late for that, then begin where you are now, because it is never too late to do the right thing.

Trust in Him On a scale of 1 to 10, how often do you demonstrate self-control? It takes practice and encouragement from God's Word to live this way, but you can trust that God, as your loving Father, will help you get there.

June 19

We Are Nothing Without God

God chose the foolish things of the world to shame the wise; God chose the weak things of the world to shame the strong. He chose the lowly things of this world and the despised things—and the things that are not—to nullify the things that are, so that no one may boast before him. 1 CORINTHIANS 1:27–29 NIV

It amazes me that God chooses weak and foolish men and women to work through, but He does. He chooses what the secular world would throw away as trash and consider useless. When God is looking for someone to fill a position or to promote, He often passes over those who would be naturally qualified if they are the type to be proud of themselves and not give Him the credit and glory for their abilities. God works through the humble, but He frustrates and defeats the proud (see 1 Pet. 5:5).

God loves to lift up those whom life has pressed down. You are special to God and He has a promotion in mind for you. He desires that we live amazed at what He can do through a submitted vessel. God is not looking for ability, but He is looking for availability. Humble yourself under the mighty hand of God, and in due time He will exalt you and lift you up. Don't discount yourself from being used by God because of your natural weaknesses or disadvantages. He is more than happy to show Himself strong in those who will trust Him.

Pride comes before destruction, so always remember to give God the credit for any good things that He does through you. Our gifts, talents, and abilities all come from Him. What do we have that He did not give us? Absolutely nothing! Therefore, all the praise goes to Him.

Trust in Him Even though you don't deserve it and may not be naturally qualified, trust God to use you for His glory.

June 20

It Is What It Is, So Be Happy Anyway

Do not conform any longer to the pattern of this world, but be transformed by the renewing of your mind.

ROMANS 12:2 NIV 1984

I used to weigh 135 pounds, and then at some point in my late fifties I gained a few pounds and have been that way ever since. My metabolism slowed down and those few pounds stuck. I'm not thrilled about it, but I finally accepted it. I would have to seriously deprive myself to lose those few pounds and keep them off. My body and health seem very good where I am, so I have decided that I would rather live with a little more weight than constantly worry about my weight and never eat the things I enjoy.

My body is also shaped so that I wear a size eight top and a size ten bottom. I have always been that way. There are lots of beautiful suits I can't buy because they don't come in split sizes. I could buy two suits and take what I needed, but then I'd feel like I had to find someone who was a size eight bottom and a size ten top so I wasn't being wasteful! The whole situation used to frustrate me until I decided "*It is what it is!*" Now I mostly laugh about it—and laughing is a very important habit to have, especially as you age.

If your feet are larger than you would like them to be, or your body is not proportioned perfectly, or you are shorter than you wish you were, don't ever let it frustrate you again. Decide right now, "*It is what it is! I am going to be happy with what I have and do the best I can with it.*"

I want to encourage you to see yourself as God sees you; then not only will you love yourself, but you will have the confidence and faith to be a powerful force for good in the world.

Trust in Him **Look in the mirror at the part of you that causes you the most frustration and say out loud, *"It is what it is! I am going to be happy with what I have and do the best I can with it."***

June 21

God Celebrates Your Progress

But the path of the [uncompromisingly] just and righteous is like the light of dawn, that shines more and more (brighter and clearer) until [it reaches its full strength and glory in] the perfect day [to be prepared]. PROVERBS 4:18

Our youngest grandson recently stood by himself for the first time. We were out of town on this joyous occasion, but we received a phone call telling us the great news. I vividly remember that there were four adults in the car when we received the news and three of us acted fairly ridiculous about the event. I actually clapped my hands together. Dave grinned from ear to ear and in a very surprised tone said, *"REALLY!"* A good friend was also in the car and she got excited. I heard questions like, *"How long did he stand there?"* and *"Has he done it more than once?"* Nobody asked if he sat down again, although we all knew that he did. We were even aware that he could have fallen down, but we did not care about anything other than his progress.

We had a similar scene at our house when he smiled for the first time, ate his first solid food, crawled, and said *"mama"* and *"da-da."* We get really excited about any little progress that he makes and we all express it to him to encourage him. Dave and I just spent several days with the baby, and, to be honest, we probably encouraged him hundreds of times during those few days. I don't remember even one time that we chastised him for what he could not do yet. God used this example to help me understand that He celebrates our progress just like we celebrate the progress of our children and grandchildren.

God isn't keeping a record of each time we fall, but He is excited about our progress, and we should be excited, too! I spent way too many years mourning over my faults and weaknesses. I was taught to grieve over my sins, but nobody in the church I was in at the time ever told me to celebrate my progress, and I think that is tragic. If you missed this important lesson like I did, then today I am telling you to celebrate, celebrate, and then celebrate your progress some more.

Trust in Him Think about an area in your life that you are making progress in. Don't focus on how far you have to go to reach your goal, but celebrate how far you have already come. Remember, God's celebrating as a proud parent every step you make—you can trust He's excited for you!

June 22

Don't Let Your Emotions Vote

Do not be misled, my beloved brethren. JAMES 1:16

If we desire to walk after the Spirit, all our actions must be governed by God's principles. In the realm of the Spirit, there is a precise standard of right and wrong, and how we feel does not alter that standard. If doing the right thing requires a "yes" from us, then it must be "yes" whether we feel excited or discouraged. If it is "no," then it is "no." A principled life is enormously different from an emotional life. When an emotional person feels thrilled or happy, he may undertake what he ordinarily would not do. But when he feels cold and emotionless or melancholy, he will not fulfill his duty, because his feelings refuse to cooperate.

All who desire to be truly spiritual must conduct themselves daily according to godly principles. A good sign to show you're growing and maturing in Christ is when you consistently obey, even when you don't feel like it.

Learn not to ask yourself how you feel about things, but instead ask yourself if doing or not doing something is right for you. You may know that you need to do something, but you don't feel like doing it at all. You can wish you felt like it, but wishing does no good. You must live by principle and simply choose to do what you know is right. There may be a certain thing you want to do badly. It might be a purchase you want to make that you know is too expensive. Your feelings vote "yes," but your heart says "no." Tell your feelings they don't get to vote. They are too immature to vote and will never vote for what is best for you in the long run.

We don't allow people to vote in political elections until they are eighteen, because we assume they would be too immature to know what they are doing. Why not look at your emotions the same way? They have always been a part of you, but they are very immature. They are without wisdom and cannot be trusted to do the right thing, so just don't let them vote. We mature but our emotions don't, and if they are left unchecked, our lives will be a series of unfinished and disappointing ventures.

Trust in Him Pray and ask God to help you trust Him more than you trust your emotions.

June 23

Stop Saying, "That's Just the Way I Am!"

I have [in short] become all things to all men, that I might by all means (at all costs and in any and every way) save some [by winning them to faith in Jesus Christ]. 1 CORINTHIANS 9:22

Some people are quiet, shy, and more laid-back simply because of their personalities. I am a talker and my husband is not, and there is nothing wrong with either of us. But when anything becomes excessive to the point that it is hindering our freedom or hurting other people, we cannot say, "*That's just the way I am.*" Dave needs to talk to me more than he might prefer to at times because that's what I need, and love requires that we make sacrifices for the sake of other people. There are also times when I would like to rattle on and on in conversation, but I notice that Dave isn't really enjoying it so I decide to be quiet or I go find someone else to talk to.

We must work with God to find the balance between being who we are and not excusing unloving behavior by saying, "*That is just the way I am.*" God is in the business of changing us into His image, and that means He helps us control our weaknesses and He uses our strengths.

Dave and I have very different personalities, and yet we get along fabulously. It was not always that way, but we've learned to be what the other needs and yet not go so far that we lose our own freedom. I try to meet Dave's needs and he does the same thing for me. Dave likes to do things that I don't enjoy, but I still encourage him to do them so he can feel fulfilled, and he treats me the same way. When a friend or spouse needs you to adapt in some area to make the relationship better, it is foolish and selfish to say, "*Sorry, that is just the way I am.*" We may be more comfortable and find it easier to do what we feel like doing, but we can make adjustments and still not lose our individuality.

We can make ourselves very miserable and have stress-filled lives by never being willing to change or adapt. We are all different, but we can get along peacefully if we are willing.

Trust in Him Ask God to help you be sensitive to the needs of those around you and give you the grace to adapt in whatever way you need to in order to walk in love with them. Trust God to help you be all things to all people.

June 24

Eat for God's Glory

And the Lord God commanded the man, saying, You may freely eat of every tree of the garden. GENESIS 2:16

After God created Adam and Eve, He gave them some very simple dining instructions. "You may freely eat of every tree of the garden," He said in Genesis 2:16.

Did He say, "You may freely eat of every Krispy Kreme on the street"? No. Did He say, "You may freely eat of every chip in the bag"? No. He did not tell them to freely eat fast food, frozen pizza, or even low-fat cookies.

God told Adam and Eve to eat from the garden, and we'd do well to stick to His advice. We've been inundated with an overwhelming amount of bad diet information from past decades that has clouded the very simple truths of healthy eating: eat the foods that come from God, in as close a state as possible to how God made them, and you can't go wrong.

Learn to do everything for God's glory, including eating. Look at your dinner plate and ask if what you are about to eat is mostly what God created for you. Don't view eating as a secular event that has nothing to do with your relationship with God. Don't forget that God put Adam and Eve in the Garden of Eden and told them what they could eat. If eating had nothing to do with their walk with Him, He probably would not have mentioned food.

This advice isn't a diet I am recommending—it's simply godly wisdom to live a balanced life. There's nothing wrong with enjoying a treat in moderation. Each time you choose good, healthy foods, you are choosing life, which is God's gift to you. He wants you to look great and feel great. Keep in mind that your body is the temple of God, and the fuel you put into it determines how it will operate and for how long.

Make sure that you are not hurting yourself by eating junk food excessively. Remember, good choices will reap good benefits.

Trust in Him Take a step of faith and begin to trust God to lead you in your eating habits. Ask Him to teach you how to eat healthily, and watch to see how much better you feel.

June 25

Be Kind and Encouraging

It [Love] is not conceited (arrogant and inflated with pride); it is not rude (unmannerly) and does not act unbecomingly. Love (God's love in us) does not insist on its own rights or its own way, for it is not self-seeking; it is not touchy or fretful or resentful; it takes no account of the evil done to it [it pays no attention to a suffered wrong].

1 CORINTHIANS 13:5

I have learned that one of the secrets to my own personal peace is letting people be who God made them to be, rather than trying to make them be who I would like them to be. I do my best to enjoy their strengths and be merciful toward their weaknesses because I have plenty of my own. I don't need to try to take the speck out of their eye while I have a telephone pole in my own.

A woman I know was widowed not long ago, and she was telling me about her relationship with her husband. This woman is pretty strong-willed and likes things to go her way. She told me that when she was first married, she noticed a lot of things about her husband that annoyed her. Like any good wife, she told her husband about his annoying traits and habits so he could change.

Gradually it dawned on her that although she was very good about telling her husband all the things about him that needed to change, he never returned the favor! As she wondered why, she realized that somewhere along the line her husband had made a decision not to look at—or for—her flaws. He knew she had plenty! But he wasn't going to focus on them. It occurred to her that she could continue to point out all his annoying traits—or she could choose not to, just as her husband had done.

At the end of our conversation, she told me that in the twelve years they were married, her husband never said an unkind word to her. I think we can all take a lesson from that.

Trust in Him Ask God to help you be kind to everyone. Don't say an unkind word today—focus on the strengths of the people you come in contact with, and do all that you can to encourage them.

June 26

Comfort and Encouragement

Praise be to the God and Father of our Lord Jesus Christ, the Father of compassion and the God of all comfort, who comforts us in all our troubles, so that we can comfort those in any trouble with the comfort we ourselves have received from God.

2 CORINTHIANS 1:3–4 NIV

When you need comfort and encouragement, whom do you go to? Have you ever had the experience of going to a friend or family member for encouragement and went away disappointed because they didn't seem to understand your need? I think we have all had that experience, but there is a better way. Learn to go to God first because He is the God of all comfort. When we go to God first He is honored, but when we run to people and leave Him out it can be offensive to Him. Remember: when we go to God, He quite often uses people to comfort or encourage us, but He chooses who to use and when to use them.

I wasted a lot of time and emotional energy over the years getting angry at Dave and other people because they didn't understand some of my emotional needs, and finally I learned that I needed to go to God first. Sometimes God uses someone we don't even know and sometimes it is someone we would have never thought to go to. But, quite often He divinely comforts us Himself.

I recall a time when my father really made me feel rejected by something he said. There were people with us, but most of them wouldn't have even understood or been able to make me feel better, so while still in my father's presence, I quietly asked God to comfort me and heal my feelings. I continued to pray for a while and soon felt better. He helped me realize that my father was not a sensitive man and didn't even realize what he had done, and I was able to let it go.

Another thing we do at times is run to food, shopping, or some other substance for comfort and we create other problems in our lives. God desires to comfort us, but we must go to Him. If you need comfort or encouragement, take some time right now and ask God specifically to minister to you in that area.

Trust in Him Going to God first shows that we trust Him. When you're hurting, run to God, not away from Him.

June 27

Cast Your Care

Casting the whole of your care [all your anxieties, all your worries, all your concerns, once and for all] on Him, for He cares for you affectionately and cares about you watchfully. 1 PETER 5:7

Obeying this Scripture is a bit more difficult for some of us than others. Because I care about most things in life and want them to go a certain way, my care can easily turn into worry if I am not careful.

For example, I really can't do anything about what people think of me, so being overly concerned about it is a total waste of time and energy, but that has not always stopped me from worrying. My husband certainly does not care what people think of him. On occasion when I have asked him how he feels about some negative thing someone has said about us, he tells me he doesn't feel anything, but instead he just trusts God to take care of it. I have gotten very upset at times when unkind articles have been written about me in the newspapers or we have been judged unfairly, but Dave just says, "*Cast your care.*"

We have had a lot of arguments in the past over that statement. I want him to share my feelings, but he really can't because he simply isn't bothered by the things that bother me. I know he is right when he tells me to "*cast my care,*" but since I am already in the midst of caring, that is not the answer I want. Thankfully, God has helped me and continues to do so, and Dave has been a good example to me.

If you are a more emotional person, I'm sure the less emotional people in your life have frustrated you at times. Nothing seems to bother them and lots of things bother you. I get it! I have been there and I do know how you feel, but I have also lived long enough to realize that living by feelings is a big mistake. It is true that the best way to live is to learn to cast your care and let God care for you.

Trust in Him Do you trust God enough to cast your cares? What burden are you carrying today? Cast it on Him—He wants to take it from you because He can carry any load.

June 28

Don't Fight Correction, Celebrate It

Those whom I [dearly and tenderly] love, I tell their faults and convict and convince and reprove and chasten [I discipline and instruct them]. So be enthusiastic and in earnest and burning with zeal and repent [changing your mind and attitude]. REVELATION 3:19

God views conviction, correction, and discipline as something to be celebrated rather than something to make us sad or frustrated. Why should we celebrate when God shows us that something is wrong with us? Enthusiasm sounds like a strange response, but the fact that we can see something that we were once blind to is good news. For many years of my life I was able to be rude, insensitive, and selfish and not even know it. I had a master's degree in manipulation, but actually had myself convinced that I was only trying to help people do what was right. Of course I did not see the pride I had that caused me to think my way was always the right way. I was greedy, envious, and jealous, but I did not see any of it. That is a sad condition to be in, but people who have no relationship with Jesus and who do not study God's Word are blind and deaf in the spiritual sense.

My heart was hard from years of being hurt by people, harboring bitterness, and doing things my own way. When our heart is hard we are not sensitive to the touch of God. When He convicts us, we don't feel it. Therefore, when we make enough progress in our relationship with God that we begin to sense when we are doing something wrong, that is good news. It is a sign of progress and should be celebrated joyfully. The longer we serve God and study His ways, the more sensitive we become. We eventually grow to the place where we know immediately when we are saying or doing something that is not pleasing to God and we have the option of repenting and making a fresh start.

How do you respond when the Holy Spirit convicts you that you're doing something wrong? Do you feel bad and guilty, or do you realize that the very fact that you can feel God's conviction is good news? It means that you are alive to God and growing spiritually.

Trust in Him Lift your hands in praise and say, "Thank You, God, that You love me enough not to leave me alone in my sin." Trust that His correction is always a sign of His love.

June 29

Believing When Your Back's Against the Wall

Then Moses stretched out his hand over the sea, and the Lord caused the sea to go back by a strong east wind all that night and made the sea dry land; and the waters were divided. EXODUS 14:21

A thorough study of the Bible shows us that the men and women God used in mighty ways always had the attitude of celebrating what God had done. They did not take His goodness for granted, but they openly showed appreciation for little things as well as big ones.

Have you ever had a time when you felt that your back was against the wall: you had a big problem and no solution, and then suddenly God did something amazing and enabled you to escape safely from your problem? Most of us can think of a time like that. When the Israelites were being led out of Egypt by God working through Moses, their backs were against the wall. The Red Sea was in front of them and the Egyptian army was behind them. They had no place to go; they were trapped! God had promised their deliverance, and what He did was amazing indeed. He actually parted the Red Sea, and the Israelites walked across on dry ground, but as the Egyptian army followed, the sea closed up over them and they drowned.

When the Israelites reached the other side, the first thing they did was start to celebrate. They sang a song that came straight from their hearts, recorded in nineteen verses in the Bible (see Exod. 15:1–19). After the song, two of the women took out a type of tambourine, and all the women followed them with their tambourines and they danced and sang some more. The entire song talked of what God had done, how great He was, how He had redeemed them and dealt with their enemies. We would probably experience more victory in life if we would take time to celebrate the ones we have already had. Once again, it is about operating on the principle of being grateful for what we have instead of taking an inventory of what we do not have yet.

Trust in Him Think of a time that your back was against the wall and God delivered you. Celebrate that victory all over again—and trust that God will deliver you the next time!

June 30

Revelation Sets You Free

For as he thinks in his heart, so is he. PROVERBS 23:7

If we become what we think about, as this Scripture attests, it's no wonder that the Bible teaches us we must learn how to meditate on the Word of God—to roll it over and over in our mind until it becomes a part of us. Meditation takes information and turns it into revelation. One of the problems I think we can have as Christians is that there is so much information available to us today that we can get stuck at *information* and never really study any one thing long enough for it to become *revelation*. It's not information that sets you free. It's revelation. It's not what somebody else knows that's going to help you; it's what *you* know. It's not even what you know; it's what you *know* that you *know* that you *know* that you *know*—it is that kind of deep-rooted revelation knowledge that Satan cannot steal from you with his lies.

Romans 12:2 says not to be conformed to this world but to be transformed by the renewing of your mind. Fear, guilt, insecurity, and worry can be let in or kept out by right or wrong thoughts. You can open your mind to fear and let it in, or you can close your mind to fear and not let it in. The mind is like a doorway. When the enemy tries to sneak in with a thought that is going to be detrimental to us or against the Word of God, we need to learn how to close our minds against that and say, "*no.*" No is a great word for Christians to learn.

"But refuse (shut your mind against, have nothing to do with) trifling (ill-informed, unedifying, stupid) controversies over ignorant questionings, for you know that they foster strife and breed quarrels" (2 Tim. 2:23). Shut your mind to gossip, slander, and to the idea that someone with an opinion different from yours must be wrong, and to other unedifying thoughts that will lead to strife. Fix your mind on things that are worthy: love, kindness, thinking the best about people, grace, mercy, and other edifying thoughts that are found in the Word of God (see Phil. 4:8).

Trust in Him As you think in your heart, so are you, so shut the door on any thought that is not from God. If you are trusting God, there is no need for fear.

July 1

Be Open and God Will Teach You

Jesus saw Nathanael coming toward Him and said concerning him, See! Here is an Israelite indeed [a true descendant of Jacob], in whom there is no guile nor deceit nor falsehood nor duplicity! JOHN 1:47

In some instances I think we need to open our minds. I think we should be single-minded (focused on the will of God), but not narrow-minded (unwilling to be open to new teachings).

There is a man in the Bible, in John 1:45–51, who Jesus had some very complimentary things to say about. His name is Nathanael. When we first meet Nathanael, Philip tells him that they'd found the Messiah and he was Jesus of Nazareth. Nathanael replied, "Can anything good come out of Nazareth?" (v. 46). He was saying that he *knew* what the people were like in Nazareth and no Messiah would be born of that stock. To which Philip tells him simply, "Come and see!" (v. 46). In other words, don't make a judgment before you've seen for yourself. So Nathanael went to see (v. 47).

God showed me that one of the reasons Jesus liked Nathanael so much was because even though he had a preconceived opinion that nothing good could come out of Nazareth, especially not the Savior, he was open-minded enough and humble enough to at least go see. I think a lot of people would get a lot further in their walk with God if they wouldn't have so many preconceived ideas. What we all *really* need is to believe the Word of God.

You should read your Bible and see what it says. Be open to letting God teach you and to learning. It's amazing what we could learn from God and other people He places in our paths if we didn't already think we knew it all.

Trust in Him Don't spend too much time listening to what other people say and miss out on the great blessings God has for your life. Let go of your preconceived notions and be humble enough to see for yourself. Trust God to teach you—and keep teaching you—through His Word.

July 2

You Don't Have to Fear

For the thing which I greatly fear comes upon me, and that of which I am afraid befalls me. JOB 3:25

Take a look at the verse above from the book of Job. I don't think this Scripture means that every time you have a fearful thought in your mind, the thing you fear is going to happen. But if you get a great fear in your life and it's something you meditate on over and over and you begin to speak it, you are putting yourself in danger of opening a door to have that thing in your life. Not just you, but me, too. We need to be very careful about our thoughts and our words, and we need to keep our minds set in the right direction. The only acceptable thought about fear a Christian can have is, *I will not fear because God is with me.*

If you have a problem with fear, with excessive timidity, with cowardice, even with extreme shyness, you will have to work at combating those things and choose instead to have faith. I think there are some things that people accept as their personality when really it's just the devil trying to take advantage of them. There are people who are more naturally bold and some who are more naturally shy than others, but if you are so shy that you can't participate in life and you won't speak your heart or your mind even when you know God is trying to get you to, then it's time for you to come against that thing and say, *"No, that's not the real me. That's not the way God wants me to be. That's not the way He created me to be."*

From cover to cover, I can show you in God's Word that He wants us to be bold and courageous, and He wants us to be confrontational when we need to be confrontational. He wants us to take new ground. He doesn't want us to be afraid of the enemy. He wants us to exercise authority, and He wants us to do great things in our lives. Be bold and courageous and fear not, for God is with you.

Trust in Him As you begin to confront the fears that have kept you in bondage, put your whole trust in God and believe you can do whatever you need to do through Him.

July 3

Seeing Yourself Properly

For whatever does not originate and proceed from faith is sin [whatever is done without a conviction of its approval by God is sinful]. ROMANS 14:23

If I get off track, it helps me get things straightened out in my life when I go back to Romans 14:23 and I say, "*You know what, Joyce, this attitude you've got—how you see yourself—is not faith, and thus it is sin and does not bring glory to God.*"

I think one of our biggest problems is that we battle with seeing ourselves properly. We have to learn to see ourselves, not in ourselves, but *in Christ*. The number one need that we have is to know God. And the number two need we have is to know who we are in Christ. Until I began to know who I was in Christ, meaning that until I began to believe what the Bible said about me rather than the way I felt or the way I thought or what other people said about me, my life wasn't going forward. Once I began to know who I was in Christ, everything changed. Now I don't care what I think; if it doesn't line up with the Word of God, then I'm wrong. And I don't care what I feel; if it doesn't line up with the Word of God, then what I feel is wrong.

We have to make a decision that we are going to see what God says about us: He says that you have gifts and talents and abilities; you are capable; anything He asks you to do you can do; you are strong in the Lord and not weak; you are forgiven; and on and on and on. It has to be more than just someone preaching that to you, however. You have to meditate and study and read it until you believe it. When you can differentiate between who you are in the flesh and who you are in Christ, things start to get really, really, really good.

Trust in Him If you see yourself *in Christ*, no matter how you feel, you can trust that you are redeemed and justified and God is living and working in you. Say, *"I'm not where I need to be, but thank God I'm not where I used to be. I'm okay and I'm on my way!"*

July 4

Confrontation Can Be Loving

If your brother wrongs you, go and show him his fault, between you and him privately. If he listens to you, you have won back your brother. MATTHEW 18:15 AMP

When Dave and I got married, I was a nightmare to get along with. I just wanted to stay in control because I thought that was the only way I could keep from being hurt. Plus I have a pretty aggressive personality to begin with, so that combined with a lot of dysfunction in my background did not make me a very nice woman.

Dave, on the other hand, is a real peace-lover and very easy to get along with. For a lot of years, he went about being happy and didn't really say too much to me while I acted badly. I believe God gave him extra patience with me because He knew the hurt I had in my life. Sometimes God calls us to put up with some things for a while, while we are praying and waiting on Him. To be honest, if Dave had confronted me in the first month we were married I would have just left him because I didn't know any better. So there was a purpose in God not asking him to confront me right away. But you need to confront when God tells you to.

After a few years, God showed Dave it was time to confront me. Dave explained to me, *"God has dealt with me that I can no longer let you get by with talking to me the way you do and acting the way you do. You're not going to get everything your way, and things must change."* And they did. It took time, but little by little, I changed.

I was very angry when Dave confronted me. But by then I was loved by Jesus enough and I knew enough of His Word to know that Dave was right—I knew that my behavior was wrong—but if he would have never confronted me, even though I knew that it was wrong, I don't know if I would have ever changed. So sometimes you are not doing somebody else a favor by not confronting them. It was the right thing for Dave to do for me. And even though I didn't like it and I got mad, Dave was right to listen to God. And we are doing the work we do today because of it.

Trust in Him Confrontation is usually not easy for the one doing the confronting, or the one being confronted, but it is an important part of spiritual growth. Follow God's lead and confront when He shows you it is time, and do it in love!

July 5

Confidence Leads to Reward

Do not, therefore, fling away your fearless confidence, for it carries a great and glorious compensation of reward.

HEBREWS 10:35

Anytime I talk about fear, I think back to my first really sizable speaking engagement. I actually got to stand in front of what would now be a small group of people, but then looked like a million people to me. One of the workshop leaders for this event canceled and because somebody knew somebody who knew somebody who knew somebody who knew me—I was asked to speak at the event. I was not their first choice, but God opened a door of opportunity and I gladly took it.

On opening night all of the speakers were sitting together. It was Dr. So-and-So, and Bishop So-and-So, and Reverend So-and-So, and Joyce. The devil was screaming in my ears, "*What are you doing here?! Why don't you go back to Fenton where you came from? You are going to make a fool out of yourself!*" I listened so much to what the devil was telling me that when it was my time to go up front and introduce myself and tell everybody what my workshop was going to be about, all I got out was a squeak. I was so scared; I was a mess. And I'm not even a really fearful person! But I let the fearful thoughts in.

Think about how much calmer you can be by just stopping your thinking about some of the things you're thinking about. If you believe you're doing what God wants you to do, then just do it. Now I just show up and trust God. Recently I spoke to nearly half a million people in India and I wasn't nervous at all. It gets easier when you have more experience trusting God; there is no doubt about that.

I remember having to make a decision the night of that first speaking engagement, to either open my mouth and try again or to run. Obviously, I tried again because here we are. What makes me sad is wondering how many people never try again.

Trust in Him Conquer your fear by trusting God and doing what He tells you to do, even if you have to do it again and again and again before you succeed.

July 6

There Is Always a Way

Some men were bringing on a stretcher a man who was paralyzed, and they tried to carry him in and lay him before [Jesus]. But finding no way to bring him in because of the crowd, they went up on the roof and lowered him with his stretcher through the tiles into the midst, in front of Jesus. LUKE 5:18–19

The Scripture above says there was "no way" to get through the crowds to Jesus... but with God there is always a way, and these men did not give up until they found it! Have you ever faced a situation and said, "There is '*no way*'..."? Maybe some of these thoughts have weighed on your mind:

- There is no way I can handle the pressure at work.
- There is no way I can pay my bills at the end of the month.

- There is no way to save my marriage.
- There is no way my children will ever grow up to be responsible adults.
- There is no way I can lose the weight I need to lose.

I want you to know there is *always* a way. It may not be easy; it may not be convenient; it may not come quickly. You may have to go over, under, around, or through, but if you will simply refuse to give up, you *will* find a way.

I know a young woman who was once working at a job she did not particularly like and was single but wanting to be married. Within one month she became engaged and was hired for her dream job. She had waited for what seemed an eternity before this time, but at the right time God made a way.

God has a plan for you and He has heard your prayers; you may not realize how close you are to your breakthrough. Even if you have to wait three, four, or five more years, if you will keep pressing on, you will have the victory you need. Whatever you do, do not give up on the brink of your breakthrough. Do not stop hoping, believing, and trying. Instead, say, *"I will never quit; I will never give up; I will never say, 'No way.' "*

Trust in Him Are you in a situation you see "no way" out of? Think again! God's ways are not our ways, but His way is always best. Do not stop trusting Him, and He will show you the way through to your breakthrough.

July 7

Never Give Up on Those You Love

Love never fails [never fades out or becomes obsolete or comes to an end].

1 CORINTHIANS 13:8

Years ago my oldest son, David, and I were so much alike we could hardly stand each other. He worked in the ministry, and the two of us clashed so intensely, I finally decided to tell him to find another job. I did not want to let him go and hurt him, but I did not believe I could endure the conflict that characterized our relationship. I planned to let him know his presence in the ministry simply was not working, but God spoke to my heart: *"Don't give up on David."*

Over time, David and I learned to get along well. Now he runs our world missions department, has opened eighteen foreign offices, and oversees numerous international outreaches. I am very thankful for his good work and glad God told me to not give up on him.

When you are tempted to give up on your loved ones, remember David and me. Whether you are believing for someone you love to become a Christian, change their behavior, leave a bad relationship, stop using drugs, go back to school, come home, or get a job, keep believing change is possible. Do not give up on the ones you love; as long as you continue believing, God can keep working. Your love and patience may be exactly what they need to make a complete turnaround.

Love never fails. In other words, it never gives up on people. The apostle Paul describes what love is in 1 Corinthians 13 and mentions that love always believes the best; it is positive and filled with faith and hope. While Jesus was on earth, He gave a new commandment to His followers: that we love one another (see John 13:34). I believe walking in love should be the main goal of every Christian.

God is love (see 1 John 4:8), and He never gives up on us. Let's choose to live with that same attitude. Believe in the power of love to change and transform anything and anyone.

Trust in Him If you are tempted to give up on something or someone, put your trust in God and believe that even if you don't have the power to change the circumstances, He does.

July 8

You Were Made for Something More

But those who wait for the Lord [who expect, look for, and hope in Him] shall change and renew their strength and power; they shall lift their wings and mount up [close to God] as eagles. ISAIAH 40:31

Do you ever feel you are like an eagle in a chicken yard—grounded and pent up when you should be soaring? You know there is much more within you than you are experiencing and expressing in your life right now. You know God has a great purpose for your life—and you cannot escape or ignore the inner urge to "go for it."

Know this: all eagles are uncomfortable in a barnyard; they all long for the clear, blue, open skies. When you are living in a place that keeps you from being who you were made to be and doing what you are meant to do, you will be uncomfortable, too. But also realize that people around you may not understand your desire to break out of the box. They may want to clip your wings. When you hear their comments and questions, something inside of you may ask, *"What is wrong with me? Why do I think as I think? Why do I feel this way? Why can't I just settle down and live a normal life like everybody else?"* The reason you cannot just settle down is that you are not a chicken; you are an eagle! You will never feel at home in that chicken yard, because you were made for something bigger, more beautiful, and more fulfilling.

I encourage you today to fan the flame inside of you. Fan it until it burns brightly. Never give up on the greatness for which you were created, never try to hide your uniqueness, and never feel you cannot do what you believe you were made to do. Realize that your hunger for adventure is God-given; wanting to try something new is a wonderful desire, and embracing life and aiming high is what you were made for. You are an eagle!

Trust in Him Is there a longing inside of you for more? Begin to value yourself, because God values you. Walk out of any "chicken mentality" you may have, trust Him, and soar like the eagle you were created to be.

July 9

The Right Perspective on Fear

Fear not [there is nothing to fear], for I am with you; do not look around you in terror and be dismayed, for I am your God. I will strengthen and harden you to difficulties. ISAIAH 41:10

What does this Scripture mean when it says, "Fear not...for I am with you...I will strengthen and harden you to difficulties"? It means God makes us stronger and stronger as we go through things. It also means that over time, we become less affected by the difficulties and challenges we face. It is like exercise. When we first do it, we get sore, but as we press through the soreness, we build muscle and gain strength. We must go through the pain to get the gain.

Consider your life. Are there situations you now handle well that would have previously made you feel fearful and anxious? Of course there are. As you have been walking with God, He has been strengthening you and hardening you to difficulties. In the same way, I can also assure you and encourage you that some of the things bothering you right now will not affect you the same way in five years.

If God removed all challenges, we would never grow and overcome obstacles. He often permits difficulty in our lives because He is trying to reveal something that needs to be strengthened or changed in us. Our weaknesses are never revealed in good times, but they quickly show up in times of trial and tribulation.

Sometimes He shows us what we are afraid of because He wants to deliver us from that fear and strengthen us for things that will come in the future. In those times, we need to say, "*Thank You, God, for allowing me to see that fear in my life. It reveals an area that needs to be dealt with in me.*" Once that particular area of fear is dealt with, then the enemy will have a very hard time bothering you—and succeeding—in that area again. This is one way God hardens us to difficulties and teaches us to not be afraid.

Trust in Him Think of a situation that once made you fearful but you now handle without fear. Some things you go through in life may not feel good initially, but they will work out for your good if you keep going forward and trust God to strengthen you each step of the way.

July 10

God Is with You

Be strong, courageous, and firm; fear not nor be in terror before them, for it is the Lord your God Who goes with you; He will not fail you or forsake you. DEUTERONOMY 31:6

If we know by faith that God is with us, we can take on any challenge with confidence and courage. We may not always feel God's presence, but we can trust His Word and remember that He said He would never leave us or forsake us.

In Joshua 1:1–3, God called Joshua to a great challenge of leadership—taking the children of Israel into the Promised Land: "After the death of Moses the servant of the Lord, the Lord said to Joshua son of Nun, Moses' minister, Moses My servant is dead. So now arise [take his place], go over this Jordan, you and all this people, into the land which I am giving to them, the Israelites. Every place upon which the sole of your foot shall tread, that have I given to you, as I promised Moses."

The Bible simply tells us in this passage that Moses had died and

Joshua was going to take his place as the leader of God's people. As soon as God gave this news to Joshua, He immediately assured him: "No man shall be able to stand before you all the days of your life. As I was with Moses, so I will be with you; I will not fail you or forsake you. Be strong (confident) and of good courage..." (vv. 5–6).

Later in this same scene, God encouraged Joshua again, saying, "Be strong, vigorous, and very courageous. Be not afraid, neither be dismayed, for the Lord your God is with you wherever you go" (v. 9). Basically, God was saying to Joshua, *"You have a big job to do, but don't let it intimidate you. Fear not. Do not be afraid, because I will be with you."*

In the Bible, the basis for not fearing is simply this: God is with us. And if we know God's character and nature, we know He is trustworthy. We do not have to know what He is going to do; simply knowing He is with us is more than enough.

Trust in Him Are you tempted to be afraid when you see the awesome responsibility God has given you? I encourage you not to run, but to stand firm, trusting God because He is with you.

July 11

You Were Created for Adventure

...Here am I; send me. ISAIAH 6:8

God has put a craving for adventure in us, and adventure means trying something we have never done before. Adventure means stepping out, doing something different, doing something a little bit on the edge, and not always living in a zone that we consider "safe."

I remember a particular Sunday in my church many years ago that I believe was a life-changing day for me. At that time of my life I truly loved God, but there were many biblical truths and principles I did not know. I knew a little bit about what a person needed to do to be saved, but I did not understand victory, overcoming obstacles, power, authority, or being used by God. I had no real hope that my life would ever be any better than it was at the time.

In that church, we had Missions Sunday once a year, and on that day, we always sang the song "Here Am I, Send Me." I remember one specific time, something welled up in me from the bottom of my heart and I sang the words with every fiber of my being: *"God, here I am! Send me! Send me!"* I do not know where I thought He would send me because I had a husband and three small children at home. But in my heart, I sensed I wanted Him to use me. I may not have had a lot of ability, but I was available to God. I was willing to say, *"I may fall flat on my face, God, but if You want to use me, I am willing to try."* Many years after that Sunday, God did call me to teach His Word, but it began the day I boldly said, *"Here am I; send me."*

If you want God to use you, offer yourself to Him and do not let the fear of failure stop you from obeying Him as He leads you. God not only sees where you are, He sees where you can be. He not only sees what you have done, He sees what you will do with His help.

Trust in Him Do you have a sincere desire deep in your heart to be used by God? If you do, just offer yourself to Him in faith and don't worry about your inabilities. God is looking for availability, not ability. Trust Him to give you all the ability you need when you need it.

July 12

The Stepping-Stones to Your Success

I call heaven and earth to witness this day against you that I have set before you life and death, the blessings and the curses; therefore choose life, that you and your descendants may live.

DEUTERONOMY 30:19

We all want to succeed in life. No one sets out to fail or wants to fail. But I do believe failure can be an important stepping-stone on the way to success. Failure certainly teaches us what *not* to do, which is often as important as knowing what we *are* to do! So-called failure is all about how we look at it.

Many stories have circulated about how many times Thomas Edison failed before he invented the incandescent lightbulb. I have heard he tried 700 times, 2,000 times, 6,000 times, and 10,000 times. No matter how many attempts he made, the number is staggering. But he never gave up. Edison is reported to have said in all his efforts he never failed—not once; he just had to go through many, many steps to get it right! It takes that kind of determination if you are really going to do anything worthwhile.

I have often pondered why some people do great things with their lives while others do little or nothing at all. I know that the outcome of our lives is dependent not only upon God but also upon something in us. Each of us must decide if we will reach down deep inside and find the courage to press past fear, mistakes, mistreatment at the hands of others, seeming injustices, and all the challenges life presents. This is not something anyone else can do for us; we must do it ourselves.

I want to encourage you to take responsibility for your life and its outcome. What will you do with what God has given you? I truly believe God gives everyone equal opportunity. He said, "I have set before you life and death . . . choose life." Fear is in the category of death; faith and progress fill us with life. It is your choice, and I believe you will make the right one!

Trust in Him What have you succeeded at that took many steps to get to victory? There is no such thing as failure if you simply refuse to quit. Trust God to teach you through each stepping-stone on your way to success.

July 13

You're Not Stuck—You're Going Through!

The Lord God is my Strength, my personal bravery, and my invincible army; He makes my feet like hinds' feet and will make me to walk [not to stand still in terror, but to walk] and make [spiritual] progress upon my high places [of trouble, suffering, or responsibility]!

HABAKKUK 3:19

We will all go through situations in life—some bad, some good. Many times, we think the phrase *"I'm going through something"* is bad news, but if we view it properly, we realize "going through" is good; it means we are not stuck! We may be facing difficulties, but at least we are moving forward.

Isaiah 43:2 says: "When you pass *through* the waters, I will be with you, and *through* the rivers, they will not overwhelm you. When you walk *through* the fire, you will not be burned or scorched, nor will the flame kindle upon you" (emphasis added). God's Word here is clear: we *will* go through things. We *will* face adversities in our lives. That's not bad news; that's reality.

Let me repeat: we *will* go through things in life, but the things we go through are the very circumstances, challenges, and situations that make us people who know how to overcome adversity. We do not grow or become strong during life's good times; we grow when we press through difficulties without giving up.

Growth is not an automatic result of difficulty. Hardships do not necessarily produce growth or strength in us; it is not that simple. We must choose the right attitude toward our challenges and refuse to quit or give up. We may have to do what is right for a long time before we feel it is "paying off," but if we stay faithful and refuse to give up, good results will come. Once we get *through* the adversities and challenges we face, we emerge as better people than we were when we went into them.

Trust in Him Determine that you will go all the way through every difficulty you face in life. Make a decision now to keep going forward, trusting God no matter how difficult it is because you know He will be with you and you will grow in faith as a result.

July 14

Press In and Press On

I press on toward the goal to win the [supreme and heavenly] prize to which God in Christ Jesus is calling us upward.

PHILIPPIANS 3:14

An important part of never giving up is making right choices while you are hurting, discouraged, frustrated, confused, or under pressure. The right choice is often the harder choice. And when we're in the middle of terrible stress, we naturally want to take the path of least resistance. But those are exactly the moments when you need to discipline yourself to make the tougher choice. In order to reap "right" results in life, you have to do right when you do not feel like it. I call this "pressing in and pressing on," and knowing how to do it is one of the most important components of becoming a person who never gives up.

You will never get where you want to be in life without being willing to sacrifice and push through the obstacles and adversities that stand in your way. Your obstacle may be an attitude, a set of circumstances, a relationship, an issue from your past, a thought or mind-set, a feeling, or a bad habit. Whatever it is, you are the only one who can press through it; no one else can do your pressing for you. You may have tried to overcome your challenges in the past. Perhaps you have tried to the point that you are weary, exhausted, or discouraged. This is precisely the point where you have to summon fresh strength from God and press in one more time.

One of the definitions I like for the word *press* is: "to exert steady force or pressure against something." I often say, *"You have to press against the pressure that's pressing against you!"* When something is pressing against you, you must be determined to press against it with greater force, because very little that is truly worthwhile or worth having in life happens without this kind of effort.

Trust in Him If you are tempted to take the easy road, instead press against your pressure and trust in God. Lean on and rely on Him to give you the strength to make the right choices in hard times. In the long run, you'll be glad you did.

July 15

Look to the Future for Your Reward

For the time being no discipline brings joy, but seems grievous and painful; but afterwards it yields peaceable fruit of righteousness to those who have been trained by it [a harvest of fruit which consists in righteousness—in conformity to God's will in purpose, thought, and action, resulting in right living and right standing with God]. HEBREWS 12:11

We should look to the future, determine what we want to see happen, and then discipline ourselves in order that we may have it. We must not buy into the lie that we should only live for the moment or that the present is all we have. We also have a future to consider, and we need to begin to live with an eye toward "afterward," toward the "later on" times. We have to begin to care just as much or more about later on than we care about right now.

If you want to be thinner when the time comes to wear your swimsuit in June, you need to start eating healthily and exercising before summer arrives. If you want to be able to afford a new car next year, you need to work toward getting out of debt right now. If you dream of living in a nice, clean, orderly home, you have to clear out the clutter and clean it up!

Discipline may not be pleasant for your flesh while you're doing it, but it will give you a tremendous sense of satisfaction in your soul—the satisfaction that comes from knowing you are making good choices. If you will pay the price to be disciplined now, you will enjoy rewards later. If you don't pay the price now to do what is right, then you'll suffer the consequences of an undisciplined life later. You can pay now or you can pay later, but at some point, we all reap the harvest of the choices we've made. We can't simply wish our lives were different; we have to press through laziness, fleshly desires, and bad attitudes and refuse to give up on the discipline that will yield good fruit later on. If there is something you want to see happen in your future, start disciplining yourself toward it now, and later on you will enjoy the fruit of it.

Trust in Him God's Word in Hebrews 12:11 says "no discipline brings joy... but afterwards..." If you discipline yourself now, you can trust that He'll bring you great reward afterward.

July 16

Don't Settle for Less Than God's Best

And Terah took Abram his son, Lot the son of Haran, his grandson, and Sarai his daughter-in-law, his son Abram's wife, and they went forth together to go from Ur of the Chaldees into the land of Canaan; but when they came to Haran, they settled there. GENESIS 11:31

You may know about Abram and Sarai and Lot, but you may not have ever heard much about this man named Terah. I believe Terah, Abram's father, failed to take an opportunity God wanted him to take.

I believe God wanted Terah to go all the way to Canaan, the Promised Land, but look at the words in the Scripture: "but when they came to Haran, *they settled there*" (emphasis added). In other words, Terah stopped short. He was supposed to go from Ur all the way to Canaan, but he stopped when he reached Haran. Terah settled for much less than God had for him. Abram ended up receiving a phenomenal blessing, but I think God also offered it to his father. His father simply quit before he reached the place where he could receive it.

I urge you today to not settle for less than the best God has for you. Don't allow yourself to get into a position where you wonder why someone else ends up with something, and then realize that you had the same opportunity and passed it up.

If we read on in Genesis 11, we learn that "Terah lived 205 years; and Terah died in Haran" (v. 32). He died where he settled. I think many people just settle somewhere and die in that place. They may not die physically, but their dream dies; their vision dies; their passion dies; their zeal dies. Their enthusiasm for life dies. Why? Because they gave up and did not press into the best God had for them.

You will face different types of pain and encounter difficulties as you go through life. You simply have to choose which kind of pain you want—the pain of pressing through or the pain of giving up. Only the pain of pressing through brings reward.

Trust in Him God has tremendous blessings for you. Commit right now to trust Him, to go all the way with Him, to press through the challenging times and never settle for less than His best for you.

July 17

Start Strong, Finish Well

Jesus, Who is the Leader and the Source of our faith [giving the first incentive for our belief] and is also its Finisher [bringing it to maturity and perfection]. HEBREWS 12:2

Everything we undertake in life has a beginning and an end. Typically, we are excited at the beginning of an opportunity, a relationship, or a venture; we're also happy when we can celebrate our achievement and have the satisfaction of a fulfilled desire. But between the beginning and the end, every situation or pursuit has a "middle"—and the middle is where we often face our greatest challenges, hurdles, roadblocks, obstacles, detours, and tests.

You may be in the middle of a lot of things right now. Perhaps you're in the middle of getting out of debt. You have paid off all but one of your charge accounts and you're starting to think, *I've done pretty well. I think I will go shopping today because I read about a huge sale at the mall.* It's easy to feel this way but I want to encourage you—keep pressing all the way through! Don't slow down when you're starting to see real progress. Discipline yourself a little while longer; you will be so glad you did when you pay off that last charge account and you are completely out of debt.

Maybe debt isn't what you are in the middle of. Maybe it is writing a term paper or training for a marathon. Maybe you are trying to adopt a child and are running into roadblock after roadblock. Or you are trying for a promotion at work. Whatever you find yourself in the middle of, determine to see it all the way through to the finish.

Between our beginnings and our endings, we must develop the boldness and determination necessary to overcome the overwhelming circumstances we encounter in the middle. The enemy wants us to settle for less than God's best for our lives and to stop short of receiving and enjoying everything God has for us. The devil hates progress and pushes us to give up. God, on the other hand, wants the very best for us; He wants us to finish the races set before us and finish them with joy (see Heb. 12:1–2). Ask yourself if you are willing to pay the price to finish.

Trust in Him Whatever you are in the middle of, don't stop short of finishing your race. God wants to be with you to the finish.

July 18

You Are More Than a Conqueror

Yet amid all these things we are more than conquerors and gain a surpassing victory through Him Who loved us. ROMANS 8:37

A person with the spirit of a conqueror must confront and deal with the adversities he or she will face, not run from them. We simply cannot keep trying to escape or avoid situations that are difficult. Anytime we run from a situation, we can almost be sure we will have to go back and face it, or something very similar, at a later time in our lives.

Think about Moses. He ran from Egypt and spent forty years in the desert, where God prepared him to be a great leader. When God appeared to Moses in the burning bush, He basically said: *"Now I want you to go back to Egypt"* (see Exod. 3:2–10). Yes, God sent Moses right back to the place he tried to escape!

The Bible is full of similar stories—enough to convince me that running from adversity doesn't do anyone any good. I used to have an extremely difficult time with people whose personalities were similar to my father's. Because he abused me, I didn't want to be around people who spoke the way he spoke, acted the way he acted, or reminded me of him in any way. But over a period of time I began to notice God was surrounding me with people who reminded me of my dad. Every time I encountered someone who reminded me of him, I felt insecure and fearful, and I slipped into old behavior patterns. I didn't like my responses, but I was asking God to change me and show me truth.

He put me in situations where I would have to deal with the fears from my past. He was trying to get me to grow up and be a stronger, more mature Christian. We often ask God to deliver us from the wrong things. We want to be delivered from our trials, but we need to ask Him to deliver us from the things in our hearts that hinder His purposes for our lives.

Trust in Him If you are tempted to run from adversity, remember Moses. He spent forty years trying to run away only to end up right back where he started. Getting away from trouble should never be your goal; your goal needs to be to trust God to help you conquer difficulties with a Christlike attitude.

July 19

Do It for God

And this is love: that we walk in obedience to his commands. As you have heard from the beginning, his command is that you walk in love.

2 JOHN 1:6 NIV

I remember one Sunday years ago when my church's pastor encouraged the congregation to take a moment to say hello to other people and even give them a hug and tell them we loved them. I looked down the row where I was sitting and saw a woman who had hurt me in a significant way. I strongly sensed the Spirit of God impressing me to give her a hug and let her know I loved her. Walking over to her and saying, "*I love you*" took everything I had! I can't guarantee I was totally sincere, but I know I was obedient to God.

Several months later, God led me to give one of my favorite possessions to that woman. *"Now God,"* I responded, *"I don't mind giving it away. I mean, I really would like to keep it, but if You are going to make me give it away, at least let me give it to someone I like so I can enjoy seeing her with it!"* God responded to me: *"Joyce, if you can give her that, if you can give your favorite possession to someone who really hurt you and is least deserving of it, you will break the power of the enemy. You will destroy his plan to destroy you."*

We do not take steps of obedience and overcome difficult times because we feel like doing so or think obedience is a good idea. We do it because we love God, we know He loves us, we want to obey Him, and we know His ways are always best for us.

Whatever adversities you are facing right now or will face in the days to come, I urge you to confront them, embrace them, and deal with them. Face them like a conqueror. Remember, they are working for your good, and God will use them to strengthen you. Embrace them with a conqueror's attitude, and you will find yourself in a place of greater maturity, wisdom, and ability than you have ever known.

Trust in Him If God asks you to do something, you know He is asking because it is what's best for you. Even if you don't want to do it, do it for God because you trust Him and He knows best.

July 20

Always Start with Prayer

[And Nehemiah prayed] Hear, O our God, for we are despised. Turn their taunts upon their own heads, and give them for a prey in a land of their captivity. NEHEMIAH 4:4

In Nehemiah 4:4, we find three words that are vitally important to remember when we are trying to stand through a storm: "And Nehemiah prayed." How did he respond to all the attacks that came against him—the laughing, the anger, the rage, the judgment, the criticism, being told his desired goal was impossible? He prayed!

Let me ask you: What would happen if you prayed every single time you felt afraid or intimidated? What if you prayed every time you were offended, or every time someone hurt your feelings? What if you prayed immediately every time some kind of judgment or criticism came against you? Would your life be different? Would you be able to withstand those storms better? Of course you would.

We can learn an important lesson from Nehemiah's prayer: "Hear, O our God," he said, "for we are despised. Turn their taunts upon their own heads, and give them for a prey in a land of their captivity." Notice that Nehemiah didn't go after his enemies himself; he asked God to deal with them. His attitude was, *"I'm doing Your will! You told me to build this wall and I am busy building it. You will have to take care of my enemies!"*

Many times, God tells us to do something or gives us an assignment and we begin doing it. But then the enemy comes against us, and when we turn to fight him, we turn away from God. Suddenly, the enemy has all of our attention. We spend our time fighting him instead of praying and asking God to intervene.

Nehemiah knew better than to let his enemies command his focus. He was aware of them, but he kept his eyes on God and the job God called him to do. And he simply prayed and asked God to deal with those who were attacking him.

Trust in Him What do you need to pray about? When the enemy attacks, don't take your focus off the task God has placed before you. Pray! And trust God to take care of the enemy.

July 21

Love Finds a Way

But when the unclean spirit has gone out of a man, it roams through dry [arid] places in search of rest, but it does not find any. Then it says, I will go back to my house from which I came out. And when it arrives, it finds the place unoccupied, swept, put in order, and decorated.
MATTHEW 12:43–44

It is very important that we fill our lives with godly activity and make decisions to work for God, making a positive difference in the world. Many people don't realize that indifference is a decision. Right and wrong are not the only decisions we make. A decision to do nothing is still a decision, and it is one that makes us weaker and weaker. It gives the devil more and more opportunities to control us.

Empty space is still a place, and the Word of God teaches that if the devil comes and finds emptiness he quickly occupies the space. Inactivity indicates that we are in agreement with and approve of whatever is going on. After all, if we are doing nothing to change it, then we must think whatever is happening is fine.

We have taken various people on mission trips to minister to desperately needy people, but they don't all respond the same way. Everyone feels compassion when they see the terrible conditions in which people live while in the remote villages in Africa, India, or other parts of the world. Many cry; most shake their heads and think these situations are terrible, but they don't all decide to do something to change the conditions.

Many pray for God to do something and are glad that our ministry is doing something, yet they never think to seek God aggressively about what they can personally do. I would venture to say that most of them return home, get busy with their own lives again, and soon forget about what they saw. But thank God there are some individuals who are determined to find ways to make a difference. Indifference makes an excuse, but love finds a way. Everyone can do something!

Trust in Him When have you seen a need and decided to do nothing? Don't settle for the status quo any longer. Trust God to show what you can do to make a change.

July 22

Pray Prayers God Can Answer

So we are Christ's ambassadors, God making His appeal as it were through us. We [as Christ's personal representatives] beg you for His sake to lay hold of the divine favor [now offered you] and be reconciled to God. 2 CORINTHIANS 5:20

Learning how to pray prayers God can answer is very important. I spent lots of years in my morning prayers telling the Lord what I needed Him to do for me, but finally I learned to also pray: *"God, what can I do for You today?"* We are Christ's ambassadors, His partners in helping people and bringing them to know Him.

I would like to suggest something for you to add to your daily prayers. Each day, ask God what you can do for Him. Then as you go through your day, watch for opportunities to do what you believe Jesus would do if He were still on earth in bodily form. He lives in you now if you are a Christian, and you are His ambassador...so make sure you represent Him well.

Recently, I was asking God to help a friend who was going through a very difficult time. She needed something, so I asked God to provide it. To my surprise, His answer to me was, *"Stop asking Me to meet the need; ask Me to show you what you can do."*

I have become aware that I often ask God to do things for me when He wants me to do those things myself. He doesn't expect me to do anything without His help, but neither will He do everything for me while I sit idly by.

God wants us to be open to being involved. He wants us to use our resources to help people, and if what we have isn't enough to meet their needs, then we can encourage others to get involved so that together we can do what needs to be done.

I encourage you to pray prayers God can answer. You and He are partners, and He wants to work *with* and *through* you.

Trust in Him Don't expect God to do everything for you. He made you His ambassador so that He could work through you. Ask Him to show you what you can do for Him, and trust in and depend on Him to give you not only the creativity, but also the resources to do it.

July 23

10 Minutes to "the Good Life"

. . . He knows [enough] to refuse the evil and choose the good.

ISAIAH 7:15

I believe in having a "think session" every day. If we were to sit down regularly and say to ourselves, "*I am going to think about a few things for ten minutes,*" and then deliberately think about some of the things the Bible tells us to think about, our lives would improve dramatically. In just ten minutes we'd experience more of "the good life" that God has for us.

Disciplining ourselves to think properly by having on-purpose "think sessions" will train us to begin thinking properly in our everyday lives. One of the things all believers need to think every day is this biblical truth: *I am in right-standing with God, through Christ*. Thinking this will help you live in the reality of who God has made you to be. Why not think something on purpose that will benefit you rather than merely meditating on whatever happens to fall into your mind?

We use our thinking abilities every day, but most of us need to change the content of our thoughts. Instead of thinking, *I'm no good; I mess up everything; I never do anything right*, we can use our mental energy to think about how much God loves us and how we are in a right relationship with Him through Jesus Christ.

As you spend more time thinking correctly, great transformation will take place in your life. You might have to put notes around your house that say, "*What have you been thinking today?*" You might have to put a note in your car to remind you to think right thoughts today—or even write out what those thoughts are and post them on a mirror or on your computer screen.

This type of exercise would not be uncommon for a college student facing final exams. They do everything they can to keep the right answers in front of them prior to the test to assure that they pass. If you will discipline yourself to remind yourself to spend time thinking right thoughts on purpose each day, you will find things improving so radically you will be absolutely amazed. Before you know it, you'll be enjoying the good life God has predestined for you. It is important to think thoughts that are in agreement with God's will for your life.

Trust in Him How can you work a ten-minute "think session" into your daily routine? Trust God to radically transform your life by thinking about His word on purpose.

July 24

Break Up with Bad Habits

But his delight and desire are in the law of the Lord, and on His law (the precepts, the instructions, the teachings of God) he habitually meditates (ponders and studies) by day and by night.

PSALM 1:2

Habits are actions we do repeatedly, sometimes without even thinking about them, or things we have done so often that they become our natural responses to certain situations.

I found thirty-four references in the Amplified Bible for the word *habitually*. That tells me that God expects us to form good habits. The psalmist David said the man who wants to prosper and succeed needs to *habitually* ponder and meditate on God's Word by day and by night (see Ps. 1:2, emphasis mine). This tells me that establishing the habits necessary for success takes discipline and consistency, especially in our thought lives. With enough discipline and consistency, we can break bad habits and new ones can be formed.

Think about breaking a bad habit like you would break up with a bad boyfriend or girlfriend. Interestingly enough, we could miss the boyfriend or girlfriend even though we knew we did the right thing in breaking up with them. We might feel lonely for a while and be tempted to go back to that person, but if we remain firm in our resolve, we will eventually no longer miss that person and find someone else that provides a healthy relationship for us.

In like manner, we may break a bad habit and might miss it for a while, even being tempted to go back to old ways. This is the time to set your mind and keep it set in the new direction because you don't want to remain in bondage to the old thing and miss the good, new thing God has for you.

Doing the right thing once or even a few times does not equal success, but *habitually* doing right will produce a life worth living. It may not be easy, but it will be worth the effort. The person who never gives up always sees victory.

Trust in Him What good habits do you need to develop in your life? Trust God to help you break bad habits and form good ones.

July 25

You Can Do All Things Through Christ

I have strength for all things in Christ Who empowers me [I am ready for anything and equal to anything through Him Who infuses inner strength into me; I am self-sufficient in Christ's sufficiency].

PHILIPPIANS 4:13

One thought that has the power to transform your life is simple: *I can do whatever I need to do in life through Christ.* In other words, I can handle whatever life hands me. I wonder—do you believe you can do whatever you need to do in life? Or are there certain things that trigger dread, fear, or cause you to say, "*I could never do that!*" when you think about them?

Whether it's suddenly losing a loved one, facing a serious unexpected illness, having your adult child with two toddlers move into your clean and quiet house after you've had an "empty nest" for years, going on a strict diet because your life depends on it, putting yourself on a budget to avoid foreclosure on your home, or suddenly having to care for a disabled elderly parent—most people have some kind of circumstance that truly seems impossible to them, something they aren't sure they can or could handle.

The fact of the matter is, while some situations may be intensely undesirable or difficult for you, you *can* do whatever you need to do in life. I know this because God tells us in His Word that we have the strength to do all things because Christ empowers us to do so. He doesn't say everything will be easy for us, He doesn't promise we will enjoy every little thing we do, but we can enjoy life in the midst of doing them.

We must understand that Philippians 4:13 does not say we can do anything we want to do because we are strong enough, smart enough, or hardworking enough. No, in fact, it leaves no room at all for human effort or striving of any kind. The secret to being able to do what we need to do is realizing that we cannot do it alone; we can only do it in Christ.

Trust in Him What in your life do you need to begin to believe you can do? Remember, you can do *all* things *in Christ*. You can trust Him to empower you to do anything He asks you to do.

July 26

Christ Is Your Strength

How can you speak good things when you are evil (wicked)? For out of the fullness (the overflow, the superabundance) of the heart the mouth speaks. MATTHEW 12:34

The Bible says that out of the heart the mouth speaks. We can learn a lot about ourselves by listening to ourselves. Do your thoughts and words reflect your complete dependence on God, realizing that His abilities (not your own) empower you to do anything you need to do in life?

I had to examine my own thoughts and words and ask myself if I portrayed a person who had faith in God, and I encourage you to do the same. I didn't like all of my answers, but the exercise in self-examination did open my eyes to understanding that I needed to make some changes. Realizing we are wrong in an area is never a problem. The problem comes when we refuse to face truth and continue making excuses.

Be willing to face anything God wants to show you and ask Him to change you. If you are trusting in your own strength, begin to trust God instead. If you are trying to do things out of your own human abilities and growing frustrated, tell God you want Him to work through you and let His sufficiency be your sufficiency (see Phil. 4:13).

When challenges arise, I encourage you to develop a habit of immediately saying, *"I can do whatever I need to do through Christ Who is my strength."* Remember that words are containers for power, and when you say the right thing, it will help you do the right thing. Don't fill your containers, (words) with things that disable you, for truly you are able to do all things through Christ. God will ask you to do things you'd never be able to do in your own strength, but He will give you His strength to do them.

As you meditate over and over on the thought, *I can do whatever I need to do in life through Christ*, you will find that you are not as easily overwhelmed by situations that arise. Each time you roll that thought over in your mind or speak it, you are developing a healthy mind-set that enables you to be victorious.

Trust in Him How often do you say, *"This is too hard for me"* or *"I just can't do this"*? What will you now begin to say to reflect your trust in God's ability to help you do whatever you need to do?

July 27

Yes You Can

Now may the God Who gives the power of patient endurance (steadfastness) and Who supplies encouragement, grant you to live in such mutual harmony and such full sympathy with one another, in accord with Christ Jesus, that together you may [unanimously] with united hearts and one voice, praise and glorify the God and Father of our Lord Jesus Christ (the Messiah). ROMANS 15:5–6

This Scripture says God supplies us with encouragement. Encouragement says, *"You can do it!"* But perhaps you have heard the words *"You can't"* repeatedly throughout your life. Many people are good at telling us what we cannot do. Other people may not be against us, and may even have good intentions, but they're not so sure we can do it, either.

Parents, teachers, coaches, friends, family members, and leaders of church groups or social activities often fail to realize the power of their words over young lives. Many children and teenagers grow up thinking, *I can't*, when that isn't true at all! No matter how many times you have heard someone say to you, *"You can't,"* I want to say to you, *"Oh, yes, you can!"* I believe miracles come in "cans"—our belief that we *can* do whatever we need to do through Christ Who is our strength.

I believe in you; God believes in you; and it's time for you to believe in yourself. Today is a new day! Put the past and all of its negative, discouraging comments behind you. Negative words and words that speak of failure come from the enemy, not from God. So decide right now to not allow the power of *"you can't"* to influence you anymore.

God tells you to have courage, so always remember if you feel "discouraged," that is from the enemy and if you feel "encouraged," that is from God. Choose to agree with God and say to yourself, *"I can!"* And let the power of your positive thoughts and words outweigh the power of the negative words anyone else has ever spoken to you.

Trust in Him Complete this sentence: Yes, I can __________________. Trust God to give you the strength and encouragement to see your situation through.

July 28

Exchange Your "I Can'ts" for "I Cans"

No temptation has overtaken you that is not common to man. God is faithful, and he will not let you be tempted beyond your ability, but with the temptation he will also provide the way of escape, that you may be able to endure it. 1 CORINTHIANS 10:13 ESV

Have you ever walked into a store before with something to exchange? Maybe it was an article of clothing that you decided you didn't like, a pair of shoes that were uncomfortable, or a gadget that didn't do what you'd expected. You entered the store with something that didn't work for you, exchanged it, and left with something that did work for you. You had to trade what was not effective for something that was.

The same principle applies to your thinking. If you exchange your "I can't" thoughts for "I can" thoughts, you will see remarkable changes begin to happen. If you build into your character the thought that, with God's help, you can do whatever you need to do in life, you will have more zeal and enthusiasm about facing every day. I have found that I even have more physical energy when I think "I can" thoughts. It helps me to not dread anything, because dread is an energy drainer.

It's never too late to begin saying, "I can." Say things like: *"My marriage has problems, but it can work"*; *"My house is a mess, but I can clean it so it will bring me joy and relaxation when I come home from work"*; *"I can get out of debt"*; *"I will own a home or have a new car"*; or, *"I have some problems right now, but I can still enjoy my life."*

Some of the challenges you face may be very difficult ones; however, God never allows more to come on us than we can bear. With every temptation, He always provides a way out. I challenge and encourage you right now to consistently believe you are able to do anything that comes your way, with God's help.

Trust in Him Which "I can't" belief in your life do you need to exchange for an "I can"? Trust God to not allow you to be tempted beyond your ability and to always provide a way out.

July 29

Meet Life Head-On

Get ready; be prepared... EZEKIEL 38:7 NIV

Everyone faces challenges in life. Some people are completely overwhelmed by their challenges, whereas others refuse to give up. My question to you is: Do you want to be able to meet all challenges head-on and overcome them? If so, then get mentally prepared for whatever comes.

According to Colossians 3:2, the way to be prepared is to "set your mind and keep it set." Don't be caught off guard and unprepared. Repeatedly thinking and saying *"I can do whatever I need to do in life through Christ"* will help you set your mind and keep it set in that direction, and it will set you up to win in life. Remember, where the mind goes, the man follows!

Do not allow yourself to think thoughts such as, *I just cannot take any more trouble!* Or, *If one more thing happens, I am going to go over the edge!* Or, *If things don't change soon—I am giving up!* There are many varieties of this kind of thinking—and you may have a favorite thought or saying of this type that you use when you feel overwhelmed. But do you realize these thinking patterns actually prepare you to be defeated before you even encounter the problem?

There is nothing strong, powerful, enabling, or victorious in thinking you will *"go over the edge"* or deciding to quit. Those are losing attitudes, not winning attitudes. Don't say things like *"I feel like I am losing my mind,"* or *"This is going to kill me."* Instead you can say, *"I have the mind of Christ,"* and *"This trial is going to work out for my good."*

Be a person who is mentally prepared for any challenge that crosses your path, and do not allow yourself to be easily discouraged and defeated. Always remember that apart from Jesus you can do nothing (see John 15:5), but in Him you can do whatever you need to do in life (see Phil. 4:13).

Trust in Him Be encouraged—God's given you everything you need in order to do what He's called you to do. So get ready and be prepared. Trust God to help you stand up to whatever challenge comes your way.

July 30

Trade Your Excuses for "I Can's"

And I am convinced and sure of this very thing, that He Who began a good work in you will continue until the day of Jesus Christ [right up to the time of His return], developing [that good work] and perfecting and bringing it to full completion in you. PHILIPPIANS 1:6

One of the reasons many people do not enjoy life, miss out on some of the blessings God wants to give them, or feel badly about themselves is that they do not finish what they start. They never taste the joy of accomplishing a goal or fulfilling a desire because they do not press past the challenges that arise. Most of us wouldn't say, *"I'm a quitter,"* so we make excuses or we blame the failure on someone or something else.

Every single one of us has an "excuse bag." It's a little invisible accessory we carry around with us all the time. Then, when something difficult comes along that challenges us or gives us more than we want to deal with, we pull out an excuse like this:

- *"That is just too hard."*
- *"I don't have enough time."*
- *"I hadn't planned on this today."*

- *"I have too many personal problems and too much going on in my life right now."*
- *"I have never done this. I don't even know anybody who's ever done this."*
- *"I don't have anyone to help me."*

I urge you today to throw away your excuse bag! Don't be limited by your excuses. Trade them for a confident attitude that says, "I can *do what God's called me to.*" Whenever you feel like reaching for an excuse, instead say, "I can *do this.*"

Stop looking at all your weaknesses, because His strength is made perfect in our weakness. It is through our weakness that God shows His strength. God actually chooses people on purpose who absolutely cannot do what He is asking them to do unless they allow Him to do it through them. You don't need ability; you need to be available to God and a "can-do" attitude.

Trust in Him What excuse do you use most? Will you determine today that you will stop making excuses and start trusting God to give you the strength to do what you need to do?

July 31

Do Everything You Can to Help Others

Let each of you esteem and look upon and be concerned for not [merely] his own interests, but also each for the interests of others.

PHILIPPIANS 2:4

A friend of mine lives in a large city where homelessness is a huge problem. One winter night she was coming home from work and walked by a man asking for money. It was cold and dark, she'd put in a long day, and she was anxious to get home. Not wanting to pull out her wallet in a less-than-safe situation, she reached deep into her purse fishing for change.

As her fingers searched in vain, the man started telling her that his coat had been stolen in the homeless shelter where he'd stayed the night before and described a few other troubles he was having. Still trying to come up with a couple of quarters, she nodded at the right times and said *"that's too bad"* now and then. When she finally found the money, she dropped it into the man's cup. He smiled and said, *"Thank you for talking with me."*

My friend says she realized that night that the $.50 she gave him was appreciated, but what meant the most to the man was the fact that someone had heard what he said and responded.

There is a team of people who try to help individuals living in the tunnels under the downtown bridge in St. Louis. They have found that each of these people had a life prior to the tunnels and they all have a story. Something tragic happened to them that resulted in them being in their present circumstances. They appreciate the sandwiches and the rides to church where they can shower and get clean clothes, but mostly they appreciate someone caring enough to actually talk with them long enough to find out who they are and what has happened to them.

Let me encourage you to do everything you can to help others. If they simply need you to be there, then take time to do so. Ask God what He wants you to do—and He will answer your prayer so you can do it.

Trust in Him When was the last time you took time to really listen to someone? Trust God to reveal what He wants you to do for others.

August 1

You Cannot Have Peace Without Trust

Peace I leave with you; My [own] peace I now give and bequeath to you. Not as the world gives do I give to you. Do not let your hearts be troubled, neither let them be afraid. [Stop allowing yourselves to be agitated and disturbed; and do not permit yourselves to be fearful and intimidated and cowardly and unsettled.] JOHN 14:27

Jesus made this statement after His death and resurrection, prior to His ascension into heaven. There were many things He could have taught His disciples, but He chose to talk about peace. This fact alone reminds me of how important peace is.

Some people don't have peace with God because they are not born again and still need to trust Jesus Christ as their Savior. But even some Christians still lack consistent peace because they simply have not responded to the leading of the Holy Spirit and have been led astray through prolonged disobedience, bad habits, and constant worry. Perhaps they prayed for something and it didn't happen. Perhaps somebody else got what they wanted. Perhaps somebody they loved died, and they don't understand why.

Sometimes we make ourselves unhappy because we don't *trust* enough. We always want God to change our circumstance, but He's more interested in changing *us* than He is our situation. A lot of people have faith to ask God for deliverance *from* something, but they don't have enough faith to take them *through* anything. Job said, "Even though He slay me, yet will I trust Him" (see Job 13:15).

There are many, many reasons why people don't trust God, but in order to enjoy peace, we must learn to trust Him in all things. I know it's not always easy, but we can do it. We must trust that God is totally and completely just, which means He always makes wrong things right if we continue to lean on Him. God is perfect; He never does anything wrong. He's worthy of our trust.

Trust in Him If you're asking God for something and don't get it, I encourage you to believe God knows more than you do. Trust God in all things so you can enjoy peace.

August 2

Follow Peace

And let the peace (soul harmony which comes) from Christ rule (act as umpire continually) in your hearts [deciding and settling with finality all questions that arise in your minds, in that peaceful state] to which as [members of Christ's] one body you were also called [to live]. And be thankful (appreciative), [giving praise to God always]. COLOSSIANS 3:15

Colossians 3:15 says to let the peace from Christ "rule (act as umpire continually)" in our hearts. The presence of peace helps us decide and settle with finality all questions that arise in our minds. If you let the Word have its home in your heart and mind, it will give you insight *and* intelligence *and* wisdom (see v. 16). You won't have to wonder, "*Should I or shouldn't I? I don't know if it's right. I don't know what to do.*" If you are a disciple of Christ, He has called you to follow peace.

Dave, my husband, and I were trying to make a decision on a large purchase we needed to make. We called some of our board members from the ministry and presented the need to them, asking, "*What do you think?*" They all gave their opinions, but as I listened to them, I knew suddenly that I didn't have peace about going forward with the plan. We have learned by experience to wait if we don't have peace for something. Dave and I agreed to wait on God to give us all peace before we proceeded.

Following the Lord of peace may mean that you have to make some adjustments in your life. You may not be able to do everything your friends do. You may not be able to buy everything you want. You may not be able to have something just because a friend or a sister or a brother has one. You may have to wait. But I believe peace is the most important, the most valuable thing we can have. If we follow peace, we will end up living holy lives and thoroughly enjoying them.

Trust in Him If you are trying to make a decision, choose to follow peace. Go forward if you have peace, and wait if you don't.

August 3

Learn to Keep Your Peace

...I have learned how to be content (satisfied to the point where I am not disturbed or disquieted) in whatever state I am.

PHILIPPIANS 4:11

Satan tries to cause trouble in virtually every area of our lives. He does not attack every area at one time, but eventually he gets to everything. He brings inconveniences of every kind, and it seems the right thing never happens at the right time. Problems never come when we are ready to deal with them. He may attack people in their finances, relationships, physical health, mind, emotions, jobs, neighborhoods, or projects.

We recently invited four different men from four different parts of the country to be guests on our television show. These men were all involved in the restoration of morality in America. They were all praying for revival. Dave and I are also very interested in this, and we wanted to impact the nation with some special programming along these lines.

Two of the four men had major delays with their flights: one man's flight was entirely canceled and he was very late, and another sat on the runway for two and a half hours without any real explanation from the airline except that it was raining. What was Satan trying to do? He didn't want them to come at all, but if they were going to come, he wanted them to be upset when they arrived.

Two guest speakers out of four having this type of trouble is more than coincidence. Satan sets us up to get us upset! He wants to steal our peace because our power is connected to it. I have learned that my ministry does not have much effect if I am not ministering from a heart of peace, so I strive to stay in peace at all times. Satan tries to steal my peace, and with God's help, I try to keep it.

Paul said he had learned to be content (satisfied to the point where he was not disquieted or disturbed). It sounds to me as if he always kept his peace, no matter what was going on in his life. This is an example we should seek to follow.

Trust in Him How often do you let Satan steal your peace? Regardless of your circumstances, trust God to help you keep your peace.

August 4

Choose Peace and Joy Instead of Dread

Then I said to you, Dread not, neither be afraid of them.
DEUTERONOMY 1:29

Probably one of the greatest ways we show our trust in God is by living life one day at a time. We prove our confidence in Him by enjoying today and not letting the concern of tomorrow interfere. It made a big change in my life when I began to gain insight from the Holy Spirit on this problem of dreading things. This truth about living one day at a time greatly increased my peace and joy, and it will do the same thing for you.

I learned that it really was not the event I was facing that was so bad—it was dreading it that made it bad. Our attitudes do make all the difference in the world. Learn to approach life with an "I can do whatever I need to do through Christ" attitude. Don't say that you hate things like driving to work in traffic, going to the grocery store, cleaning the house, doing laundry, changing the oil in the car, or cutting the grass. These chores are all part of life, and it is useless to dread them.

Don't let the events of life dictate your level of joy. It is the joy of the Lord that is your strength. Be joyful that you are going to heaven; be grateful that you have someone who always loves you, no matter what. Look at and concentrate on what you *do* have, not what you *don't* have.

Everyone has to attend to some unpleasant details in life. Don't dread them, but learn how valuable God's peace is in those circumstances.

Some things are certainly more naturally enjoyable and easier to do than others, but that does not mean we cannot purposely choose to enjoy the other less enjoyable tasks. We can choose to have attitudes of joy and peace. Usually, if we don't feel like doing something, we automatically assume we cannot enjoy it or have peace during that time, but that is a deception. We grow spiritually when we do difficult things with a good attitude.

Trust in Him Dreading things does not glorify God. Show your trust in Him by facing each day with a good attitude.

August 5

Bless the Lord at All Times

I will bless the Lord at all times; His praise shall continually be in my mouth.
PSALM 34:1

At times it seems like the whole world lives in fear and dread, but God's children should not. We are to behave differently from the people of the world; we should let our light shine.

Just being positive in a negative circumstance is a way to do this. The world will notice when we are stable in every kind of situation. Make up your mind right now that all of life does not need to make you feel good in order for you to face it with peace and joy. Make a decision that you will not dread anything you have to do. Do it all with a thankful attitude.

I never considered driving down the street to get a cup of coffee to be a huge privilege until after I had been hospitalized with breast cancer and had surgery. When I was released, I asked my husband to take me out for a coffee and a drive through a local park. It was amazing how much joy I felt. I was doing a very simple thing that was previously available to me every day, yet I had never seen it as a privilege.

Our son went on an outreach with a team of people who go visit the homeless each Friday evening, and after helping in this ministry, he was appalled at himself for the things he had murmured about in the past once he saw, by comparison, how some people were living. We would all feel exactly the same way. Those without a place to live would love to have a house to clean, while we dread cleaning ours. They would delight in having a car to drive, even an old one, while we complain about needing to wash ours or take it in for an oil change.

The point is, most of the time we lose sight of how blessed we are, but we should work at keeping it in the front of our thinking. Be thankful you can do anything in Christ, and don't dread things you have to do.

Trust in Him What are you thankful for? If your trust is in Him, you can face anything with peace and joy and gratitude in your heart.

August 6

Face Life with Boldness and Courage

Then you will prosper if you are careful to keep and fulfill the statutes and ordinances with which the Lord charged Moses concerning Israel. Be strong and of good courage. Dread not and fear not; be not dismayed. 1 CHRONICLES 22:13

Recently a group of pastors asked me a question: Besides God Himself, what one thing had helped me get from where I started in ministry to the level of success I currently enjoy? I immediately said, *"I refused to give up!"* There were thousands of times when I felt like giving up, thought about giving up, and was tempted to give up, but I always pressed on.

Don't let life defeat you. Face it with boldness and courage, and declare that you will enjoy every aspect of it. You can do that because you have the awesome power of God dwelling in you. God is never frustrated and unhappy. He always has peace and joy, and since He lives in us and we live in Him, surely we can attain the same thing.

When you are in pain, you don't have to dwell on the pain and let it ruin your day. You can still accomplish what you need to do by God's grace, and you don't have to fear and dread that you may feel that same way tomorrow. I have ministered to others many times while I was in pain myself. Whatever we go through, God will always be with us. Choose to believe that Jesus is your Healer and that His healing power is working in your body right now!

When tempted to worry, Dave always says, *"I am not impressed."* He believes we should be more impressed by God's Word than our problems. He says if we don't get *impressed*, we won't get *depressed*, then *oppressed*, and ultimately perhaps even *possessed* by our difficulties.

No matter what you are facing right now, God has a great life planned for you. It includes prosperity and progress in every area of life. It includes great peace, unspeakable joy, and every good thing you can imagine. Refuse to settle for anything less than God's best for you!

Trust in Him Trusting God means believing He lives in you, and all that is His is yours. Be strong and courageous and never give up, and you will have everything He wants you to have in life.

August 7

A Better Way to Live

But the natural, nonspiritual man does not accept or welcome or admit into his heart the gifts and teachings and revelations of the Spirit of God, for they are folly (meaningless nonsense) to him…

1 CORINTHIANS 2:14

One year a man I worked for was helping me do my income tax. When he observed that we gave 10 percent of our income to the church each year, he promptly told me we were giving too much, that it was not necessary, and we should stop. He was looking at our giving in the natural and could find no reason why we would want to do such a thing. We, however, were looking at it according to our knowledge of God's Word. We understood spiritually what we were doing and believed that if we gave, God would always take care of us.

I tried to explain God's principles on sowing and reaping to him, but he insisted that even if we wanted to give, it did not need to be that much, especially since we didn't have an abundance left over after giving to the church and paying our bills. This is an example of a natural man not understanding the spiritual man. First Corinthians 2:14 explains that the natural man cannot understand spiritual things, because they must be spiritually discerned to do so. This simply means that spiritual things take place in the born-again spirit of the inner man, not in the natural mind.

This is the reason people who depend on their intellect have a difficult time believing in God. They don't see Him, they don't feel Him, and many of His principles don't make sense to their natural minds. Naturally speaking, what sense does it make to tell people that they will have increase if they give away some of their money? It makes no sense at all.

The Bible says that the first will be last, and the last will be first. That makes no sense to my mind, but I know by spiritual understanding that it means when we try to push ourselves forward into first place, we will end up last. When we wait on God to promote us, even if we start out last, we will end up right where we are supposed to be.

Trust in Him As a believer in Jesus Christ, filled with His Spirit, you can make decisions courageously because you can trust what is in your heart. Be grateful for the discernment and spiritual understanding that comes from trusting God.

August 8

Abide in Christ

Just as no branch can bear fruit of itself without abiding in (being vitally united to) the vine, neither can you bear fruit unless you abide in Me. JOHN 15:4

Whenever I return home from ministering at conferences, I revitalize myself by abiding in Jesus. I pray, meditate on His Word, and spend time with Him. I say, *"Thank You, Lord, for strengthening and refueling me. I need You, Jesus. I can't do anything without You."*

I know I must abide in Him if I want to bear good fruit. Abiding replenishes the energy I use in my conferences. For many years I ministered at my conferences, returned home, and went right back to the office or out on another trip without spending the time I needed with the Lord. When I did, I usually ended up worn-out, depressed, crying, and wanting to quit.

If we drive our cars without filling up the tanks, we ultimately run out of gasoline and break down. We can do the same thing as individuals. We will break down mentally, physically, emotionally, and spiritually if we don't stay full of Jesus by abiding in Him.

Dave and I have developed the habit of spending time each morning with the Lord by praying, reading, meditating, pondering, writing, resting, trusting, and abiding in Him. Sometimes people "pick on" us, and when they do, we want them to be able to pick good fruit. By the time I face my family or work responsibilities, I'm full of good fruit in case anybody has a need. I encourage you to develop what I like to call the "God Habit." Need time with Him more than you need anything else, and everything else will fall into place and work much better.

Jesus said if we dwell in Him, He will dwell in us. If we live in Him, He will live in us. He said we cannot bear fruit without abiding in Him. But if we *live*—which implies daily abiding—in Him we will bear *abundant fruit* (see John 15:4–5). Whether it is teaching or anything else I do in life, I have learned by experience that I need Him and cannot do anything of real value without Him.

Trust in Him Do you need to spend more time abiding in Christ? The more you relax and trust Him, the more you are abiding in Him.

August 9

Relax in the Keeping Power of God

For He will give His angels [especial] charge over you to accompany and defend and preserve you in all your ways [of obedience and service]. PSALM 91:11

A lady who works for me says that she doesn't have a "big" testimony. She just grew up in the church, loving God. She got married, was filled with the Holy Spirit, and then came to work for us. Through our ministry, she was moved by the testimonies of drug addicts and people who have suffered abuse. One day she asked God, *"Lord, why don't I have a testimony?"* He said, *"You do have a testimony. Your testimony is that I kept you from all of it."* God had kept her from the pain that results from being separated from Him.

The keeping power of God is a great testimony! Some people are kept from tragic things. Some people are kept as they go through tragic things. His plan for each one of us is perfect, and we can trust His keeping power!

Psalm 91 teaches that He will give His angels charge over us, and they will protect and defend us. It's true that some things happen in our lives that we don't like, but what has God kept us from that we never even knew Satan had planned against us? We need to thank God for His keeping power. We can relax knowing that He is our Keeper.

I don't know how I've done what I've done over these past years. I look back at my calendars and see how hard I've worked. I read some of my prayer journals and remember some of the things I've gone through with people, and the hurt I've felt. I think, *How did I ever get through that?* But God held me together. He strengthened me. He kept me. And I can see now that I worried about a lot of things I didn't have to worry about because they worked out okay anyway. God will do the same thing for you as you trust Him.

God has a plan, and He is working His plan. We can trust that and relax. Psalm 145:14 says, "The Lord upholds all those [of His own] who are falling and raises up all those who are bowed down."

Trust in Him The Bible says that God never sleeps nor slumbers. When you go to sleep at night, He stays up and watches over you. Relax and trust Him to strengthen you and keep you all the days of your life.

August 10

Good Attitude, Good Life

... Let there be no strife, I beg of you, between you and me, or between your herdsmen and my herdsmen. GENESIS 13:8

Genesis 12 records the covenant of peace that God made with Abraham and his heirs. Abraham became extremely rich and powerful because God blessed him. God chose him to be the man through whom He would bless all the nations on the face of the earth.

I find it interesting that in the very next chapter, Genesis 13, strife came between the herdsmen of Lot and Abraham's cattle (see v. 7). Strife is the exact opposite of peace. God gave Abraham peace, and Satan went immediately to stir up strife. God wanted to bless Abraham, and Satan wanted to steal the blessing.

Sometimes God's abundance can cause problems that lead to strife. He had blessed Abraham and Lot with so many possessions and cattle that the land could not nourish and support them both. The Bible says that Abraham went to Lot and said, "Let there be no strife, I beg of you, between you and me, or between your herdsmen and my herdsmen." He told Lot that they were going to have to separate, so Lot should choose the land he wanted, and Abraham would take what was left. Abraham took a humble position to avoid strife, knowing that if he did what was right, God would always bless him. But Lot, who would have had nothing if Abraham hadn't given it to him, chose the best part: the Jordan Valley. Abraham didn't say a thing; he just took the land that was left. He knew God would bless him if he stayed in peace.

God took Abraham up on a hill and said, "Now, you look to the north, to the south, to the east, and the west—and everything you see, I'll give to you" (see vv. 14–15). What a great deal! God honored Abraham's humility and blessed him abundantly with fruitful land.

I believe that God's got a good plan for all of us, but prideful attitudes can prevent us from having all that God wants us to have. A bad attitude is one of the most important things we can work on with God to overcome.

Trust in Him **Trust God's promises for your life, and know that the way to please God is through humbling yourself and avoiding strife.**

August 11

Enjoy God's Grace While You Wait

...My grace (My favor and loving-kindness and mercy) is enough for you [sufficient against any danger and enables you to bear the trouble manfully]; for My strength and power are made perfect (fulfilled and completed) and show themselves most effective in [your] weakness. 2 CORINTHIANS 12:9

Works of the flesh are attempts to accomplish through your own energy things that are God's job. We become frustrated when we try to achieve by *works* a life that God not only brought into being but designed to be received by *grace*. Grace is the power of God to meet our needs and solve our problems (see James 4:6).

I was living a frustrated, complicated, joyless life many years ago before I began to seriously seek God for answers to my problem of a lack of peace and joy. When I had a problem or a need, I tried to help myself and work things out in my own way, which never produced any good results. The Word of God and my personal experience have taught me that the way to avoid the frustration of fleshly works is to ask God for help. At times, all of us are guilty of trying to handle our circumstances instead of trusting God to take care of them for us. It is not a sign of weakness to admit that we cannot help ourselves—it is the truth. Jesus said, "Apart from Me [cut off from vital union with Me] you can do nothing" (John 15:5).

You may be frustrated, struggling, and unhappy simply because you are trying to fix something you cannot do anything about. Perhaps you have a situation in your life that you don't want, and you are trying to get rid of it. Maybe there is something you do want and are trying hard to get, yet nothing you try is working and it is frustrating you. In any case, the only thing you can do is cease from your own works, and trust God. While you are waiting for God to take care of the situation, I encourage you to enjoy the wait.

When you stop and consider all the ways God's blessed you through His generous grace, instead of being frustrated, you'll be filled with gratitude.

Trust in Him Trusting God to do what only He can do always leads to joy, because "what is impossible with men is possible with God" (Luke 18:27).

August 12

Only God Can Change Us—And That's a Good Thing!

And Jesus said, [You say to Me], If You can do anything? [Why,] all things can be (are possible) to him who believes! MARK 9:23

Suppose you feel you can't wait to get married, so you decide to find the perfect mate for yourself, in your own way, instead of waiting on God to work it out for you. It would be a terrible mistake to become so desperate that you settle for someone who is not right for you. It would be much better to wait until God brings you a divine connection. It is always best not to do anything that you don't have God's peace in your heart about.

Maybe you are married, and you have been thinking, *I want my spouse to change. I just can't put up with my partner anymore.* You cannot change your spouse; only God can. But God does not move in your life when you struggle and try to take matters into your own hands. He moves when you trust Him. So I suggest that you pray, cast your care on the Lord, leave your hands off the situation, trust God, and go ahead and enjoy your life.

It may not be a marital situation you want changed. You may feel that you want your kids to change, or you want more money, or you may want a different job. We all have something going on in our lives we would like to see change for the better. Desiring change is just part of living. You are always going to want something in your life to be different. So if you want an enjoyable life, sooner or later you must learn to quit trying to make things happen yourself.

Numerous times I struggled while trying to change my husband, trying to change my kids, trying to change myself, yet I failed every time. I probably struggled with changing myself more than anything or anyone else. The truth is you can't really change yourself. You can only tell God that you want to change and that you are willing to change. You can only throw open your life to Him every day by praying and studying His Word, and leave the rest to Him. The effort that we make should be made "in Christ," leaning on Him, and not in the flesh (our own strength, apart from God).

Trust in Him You can live by trying to take care of yourself, or you can live by trusting God. You can try to make things happen, or you can believe God to make things happen. The choice is yours.

August 13

Works That Don't Work

My people have committed two evils: they have forsaken Me, the Fountain of living waters, and they have hewn for themselves cisterns, broken cisterns which cannot hold water.

JEREMIAH 2:13

The Word teaches that God's people dug wells for themselves that couldn't hold water. I know what it is like to work hard with no results. I spent many years of my life digging empty wells like these, and I can tell you, it really wears you out.

You may be digging an empty well right now. You may be working on something or somebody. You may have your own little project going. You may be following your own plan, trying to make things happen in your own strength and ability. If so, it is not going to work if you have left God out of your plan. Many times we make a plan and then pray for it to work. God wants us to pray first and ask Him for His plan. After we have His plan, then He wants us to trust Him to bring it to pass, as we follow His direction and work in partnership with Him.

Our activity birthed out of the flesh actually prevents God from showing Himself strong in our lives. The Bible describes that kind of activity as "works of the flesh" (see Gal.5:19–21 KJV). I call them "works that don't work." That is not the way to live the higher life that God prepared for us.

Trust in Him When we wait on God and trust Him, He will bring to pass according to His will what we are believing for—no matter how long it takes.

August 14

Love Finds a Way

[Love] does not rejoice at injustice and unrighteousness, but rejoices when right and truth prevail. 1 CORINTHIANS 13:6

Do you think something should be done about starving children? Should somebody help the 1.1 million people who have no safe drinking water? Should people live on streets and under bridges? Should a family you have gone to church with for years experience a tragedy and not even get a phone call from anyone to find out why they have not been in church for three months? If a church of another denomination in your city burns down, is it proper to just pray and do nothing practical to help? Do you believe somebody should do something about injustices?

I think you would agree the answer is "No!" So I have one final question: What are *you* going to do? Will you be the "somebody" who does what needs to be done? We'll always be able to find an excuse as to why we can't do anything about these problems. But in the end, indifference makes an excuse, but love finds a way.

When I ask what you are going to do, do you feel afraid because you wonder what "doing something" will require? I understand that kind of panicky feeling. After all, if I really decide to forget myself and start aggressively trying to help others, what will happen to me? Who will take care of me if I don't take care of myself? God said He would, so I think we should find out if He really meant what He said. Why not retire from "self-care" and see if God can do a better job than you have done.

If we take care of His business, which is helping people who are hurting, I believe He will take care of ours.

Trust in Him Do you trust God to take care of you? Then think of a way you can demonstrate that trust by lovingly helping someone in need. And as you do, you'll experience more of God's love for you.

August 15

"God, This Is Just Not a Good Time!"

. . . Felix became alarmed and terrified and said, Go away for the present; when I have a convenient opportunity, I will send for you.

ACTS 24:25

The Bible tells a story about a man who did not follow God because doing so would have been inconvenient. This man, named Felix, asked Paul to come and preach the Gospel to him. But when Paul started talking to him about right living, purity of life, and controlling his passions, Felix became alarmed and frightened. He told Paul to go away and that he would call him at a more convenient time (see Acts 24:24–25).

I find this extremely amusing, not because it is really funny, but because it clearly depicts the way we are. We don't mind hearing about how much God loves us and about the good plans He has for our lives, but when He begins to chastise us or correct us in any way, we try to tell Him that "now" is just not a good time. I doubt He ever chooses a time we would consider "a good time," and I think He does that on purpose!

When the Israelites were traveling through the wilderness, they were led by a cloud during the day and a pillar of fire by night. When the cloud moved, they had to move. And when it hovered, they stayed where they were (see Num. 9:15–23). The Bible says that sometimes it moved during the day and sometimes it moved at night. Sometimes it rested for a few days and sometimes it rested for one day.

I seriously doubt that at night they all hung Do Not Disturb signs on the openings of their tents to let God know they did not want to be inconvenienced. When He decided it was time to go, they packed up and followed Him. And when He decides it is time for us to move to the next level of our journey in Him, we should never say, *"This is just not a good time!"*

God knows best, and His timing is always exactly right. The fact that I don't *feel* ready to deal with something in my life doesn't mean that I'm not ready. God's timing is perfect, and His ways are not our ways, but they are higher and better than our ways (see Isa. 55:9).

Trust in Him Have you ever said to God, *"This is not a good time"*? Commit to following God's will for your life in His timing. God's timing may not be your timing, but you can trust Him because He knows best.

August 16

"Do You Want It or Not?"

And He said to them, Come after Me [as disciples—letting Me be your Guide], follow Me, and I will make you fishers of men!

MATTHEW 4:19

Peter, Andrew, James, John, and the other disciples were greatly honored. They were chosen to be the twelve disciples, the men who would learn from Jesus and then carry the Gospel to the world. What I find interesting is they were all busy when Jesus called them. They had lives, families, and businesses to take care of. With no warning at all, Jesus showed up and said, *"Follow Me."*

The Bible says Peter and Andrew were casting their nets into the sea when Jesus called them, and they left their nets and followed Him (see Matt. 4:18–21). Talk about an interruption! He did not tell them they could pray about it, or consider it, or go home and talk to their wives and children. He merely said, "Follow Me," and they did.

The disciples didn't ask how long they would be gone or what the salary package would be. They didn't ask about benefits, compensation time for travel, or what kind of hotel they would be staying in. They didn't even ask Him what their job description would be. They simply left everything behind and followed Him. Even when I read this now, I must admit it seems a bit severe, but perhaps the greater the opportunity is, the greater the sacrifice must be.

I remember a time when I was complaining about some of the things God seemed to be requiring of me because I felt others didn't have the same requirements placed on them. He simply said, *"Joyce, you have asked Me for a lot. Do you want it or not?"* I asked to be able to help people all over the world, and I was learning that the privilege of doing so would frequently be inconvenient and uncomfortable.

King Solomon said if we wait for all conditions to be favorable before we sow, we will never reap (see Eccl. 11:4). In other words, we must give and obey God when it is not convenient and when it is costly if we want to reap our reward.

Trust in Him What have you asked God for? Have you thought about what it might require in order for Him to give it to you? No matter what God asks of you, you can trust that it is not more than you can bear, and you will reap what you sow from following Christ.

August 17

Be Ready to Be Interrupted

I am the Good Shepherd. The Good Shepherd risks and lays down His [own] life for the sheep. JOHN 10:11

The more I study the men and women in the Bible whom we consider to be "great," the more I see that they all made huge sacrifices and there was nothing convenient about what God asked them to do.

Abraham had to leave his country, his relatives, and his home and go to a place God would not even tell him about until he went there. Joseph saved a nation from starvation, but not before he was violently removed from his comfortable home and put in an inconvenient place for many years. Esther saved the Jews from destruction, but God certainly interrupted her plan in order for her to do so.

The list of individuals who entered into sacrificial obedience could go on and on. The Bible calls them people "of whom the world was not worthy" (see Heb. 11:38). These people we read about were inconvenienced so that someone else's life could be easier. Jesus died so we could have life and have it abundantly. Soldiers die so that civilians can remain safe at home. Fathers go to work so their families can have nice lives, and mothers go through the pain of childbirth to bring another life into the world. It seems quite obvious that someone usually has to experience pain or inconvenience for anyone to gain anything.

If you make the decision that you don't mind inconvenience or interruption, then God can use you. You can make a difference in the world. But if you remain addicted to your own comfort, God will have to pass you by for someone who is more willing to endure the hard things in life in order to do God's will.

Trust in Him Think about a situation in which God is asking you to do some things you would rather not do—stay in a situation, leave a situation, spend time with someone you don't get along with... Are you willing to trust the "interruption" from God in order to do His will?

August 18

You're a Channel, Not a Reservoir

Behold, this was the iniquity of your sister Sodom: pride, overabundance of food, prosperous ease, and idleness were hers and her daughters'; neither did she strengthen the hand of the poor and the needy. EZEKIEL 16:49

You have probably heard of Sodom and Gomorrah and the terrible wickedness in those cities. But what did they actually do that was so displeasing to God?

We often have the idea that their sexual perversion finally put God over the edge and caused Him to destroy them, but it was actually quite a different situation that caused Him to act against them. I was shocked when I saw the truth behind their destruction. I discovered it while searching Scriptures about the need to feed the poor.

The problem with Sodom and Gomorrah was that they had too much and were not sharing it with those in need. They were idle and lived excessively convenient lifestyles, which led them to commit abominable acts. We see clearly from this that idleness and too much convenience is not good for us and leads us into more and more trouble. Failing to share what we do have with those who have less than we do is not good for us, and is actually dangerous, because this selfish type of lifestyle opens the door for evil to progress.

Not only are these things not good for us, but they are offensive to God. He expects us to be channels for Him to flow through, not reservoirs that hold everything we have for ourselves.

We appreciate all the conveniences that are available to us today, but in some ways I think Satan is using them to destroy any willingness to be inconvenienced in order to obey God or help others in need. We have become addicted to ease, and we need to be very careful. Like most people, I like nice, comfortable things, but I have made an effort not to complain when I don't have things the way I want them. I also realize that inconvenience is almost always part of helping others, and I know I am called by God to help people and do so with a good attitude.

Trust in Him Are you willing to be inconvenienced for God? God wants you to be a channel of His love to the world. Ask Him to help you find balance in all things, trust Him with the resources He has given you, and keep a good attitude.

August 19

Real Relationships Are Worth It

For I have given you this as an example, so that you should do [in your turn] what I have done to you. JOHN 13:15

Jesus did not waste His time, so we can assume that everything He did was very meaningful and contains a great lesson to be learned. Let's think about the time He decided to wash His disciples' feet (see John 13:1–17). What was that all about?

Jesus was and is the Son of God. Actually, He is God manifested in the second person of the Trinity. So it suffices to say that He is really important and certainly would not have to wash anyone's feet, especially not guys who were His students. But He did so because He wanted to teach them that they could be in authority and still be servants at the same time.

Peter, the most vocal disciple, vehemently refused to let Jesus wash his feet, but Jesus said if He did not wash Peter's feet, the two of them could not be real friends. In other words, they had to be doing things for one another in order for their relationship to be healthy and strong.

I decided a few years ago that I was not willing to have any more one-sided relationships—relationships in which I do all the giving and the other person does all the taking. That kind of interaction is not real friendship, and it always eventually causes resentment and bitterness. Not only should we do things for each other, we actually *need* to do things for one another. This is part of maintaining good relationships.

Giving does not always have to be a response to a desperate need. We may be led to do something for people who don't seem to need what we can do for them at all. If there is no need, then why do it? Simply because giving of any kind prevents us from becoming greedy, and it encourages people and makes them feel loved—and we all need to feel loved, no matter how many "things" we have.

Trust in Him Trust God enough to be willing to make sacrifices in order to serve and bless others, and He will always take care of you!

August 20

Little Things Mean a Lot

So then, as occasion and opportunity open up to us, let us do good [morally] to all people... GALATIANS 6:10

We took the band Delirious? to India with us on a mission trip, and Stu, their drummer at the time, was given a little strip of leather from a poor girl who wore it as a bracelet. The small gesture of love from one who had so little was life-changing. Stu has said publicly that as long as he lives, he will never forget the lesson it taught him. If someone with so little was willing to give, what could he be doing? Yes, little things can have a huge impact.

What little thing could you do? Below is a partial list of some things the Bible says we can and should do for one another:

- Watch over one another
- Pray for one another
- Be friendly and hospitable
- Be patient with one another
- Bear with others' faults and weaknesses
- Forgive one another
- Comfort one another
- Build up one another—encourage and love them through their weakness
- Be happy for people when they are blessed
- Believe the best of one another
- Meet people's needs

This is a partial list. Love has many faces or many ways it can be seen. The ideas listed here are relatively simple things we all can do if we are willing. We don't have to make special plans for most of them, but we can do them throughout the day as we encounter opportunities.

Trust in Him What little things will you do today to be a blessing to someone? God wants you to be a blessing to others, and even little things mean a lot. Begin looking for people to be a blessing to and trust God to use these blessings to further His Kingdom.

August 21

Love Must Do Something

But if anyone has this world's goods (resources for sustaining life) and sees his brother and fellow believer in need, yet closes his heart of compassion against him, how can the love of God live and remain in him?
1 JOHN 3:17

We often think of love as a thing or a feeling, but the word *love* is also a verb. Love must *do* something in order to remain what it is. Part of the nature of love is that it requires expression. The Bible asks, if we see a need and close our heart of compassion, how can the love of God live and remain in us? Love becomes weaker and weaker if it cannot be demonstrated; in fact, it may become totally inactive. If we keep it active on purpose as we do things for others, we can keep from being selfish, idle, and unfruitful.

The quintessential act of love is that Jesus laid down His own life for us. And we ought to lay down our lives for one another. That sounds extreme, doesn't it? Fortunately, the great majority of us will never be called upon to give up our physical life for someone else. But we have opportunities every day to "lay down" our life for others. Every time you put aside your own desire or need and replace it with an act of love for someone else, you are laying down your life for a moment, or an hour, or a day.

If we are full of the love of God—and we are because the Holy Spirit fills our hearts with love at the new birth—then we must let love flow out of us. If it becomes stagnant through inactivity, it is good for nothing. God so loved the world that He gave His only Son (see John 3:16). Do you get it? God's love provoked Him to *give*!

Trust in Him Put a huge sign in your house, perhaps in several places, that asks, "*What have I done to help someone today?*" Don't go through the day without increasing someone else's joy. Trust Christ's example of laying down His life for you as a model for how to live!

August 22

Set Sail and Be Free

And because you [really] are [His] sons, God has sent the [Holy] Spirit of His Son into our hearts, crying, Abba (Father)! Father!
GALATIANS 4:6

I once read that we believers are like ships that God wants to turn out to sea to sail wherever the wind and waves carry us. That sea represents the freedom we have in God, and the wind is a symbol of the Holy Spirit. But as new believers, we are tied to the dock because that is the only place we can avoid becoming shipwrecked until we learn how to follow Him. When we learn to follow those inner promptings of the Holy Spirit, we can be untied from the dock and sail the seas of life under His leadership without the fear of becoming lost.

God's leading doesn't contradict the laws that He ordained. When we are new believers, we learn to follow God's laws that He defined in the Word. And as we mature, we develop the ability to be led by the Spirit of the living God. When the Spirit of God is in you, the law of God is written in your heart. You no longer have to memorize the law, because you can follow the leadership of the Holy Spirit, Who will lead you in the right direction.

Some people feel much safer following the law than being led by the Spirit. They think they are okay as long as they follow a prescribed plan that everyone else is following. But following the Spirit may lead people to do something a little differently from what everyone else is doing. They will need faith to leave the security of the crowd because

God doesn't lead everybody to serve Him in exactly the same place or at the same capacity.

We cannot follow the leadership of the Holy Spirit by simply obeying laws, rules, and regulations. God's law is our tutor, but it is not to be our master. To live at ease and be full of joy, we must learn to prayerfully follow the Holy Spirit.

Trust in Him God wants you to set sail and be free from captivity. To do so, you must trust the leadership of the Holy Spirit when He speaks to your heart and leads you in the right direction.

August 23

Simply Believe

Whoever will humble himself therefore and become like this little child [trusting, lowly, loving, forgiving] is greatest in the kingdom of heaven.
MATTHEW 18:4

I used to be a very complicated person. My way of seeing and doing things was so complicated that it kept me from enjoying anything. We say that we live in a complicated society, but I believe we are the complicated ones, and that we complicate life. Serving God should not be complicated, and yet it can become very complicated and complex. Worry, fear, anxiety, jealousy, resentment, and bitterness are all very complicated. Little children have none of these.

Think about the simple, uncomplicated approach a child has to life. Here are some things children seem to have in common: They are going to enjoy themselves if at all possible. They are carefree and completely without concern. And they believe what they are told. It is their nature to trust unless they have had an experience that taught them otherwise.

Remember, He told us in John 3:16, "God so loved the world that He gave His only begotten Son, that whoever *believes* in Him should not perish but have everlasting life" (NKJV, emphasis added). All He wants to hear us say is, *"I believe!"*

Believing simplifies life. It releases joy and leaves us free to enjoy our lives while God takes care of our circumstances. When God says something to you in your heart, or when you read something in the Bible, you should say, "I believe it. If God says that He wants to bless us, then we should believe it. If He says that we will reap what we sow, we should believe it. If He says to forgive our enemies, even though it doesn't make any sense to us, we should believe it—instead of being resentful. Let us diligently do what God says. If He says to pray for our enemies, let us believe it and follow through with obedience. If He says to call 'things which do not exist as though they did' (Rom. 4:17 NKJV), then we should respond as a child and simply do what He says."

Even though life can get complicated, we can simplify it by approaching it as a child would. Put all your trust in God and be obedient.

> *Trust in Him* God has a plan for your breakthrough—and your part is to trust Him. Say several times throughout each day, "Father, I trust You!"

August 24

You Can Handle Whatever Life Hands You

> *Yet amid all these things we are more than conquerors and gain a surpassing victory through Him Who loved us.* ROMANS 8:37

For years, I have pondered what being "more than a conqueror" means. I'm sure other people have other perspectives, but I have come to the conclusion that being more than a conqueror means having such confidence that no matter what comes up in your life, you know that through Christ you can handle it. You know before you are ever faced with a problem that you're going to have victory over it.

So therefore, you don't dread things, you don't fear the unknown, you don't live in anxiety about what's going to happen in uncertain situations. It doesn't really matter what the specifics of the situation are, you know you can handle it through Christ. For you, defeat isn't an option!

Begin to think every day, *I can handle whatever life hands me. I can do whatever I need to do in life. I am more than a conqueror. I am equal to anything through Him who infuses inner strength into me.* Even before you get out of bed in the mornings, let these thoughts roll over and over in your mind, and your confidence will skyrocket and you will find that indeed, you can do whatever you need to do in life.

Right thinking is the first step toward a better life. Wishing won't work. Being jealous of someone who has what you desire does no good. Self-pity is a waste of time and energy. Discovering God's will through an accurate knowledge of His Word and beginning to think as He thinks is the beginning of a new life for anyone who desires one.

Trust in Him In what specific situation do you need to believe you are more than a conqueror? Trust that through Christ, you are equal to anything.

August 25

Remember: God Loves You Unconditionally

Even as [in His love] He chose us [actually picked us out for Himself as His own] in Christ before the foundation of the world, that we should be holy (consecrated and set apart for Him) and blameless in His sight, even above reproach, before Him in love.

EPHESIANS 1:4

We frequently compare ourselves with other people, and if we are not what they are, or cannot do what they do, then we assume something is wrong with us. There is, however, an antidote for this type of thinking poisonous. It is frequently thinking, *God loves me unconditionally!*

Knowing God loves us unconditionally is an absolute necessity in order to make progress in our walk with Him. Jesus didn't die so we could be religious; Jesus died so we could have deep, intimate, personal relationships with God through Him. Religion offers us rules and regulations to follow in order to be close to God. But relationship lets us know we can be close to Him because He has chosen us.

We will not draw near to God if we are afraid He is displeased with us. It is vital that you learn how to separate how important *you* are to God from the right or wrong things you do. How can we hope to have an intimate relationship with God, His Son Jesus, and the Holy Spirit if we are not confident that we are loved unconditionally?

Good relationships must be based on love and acceptance, not on fear. All too often we are deceived into thinking that our acceptance is based on our performance.

We are loved and accepted by God, and made right with Him because we place our faith in Jesus Christ and the work He accomplished for us on the cross. He paid for our sins and misdeeds. He absolved us from guilt and reconciled us to God. Now, when we stand before God, we have "rightness," not "wrongness." And we have it because He gave it as a gift, not because we have earned it. Blessed is the man who knows he has right standing with God apart from the works he does.

Trust in Him Trust God and believe that He loves you unconditionally, and that He is not mad at you!

August 26

The Source of Your Confidence

For our sake He made Christ [virtually] to be sin Who knew no sin, so that in and through Him we might become [endued with, viewed as being in, and examples of] the righteousness of God [what we ought to be, approved and acceptable and in right relationship with Him, by His goodness]. 2 CORINTHIANS 5:21

Knowing we are loved and accepted even in our imperfection is such a relief! Serving God from desire rather than obligation is incredibly liberating and brings great peace and joy to our lives. The Bible says that we love Him because He first loved us (see 1 John 4:19). Being assured of God's unconditional love gives us confidence and boldness.

Our confidence should not be in anything or anyone but Jesus—not in education, outward privilege, positions we hold, people we know, how we look, or our gifts and talents. Everything in this world is shaky at best, and we should not place our confidence in it. He is the same yesterday, today, and forever (see Heb. 13:8). We can count on Him to always be faithful and do what He says He will do—and He says He will *always* love us. He says we are righteous in His sight, and we need to make a decision to simply believe it.

We become what we believe we are; therefore, as we become convinced that we are right with God, our behavior will improve. We will do more things right and with less effort. As we focus on our relationship with God rather than our performance, we relax, and what God has done in our spirits when we were born again is gradually worked out in our souls and finally seen through our daily lives.

No matter what other people may have told you that you are not, God delights in telling you in His Word who you are in Him—loved, valuable, precious, talented, gifted, capable, powerful, wise, and redeemed. I encourage you to take a moment and repeat those nine things out loud. Say, *"I am loved, valuable, precious, talented, gifted, capable, powerful, wise, and redeemed."* He has a good plan for you! Get excited about your life. You are created in God's image and you are amazing!

Trust in Him Do you trust God's Word, which says you are loved unconditionally?

August 27

Your Account Is "In Balance"

But all things are from God, Who through Jesus Christ reconciled us to Himself [received us into favor, brought us into harmony with Himself] and gave to us the ministry of reconciliation [that by word and deed we might aim to bring others into harmony with Him].

2 CORINTHIANS 5:18

What does it mean to be reconciled to God? It means "your account is in balance." You don't owe anything!

I once saw a bumper sticker that said, "*I owe, I owe, so off to work I go.*" I immediately realized that was the mentality I lived with for years. I felt that I owed God something for all the wrong I had done, and I tried every day to do good works to make up for my mistakes. I wanted to be blessed by Him, but felt I needed to earn His blessings. I finally learned that we cannot pay for His gifts; otherwise, they are not gifts at all.

God sees the heart of man, and how He deals with us is based on the kind of heart we have. I don't do everything right, but I do love God very much. I am very sorry for my sins, and it grieves me when I know that I have disappointed Him. I want His will in my life. Perhaps like me, you have been tormented for years by feelings of guilt and fear, but knowing that God loves you unconditionally releases you from those negative emotions and allows you to enjoy yourself while you are changing.

In 2 Corinthians 5:20, Paul emphasizes again the reconciliation and favor God extends to us and encourages us to believe these things: "So we are Christ's ambassadors, God making His appeal as it were through us. We [as Christ's personal representatives] beg you for His sake to lay hold of the divine favor [now offered you] and be reconciled to God." Paul is actually begging the believers of his day to take hold of what God is offering, and I urge you to do the same. Don't wait another moment to believe that God accepts you, views you as being in right standing with Him, and loves you unconditionally.

Trust in Him Do you really believe you are reconciled to God? Trust that He is completely satisfied and pleased with who you are; you don't owe Him a thing except your love.

August 28

Catch It Early

Be self-controlled and alert. Your enemy the devil prowls around like a roaring lion looking for someone to devour. Resist him, standing firm in the faith, because you know that your brothers throughout the world are undergoing the same kind of sufferings.

1 PETER 5:8–9 NIV 1984

In the United States, there is an over-the-counter medication advertised as the medicine to take at the first indication of a cold, to keep it from getting worse and becoming full-blown. I take a lot of vitamin C if I have a scratchy throat or a runny nose because it often keeps me from getting worse. Catching something before it goes too far is wisdom.

I recommend that anytime you even begin to feel fearful about anything that you immediately begin to pray and confess, "*I will not live in fear.*" You will see amazing results. When we pray, God hears and answers. When we confess His Word, we renew our own minds and come into agreement with His plans for us. No matter what God wants to do for us, we must agree with Him in order to receive and enjoy it (see Amos 3:3). We must learn to think like God thinks and talk like He talks—and none of His thoughts or words are fearful.

This thought—*I will not live in fear*—will help you become courageous rather than fearful. Call it to mind the instant you begin to feel fear, and meditate on it even during the times when you are not afraid.

By doing this you will be even more prepared to stand against fear when it does come.

Remember that it will take time; be committed to stick with it until you see change. I still say, *"I will not live in fear."* Say it as soon as you feel fearful about anything, and you will be able to keep fear from controlling you. You may still feel fear, but you can move beyond it by realizing that it is merely the devil's attempt to prevent you from enjoying life or making any kind of progress. Do what you believe you are supposed to do even if you have to "do it afraid."

Trust in Him What can you do to "catch it early" and not let fear control you? Trust that God does not want you to live a life of fear.

August 29

Don't Fear—Keep Going

If God is for us, who [can be] against us? [Who can be our foe, if God is on our side?] ROMANS 8:31

We must learn how to deal with fear before it goes too far because it will never completely go away. Feeling fear is part of being alive. We may feel fear when we are doing something we have never done before, or when the obstacles seem insurmountable, or when we don't have the natural help we feel we need. None of this means we are cowards; it means we are human. We can only be cowardly when we allow our fears to dictate our actions or decisions, instead of following our hearts and doing what we know is right for us.

We must accept the fact that fear will never go away completely, but also know we can live boldly and courageously because God has told us that He is always with us. Because of that knowledge we can choose to ignore the fear we feel. It's okay to feel fear; it's not okay to act on those feelings. You see, the word *fear* means "to take flight" or "to run away from," and it causes us to want to flee from what God wants us to confront.

The only acceptable attitude for a Christian to have toward fear is *"I will not fear."* Do not shrink back from anything in fear. You may be going forward with something you feel God has spoken to you to do. Then something happens to make it appear that it's not working out or that people are not in favor of it. You realize that if you do what God wants you to do, you may risk losing some friends, some resources, or your reputation.

When you feel that fear, the first impulse is to shrink back, isn't it? God knows that, and that is why He says, "Do not fear." When He tells us not to fear, what He means is, no matter how you feel, keep putting one foot in front of the other and doing what you believe He has told you to do because that's the only way to defeat fear and make progress.

Trust in Him Trust the Word of God more than you trust the lies of the devil, and keep making progress!

August 30

The Main Thing

Trust (lean on, rely on, and be confident) in the Lord and do good…

PSALM 37:3

The Lord led me to study the above Scripture, and I was startled to realize that I had only half of what I needed to know to connect properly with God. I had the faith (trust) part, but not the "do good" part. I wanted good things to happen to me, but I was not overly concerned about being good to others, particularly when I was hurting or going through a time of personal trial.

Not only was I lacking in this area, but I realized that most of the other Christians I knew were probably in the same condition. We were all occupied "believing" God for the things we wanted. We prayed together and released our faith through the prayer of agreement, but we did not meet together and discuss what we could do for others while we were waiting for our needs to be met. We had faith, but it was not being energized by love!

I don't want to sound as though I was totally self-absorbed, because that wasn't the case. I was working in ministry and wanted to help people, but mixed in with my desire to help were a lot of impure motives. Being in ministry gave me a sense of self-worth and importance. It gave me position and a certain amount of influence, but God wanted me to do everything I did with a pure motive, and I still had a great deal to learn.

There were times I did acts of kindness to help people, but helping others was not my number one motivator. I needed to be much more aggressive and purposeful about loving others; it needed to be the main thing in my life, not a sideline. God helped me change in this area, and I am much happier because of it.

Ask yourself what motivates you more than anything else, and answer honestly. Is it love? If it isn't, are you willing to change your focus to what is important to God?

Trust in Him Trusting God is only half of what He wants from you. Don't forget that He also wants you to do good for others as you wait on Him to solve your problem.

August 31

You Are a Witness

Conduct yourselves properly (honorably, righteously) among the Gentiles, so that, although they may slander you as evildoers, [yet] they may by witnessing your good deeds [come to] glorify God in the day of inspection [when God shall look upon you wanderers as a pastor or shepherd looks over his flock]. 1 PETER 2:12

I believe the world is watching Christians, and what people see Christians do is very important. In the Scripture above, Peter encouraged believers to conduct themselves properly and honorably among Gentiles, the unbelievers of the day. He said even if the unbelievers were inclined to slander the believers, the unbelievers would eventually come to glorify God if they saw the believers' good works and loving deeds.

If your neighbors know you go to church every Sunday, I can assure you that they also watch your behavior. When I was growing up, our neighbors dutifully went to church. Actually, they went several times a week, but they also did lots of things they should not have done. I recall my father often saying, "*They are no better than I am; they get drunk, use bad language, tell dirty jokes, and have bad tempers, so they are just a bunch of hypocrites.*" My dad was looking for an excuse to not serve God anyway, and their behavior just added fuel to the fire.

I certainly realize that as Christians, we don't behave perfectly, and that people who want an excuse to not believe in Jesus or practice Christianity will always watch us and criticize us. But we should do the best we can to not give them a reason to judge us.

Trust in Him Are you conducting yourself properly so that when the world looks at you it sees God's character? Ask God to help you be a good witness at all times.

September 1

The Right Reward

Give, and it shall be given unto you; good measure, pressed down, and shaken together, and running over, shall men give into your bosom. For with the same measure that ye mete withal it shall be measured to you again.

LUKE 6:38 KJV

Giving and living selflessly do produce harvests in our lives. There is nothing wrong with desiring and expecting a harvest. Our motivation for helping others should not be to get something for ourselves, but God does tell us we will reap what we sow, and we can look forward to that benefit.

God promises to reward those who diligently seek Him (see Heb. 11:6). The word *reward* in the original Greek text of the New Testament means, "wages received in this life" or "recompense." In the Hebrew language, in which the Old Testament is written, the word *reward* means, "fruit, earnings, product, price, or result." The word *reward* is used sixty-eight times in the Amplified Bible version. God wants us to look forward to rewards of our obedience and good choices.

If we care about those who are poor and oppressed, God promises that we will not want, but if we hide our eyes from their need we shall have "many a curse" in our lives (Prov. 28:27). The writer of Proverbs even says that when we give to the poor we are lending to God (see Prov. 19:17). I cannot imagine that God does not pay great interest on what is loaned to Him. I urge you to work to bring justice to the oppressed. That simply means that when you see something that you know is not right, you work to make it right.

Trust in Him Are you lending to God by taking care of the poor? Focus on giving to others and righting the injustice in the world, and you can trust God to bring a harvest of blessings into your life.

September 2

The Key to Being Satisfied

Then shall your light break forth like the morning...

ISAIAH 58:8

We all probably want more light in our lives. That would mean more clarity, better understanding, and less confusion. The prophet Isaiah declared that if we would divide our bread with the hungry and bring the homeless poor into our homes, cover the naked and stop hiding ourselves from the needs around us, our light would break forth (see Isa. 58:7–8). He also said our healing and restoration and the power of a new life would spring forth quickly. That sounds good to me, and I am sure it does to you also.

Isaiah also wrote of justice, and he said it would go before us and conduct us to peace and prosperity, and that the glory of the Lord would be our rear guard. If we are actively helping the oppressed, God goes before us and He also has our backs! I like that feeling of safety and certainty.

Isaiah further said if we would pour out that with which we sustain our own lives for the hungry, and satisfy the need of the afflicted, our light would rise in darkness and any gloom we experienced would be comparable to the sun at noon (see Isa. 58:10). The sun is very bright at noon, so it sounds to me like helping people is the way to live in the light.

The Lord will guide us continually, and even in dry times He will satisfy us. He will make our bones strong and our lives will be like a watered garden (see Isa. 58:11). All of this happens as a result of living to bring justice to the oppressed.

I hope you are seeing what I am seeing through these promises. I think most of us waste a lot of our lives trying to *get* what God will gladly *give* if we simply do what He is asking us to do: care about the poor, the hungry, the destitute, orphans, widows, the oppressed, and needy. Live your life to help others, and God will satisfy you in every way possible.

Trust in Him When you care about God's children you can trust Him to release more light into your life. If you follow His instructions, as written in His Word, for how to live a godly life—living your life to help others—He will gladly give you all He has promised.

September 3

All People Are Worthy of Respect

And Peter opened his mouth and said: Most certainly and thoroughly I now perceive and understand that God shows no partiality and is no respecter of persons. ACTS 10:34

The Bible says in several places that God is not a respecter of persons (see Acts 10:34, Rom. 2:11, Eph. 6:9). He does not treat some people better than others because of the way they dress, their levels of income, the positions they hold, or who they know. He not only treats everyone the same, it seems He goes out of His way to treat those who are hurting especially well.

The apostle Peter said this:

> Practice hospitality to one another (those of the household of faith) [Be hospitable, be a lover of strangers, with brotherly affection for the unknown guests, the foreigners, the poor, and all others who come your way who are of Christ's body]. And [in each instance] do it ungrudgingly (cordially and graciously, without complaining but as representing Him). (1 Pet. 4:9)

Before you rush past this part, take an inventory of how friendly you are with people you don't know and especially those who are entirely different from you. Some people are just naturally friendly and outgoing in temperament, but those of us who don't seem to have the "friendly gene" need to make a decision to be friendly because the Bible says to do it.

The apostle James admonished the church not to pay special attention to people who wore splendid clothes to the synagogue or to give them preferable seats when they came in. He said if people acted in these ways and wanted special treatment, they had wrong motives (see James 2:1–4). In other words, we are to treat all people as being worthy of respect.

Jesus put an end to distinction between people and said we are all one in Him (see Gal. 3:28). We simply need to see valuable people—not rich or poor, highly educated or uneducated, not the labels in their clothes, hairstyles, the cars they drive, their professions or titles—just people for whom Jesus died.

Trust in Him God knew what He was doing when He sent His Son Jesus to die for *all* of us. If He was willing to do that, you can trust that He wants you to treat each person for whom He died with equal respect.

September 4

The "Much Greater Hunger"

So let us then definitely aim for and eagerly pursue what makes for harmony and for mutual upbuilding (edification and development) of one another. ROMANS 14:19

Mother Teresa said, *"Being unwanted, unloved, uncared for, forgotten by everybody, I think that is a much greater hunger, a much greater poverty than the person who has nothing to eat."*

I have discovered that most people we meet or come into contact with in our everyday lives do not have a sense of their infinite value as children of God. I think the devil works very hard to make people feel devalued and worthless, but we can neutralize the effect of his lies and insinuations by building people up, encouraging, and edifying them. One way to do this is with a sincere compliment, which is one of the most valuable gifts in this world.

Most people are quick to compare themselves with others, and in doing so, they often fail to see their own abilities and worth. Making another person feel valuable isn't expensive and doesn't have to be time consuming. All we need to do is get ourselves off of our minds long enough to think about someone else, and then find something encouraging to say. Making people feel valuable won't cost any money, but it gives them something worth more than anything money can buy. Offering a sincere compliment may seem like a small thing, but it gives someone tremendous strength.

I believe in having goals. As I was working with God to develop good habits in the area of encouraging others, I challenged myself to compliment at least three people each day. I recommend that you do something similar to help you become a frequent encourager.

Trust in Him What are you doing to make sure that the people you come in contact with feel valuable? As a child of God, you have value, but many people you meet don't know Him or trust His love. Begin to help people see their worth by paying them a sincere compliment.

September 5

You've Been Adopted as His Own

Although my father and my mother have forsaken me, yet the Lord will take me up [adopt me as His child]. PSALM 27:10

I have come to understand that multitudes of people that we encounter daily are just trying to survive until someone rescues them—and that someone could be you or me.

My mother was deeply afraid of my father, so she was unable to rescue me from the various kinds of abuse he perpetrated against me. I felt very alone, forgotten, and abandoned in my nightmare. I finally decided that nobody was going to help me, so I proceeded to "survive" my circumstances until I could escape them.

The Bible says that in God's love, "He chose us [actually picked us out for Himself as His own] in Christ before the foundation of the world" (Eph. 1:4). He planned in love for us to be adopted as His own children.

Those beautiful words brought a great deal of healing to my wounded soul. God adopts the forsaken and the lonely and He lifts them up and gives them value. He works through His Word, through the Holy Spirit, and through Spirit-led people who live to help others.

Mother Teresa felt that each person she met was *"Jesus in disguise."* Just try to imagine how much differently we would treat people if we really looked at them the way she did.

Jesus said if we do good or bad to even "the least" of people, we do it to Him (see Matt. 25:45). In other words, He takes our treatment of others personally. If someone insulted, slighted, ignored, or devalued one of my children, I would take it as a personal insult, so why is it so hard to understand that God feels the same way? Let us all strive to build people up, to make everyone we encounter feel better, and to add value to their lives.

Trust in Him If you feel like you can't trust anyone and you have to take care of yourself in order to survive, begin to trust God, because He chose you and adopted you as His own. Once you know that truth for yourself, you can begin to help others know it for themselves as well.

September 6

God Wants You to Laugh

A happy heart is good medicine and a cheerful mind works healing, but a broken spirit dries up the bones.

PROVERBS 17:22

One of the amazing things I have noticed from teaching and ministering is that God loves to make people laugh. I don't plan to be funny when I speak, but the Holy Spirit speaks through me—and I'm amazed at how He adds funny little thoughts or illustrations. He clearly knows the value of humor and the healing effect it brings.

God wants us to laugh, and He wants us to make other people laugh. That does not mean we should all become jesters or laugh at inappropriate times, but we can certainly aid one another in taking a more lighthearted approach to life. We would all be much better off if we would learn to laugh at ourselves sometimes instead of taking ourselves so seriously.

The last three times I have worn white pants, I have spilled coffee on myself. I can either think I am a klutz who cannot hold on to anything and begin to devalue myself, or I can make a joke out of it and try harder to stay clean the next time. For years, I have listened to people downgrade themselves verbally for every mistake they make, and I believe that grieves God. If we know our value in Christ we should *never* say things about ourselves that devalue what God has created.

Why not make a habit of helping people see that we all make silly mistakes and we can choose to laugh rather than get upset? Give people permission to not be perfect! I love to be with people who do not pressure me to be perfect. God loves us unconditionally, and that means He accepts us the way we are and then helps us to be all we can be. Helping people laugh at themselves is a way of saying, *"I accept you, faults and all."*

Remember to take every opportunity to laugh—especially at yourself—because it will improve your health and you will enjoy your life much more.

Trust in Him Do you accept yourself, faults and all? God does! If you trust Him to love you just the way you are (He *is* the One Who created you!), then you can lighten up, accept that you aren't perfect, and be an example to others who need more laughter in their lives.

September 7

You Are Known by Your Fruit

Either make the tree sound (healthy and good), and its fruit sound (healthy and good), or make the tree rotten (diseased and bad), and its fruit rotten (diseased and bad); for the tree is known and recognized and judged by its fruit. MATTHEW 12:33

Jesus said we would be known by our fruit, which means that people can tell who we really are on the inside by what we produce with our lives and by our attitudes.

Jesus not only talked about love, but He showed love by His actions. Acts 10:38 says He got up daily and went about doing good and healing all those who were harassed and oppressed by the devil. His disciples saw Him daily helping people, listening to them, or letting His plans be interrupted in order to help someone who came to Him with a need. The disciples saw Him make sure they always had money set aside to help the poor. They also witnessed Him being quick to forgive and showing patience with the weak. He was kind, humble, and encouraging, and never gave up on anybody. Jesus did not merely talk about loving people, He showed everyone around Him how to love. Our words are important, but our actions carry more weight than our words.

The single biggest problem we have in Christianity is that we listen to people tell us what to do—and we even tell others what to do—and then we walk out of our church buildings or Bible studies and do nothing. It doesn't matter what we *think* we know. The proof of what we know is in what we do.

I must constantly ask myself, *"What am I doing to actually show love?"* We can be deceived by knowledge, according to the apostle Paul (see 1 Cor. 8:1). We can become blinded by the pride of what we know to the point where we can never see that we are not really practicing any of it. We should all make sure there is no gap between what we say and what we do.

Trust in Him Ask God to reveal to you if there is a gap between what you say and what you do. Whatever He reveals to you, you can trust that He is doing so in order to help you reap good and healthy fruit.

September 8

Be Difficult to Offend

Great peace have they who love Your law; nothing shall offend them or make them stumble. PSALM 119:165

People who want to live powerful lives must become experts at forgiving those who offend and hurt them. When someone hurts my feelings or is rude and insensitive to me, I find it helpful to quickly say, *"I will not be offended."* I have to say those words quietly in my heart if the person is still in my presence, but later when the memory of what he or she did returns to haunt me, I repeat them aloud. When I say, *"I will not be offended,"* I always pray for God to help me, realizing that I can do nothing without Him.

My husband, Dave, has always been difficult to offend. When he is around people who could hurt him or in situations where he could be offended, he says, *"I am not going to let negative people control my mood. They have problems and they are not going to give their problems to me."*

On the other hand, I spent many years getting my feelings hurt regularly and living in the agony of offense, but I am not willing to live that way any longer. I am busy getting a new mind-set. Are you willing to join me in becoming a person who is hard to offend? If so, you will open the door to more peace and joy than you have ever known before.

People are everywhere, and you never know what they might say or do. Why give the control of your day to other people? Being hurt and offended does not change the people, it only changes us. It makes us miserable and steals our peace and joy, so why not prepare ourselves mentally not to fall into Satan's trap? Developing the mind-set that you are a person who is difficult to offend will make your life much more pleasant.

Trust in Him Do you get your feelings hurt easily? Trust God to help you become a person who is difficult to offend.

September 9

Pray for Those Who Hurt You

But love your enemies, do good to them, and lend to them without expecting to get anything back. Then your reward will be great…

LUKE 6:35 NIV

One of the reasons we find forgiving others difficult when we are offended is because we have told ourselves probably thousands of times that forgiving is hard to do. We have convinced ourselves and set our minds to fail at one of God's most important commands, which is to forgive and pray for our enemies and those who hurt and abuse us (see Luke 6:35–36). We meditate too much on what the offensive person has done to us, and we fail to realize what we are doing to ourselves when we take Satan's bait.

Though praying for our enemies and blessing those who curse us may seem extremely difficult or nearly impossible, we can do it if we set our minds to it. Having the proper mind-set is vital if we want to obey God. He never tells us to do anything that is not good for us or to do anything we cannot do. He is always available to give us the strength we need to accomplish the task. We don't even need to think about how hard it is; we just need to do it!

God is just! Justice is one of His most admirable character traits. He brings justice as we wait on Him and trust Him to be our vindicator when we have been hurt or offended. He simply asks us to pray and forgive—and

He does the rest. He makes even our pain work out for our good (see Rom. 8:28). He justifies, vindicates, and recompenses us. He pays us back for our pain if we follow His commands to forgive our enemies and even says that we will receive "double for our trouble" (see Isa. 61:7).

As we renew our minds with thoughts such as, *I freely and quickly forgive*, we will find forgiving and releasing offenses easier than ever to do. The reason this is true is because "*Where the mind goes, the man follows.*" As we mentally and verbally agree with God by obeying His Word, we become a team that is unbeatable.

Trust in Him In what areas do you frequently take the bait of Satan and fall into his trap of being offended? Stop saying it is too hard and simply trust that if you pray and forgive, God will do the rest.

September 10

"Because I'm in Christ!"

As far as the east is from the west, so far has He removed our transgressions from us. As a father loves and pities his children, so the Lord loves and pities those who fear Him [with reverence, worship, and awe]. PSALM 103:12–13

We put a lot more pressure on ourselves than God would ever put on us. God removes all that makes us unrighteous (our transgressions) and sends it as far away as the east is from the west. How far is the east from the west? A long way!

When my son was younger, he decided to do something nice for me. He got a bowl of water and went out on the porch. Soon he came to me and said, "*Mommy, I washed the windows for you.*" The porch was wet. He was wet. The windows were smeared up. But he did it because he loved me. God reminded me of this one time. He said, "*Do you remember what you did afterward? You sent your son off to get cleaned up and then you went and cleaned up his mess when he wasn't looking."* God showed me that He does the same with us.

God is aware of our imperfections, yet He receives what we do out of love for Him. He cleans up our messes, and even works good out of them, because He loves us with a perfect love. He sees our faith in Him and through it considers us to be "in Christ."

If God asks, *"Why should I let you into heaven?"* the only right answer is, *"Because I'm in Christ."* If God asks, *"Why should I answer your prayers?"* the right answer is, *"Because I'm in Christ."* If God asks, *"Why should I help you?"* the only right answer is, *"Because I'm in Christ."*

Jesus wants us to come fearlessly, confidently, and boldly to the Father to receive mercy for our failures and grace for every need we have. He understands our weaknesses and faults. He understands that we are not going to manifest perfection every day. But we can ask God to forgive us for the mistakes we make and then go boldly before the throne to ask God to meet our needs.

Trust in Him Do everything out of love for your heavenly Father. You can trust Him to answer your prayers and clean up your messes.

September 11

Believe the Best about People

Love bears up under anything and everything that comes, is ever ready to believe the best of every person, its hopes are fadeless under all circumstances, and it endures everything [without weakening]. 1 CORINTHIANS 13:7

Believing the best about people is very helpful in the process of forgiving people who hurt or offend us. As human beings, we tend to be suspicious of others and we often get hurt due to our own imaginations. It is possible to believe someone hurt you on purpose when the truth is they were not even aware they did anything at all, and never intended to upset you.

I can remember, during the early years of our marriage, focusing on everything I considered negative about Dave and ignoring his positive traits. My thoughts went something like this: *We just don't agree about anything. Dave is so stubborn, and he has to be right all the time. He is insensitive, and he just doesn't care how I feel. He never thinks of anyone but himself.* In reality, none of these thoughts were true! They only existed within my own mind; and my wrong thinking caused a great deal of offense and disagreement that could have been easily avoided had my mind-set been more positive.

Over time, as I grew in my relationship with God, I learned the power of believing in the best about people and meditating on the things that were good. As that happened, my thinking sounded like this: *Dave is usually very easy to get along with; he has his areas of stubbornness, but then so do I. Dave loves me and would never hurt my feelings on purpose. Dave is very protective of me and always makes sure I am taken care of.* At first, I had to think these things on purpose, but now I actually feel uncomfortable when I think negative thoughts, and positive thoughts come more naturally because I have disciplined myself to think them.

There are still times when people hurt my feelings, but then I remember that I can choose whether to be hurt or to "get over it." I can believe the best or I can believe the worst, so why not believe the best and enjoy my day?

Trust in Him Do you believe the best about people? Is there someone in particular whom you need to believe the best? Trust God to help you meditate on the best of all people until positive thoughts come naturally.

September 12

Every Day Is Precious

For if you forgive people their trespasses [their reckless and willful sins, leaving them, letting them go, and giving up resentment], your heavenly Father will also forgive you. MATTHEW 6:14

I have learned that any day I spend angry and offended is a wasted day. Life is too short and too precious to waste any of it. The older people get, the more they usually realize that, but I am sad to say that some people never learn it. The society we live in today is filled with angry, easily offended people who are stressed out and tired most of the time. But Jesus teaches us a better way to live.

I want to encourage you to make the most out of today—and every day—because life is a precious gift from God. Every day is filled with wonderful promise and possibility. Enjoy this day! Don't waste it being angry or offended.

We can choose to live according to God's Word rather than to live the world's way, or to give in to fleshly thoughts or emotions. A wise person refuses to live with hurt feelings or offense in his heart. Life is too short to waste one day being angry, bitter, and resentful. The good news of the Gospel of Jesus Christ is that our sins are forgiven, and I believe we have been given the ability to forgive those who sin against us. Anything God has given us, such as forgiveness and mercy, He expects us to extend to others. If it comes *to* us, it should flow *through* us—and that should be our goal.

When we are offended, we need to quickly call to mind the fact that God has freely and fully forgiven us, so we should freely and fully forgive others.

Trust in Him Is there an offense you have been holding on to? If so, trust it to God—turn it over to Him—and forgive. Don't waste another minute that you could be enjoying life.

September 13

Do Yourself a Favor and Forgive

And should you not have had pity and mercy on your fellow attendant, as I had pity and mercy on you?

MATTHEW 18:33

In Matthew 18:23–35, Jesus tells a story about one man who refused to forgive another. At the end, he makes the clear and strong point that those who do not forgive others get "turned over to the torturers" (v. 34). If you have, or have ever had, a problem forgiving others, I'm sure you can attest to this truth. Harboring hateful thoughts and bitterness toward another person in your mind is indeed torturous.

You may have heard the saying, "*Refusing to forgive is like drinking poison and hoping it kills the other person.*" We are not hurting the one who hurt us by being angry at them. The truth is that most of the time people who offend us don't even know how we feel. They go on with their lives while we drink the poison of bitterness. When you do forgive those who offend you, you are actually helping yourself more than you are helping them, so I say, "*Do yourself a favor and forgive!*"

We think, *But, it is so unfair for me to forgive them and then they just have no punishment for what they did. Why should I have the pain while they get the freedom?* The truth is that by forgiving, we are releasing them so God can do what only He can do. If I'm in the way—trying to get revenge or taking care of the situation myself instead of trusting and obeying God—He may sit back and allow me to try to handle things in my own strength. But, if I allow Him to deal with those who offend me by forgiving them, He can work good out of it for both parties concerned.

The book of Hebrews tells us that God settles the cases of His people. When we forgive, we put God on the case (see Heb. 10:30).

Trust in Him Is there a situation in your life that you are trying to take care of instead of trusting God to work it out? If so, do yourself a favor and forgive so God can settle it.

September 14

The Benefits of Forgiveness

But if you do not forgive, neither will your Father in heaven forgive your failings and shortcomings. MARK 11:26

Mark 11:22–26 clearly teaches us that unforgiveness hinders our faith from working, so we can conclude in contrast that forgiveness enables our faith to work. The Father can't forgive our sins if we don't forgive other people (see Matt. 6:14–15).

There are still more benefits of forgiveness. For one, I'm happier and I feel better physically when I'm not filled with unforgiveness. We can be healthier when we quickly forgive. Serious diseases can develop as a result of the stress and pressure that result from bitterness, resentment, and unforgiveness.

Our fellowship with God flows freely when we're willing to forgive, but unforgiveness serves as a major block to communion with God. I also believe it is difficult to love people while harboring anger. When we have bitterness in our hearts it seeps out in all of our attitudes and relationships.

It is good to remember that even people we want to love may suffer when we hold bitterness, resentment, and unforgiveness. For example, I was very angry and bitter toward my father for abusing me, and I ended up mistreating my husband who had nothing at all to do with the pain I had encountered. I felt that someone needed to repay me for the injustice in my life, but I was trying to collect from someone who could not pay and had no responsibility to do so.

God promises to pay us back for our former trouble if we turn the situation over to Him. And if we don't, then we allow Satan to perpetuate our pain and take it from relationship to relationship. Ephesians 4:26–27 tells us not to let the sun go down on our anger or give the devil any such foothold or opportunity. Remember that the devil must have a *foothold* before he can get a *stronghold*. Do not help Satan torture you. Be quick to forgive when you are offended.

Trust in Him There is no end to the benefits in your life if you will trust God's Word that tells you to forgive, not seven times, but seventy times seven times (Matt. 18:22).

September 15

What God Tells Me Every Day

I give you a new commandment: that you should love one another. Just as I have loved you, so you too should love one another.

JOHN 13:34

The Roman philosopher Seneca made a statement we all need to remember: "*Wherever there is a human being, there is an opportunity for kindness.*" I would add to that, "*Wherever there is a human being, there is an opportunity to express love.*" Everyone on earth needs love and kindness. Even when we have nothing to offer others in terms of money or possessions, we can give them love and show them kindness.

It seems like God tells me every day, "*Get your mind off of yourself and your problems and spend today doing something to love someone else.*" From start to finish, in all kinds of ways, God's Word encourages and challenges us to love other people. To love others is the "new commandment" Jesus gave us in John 13:34, and it is the example He set for us throughout His life and ministry on earth. If we want to be like Jesus, we need to love others with the same kind of gracious, forgiving, generous, unconditional love He extends to us.

Nothing has changed my life more dramatically than learning how to love people and treat them well. Incorporate this thought into your life: *I love people and I enjoy helping them.*

Trust in Him What are you doing to show love toward others? Trust the example of God's unconditional love to be your guide.

September 16

Real Love Is More Than Words—It's Action

...Let us not love [merely] in theory or in speech but in deed and in truth (in practice and in sincerity). 1 JOHN 3:18

Some people think of love as a wonderful feeling—a sensation of excitement or gushy emotions that make us feel warm and fuzzy all over. While love certainly has its wonderful feelings and powerful emotions, it's so much more than that. Real love has little to do with gooey emotions and goose bumps; it has everything to do with the choices we make about the way we treat people. Real love is not theory or talk; it is action. It is a decision concerning the way we behave in our relationships with other people. Real love meets needs even when sacrifice is required in order to do so.

I am amazed when I think about how often we know the right thing to do, but never get around to doing it. The apostle James said if we hear the Word of God and don't do it, we deceive ourselves with reasoning that does not agree with the truth (see James 1:21–22). In other words, we know what is right but we make an excuse for ourselves. We find reason to exempt ourselves from doing what we tell others they ought to do. If we really want to walk in love, we will *do* what is right.

Would you make a commitment before God and sincerely in your heart to do at least one thing for somebody else every day? It may sound simple, but to do it, you will have to think about it and choose to do it on purpose. You may even have to move beyond the normal group of people in your life and do things for people you would not normally reach out to, or even strangers.

There are so many people in the world who have never ever had anyone do anything nice for them, and they are desperate for some words or actions of love. Let love be the main theme of your life and you will have a life worth living. The Bible says we know that we have passed over from death to life if we love one another (see 1 John 3:14).

Trust in Him What will you do to put love into action today? Trust God to bring people into your life that need to know His love, and then let them see it through you.

September 17

God Will Give You Truth When You Ask for It

He who does not love has not become acquainted with God [does not and never did know Him], for God is love. 1 JOHN 4:8

I spent many years of my life as a very unhappy, dissatisfied person, and I wasted a lot of time thinking my unhappiness was someone or something else's fault. Thoughts such as, *If I just had more money, I would be happy*, or *If people did more for me, I would be happy*, or *If I did not have to work so hard, I would be happy*, or *If I felt better physically, I would be happy* filled my mind. The list of reasons that I thought caused my unhappiness seemed endless, and no matter what I did to entertain myself, nothing worked for long.

As I grew in my personal relationship with God, I literally became desperate for peace, stability, true happiness, and joy. That kind of hunger for change usually requires facing some truth—maybe some unpleasant truth or things we don't like to admit—about ourselves, and I have learned that if we really want truth, God will give it to us. As I began seeking God for the root cause of my unhappiness, He showed me that I was very selfish and self-centered. My focus was on what others could and should do for me, rather than what I could and should do for them. That was not easy for me to accept, but doing so was the beginning of a life-changing journey with God.

God helped me begin to see myself as a person who could give and help. I had to change my thinking from, *What about me?*, to *What can I do for you?* I would like to say this was an easy change to make, but the truth is that it was very difficult and took a lot longer than I like to admit.

Everything God does is for our good; all of His commands are intended to help us have the best lives we can possibly have. He commands us to love and be kind to others, which means taking the focus off of ourselves, silencing the voice that asks, "*What about me?*" and learning to follow Jesus' example of being kind, generous, and loving toward others.

Trust in Him Ask God to show you the root cause(s) of any unhappiness in your life. Trust Him and be willing to face the truth about yourself even if you don't like it. This is the first step toward a better life!

September 18

Think About Something Good

For the rest, brethren, whatever is true, whatever is worthy of reverence and is honorable and seemly, whatever is just, whatever is pure, whatever is lovely and lovable, whatever is kind and winsome and gracious, if there is any virtue and excellence, if there is anything worthy of praise, think on and weigh and take account of these things [fix your minds on them]. PHILIPPIANS 4:8

One day I remember praying, *"God, I can't go on fighting my thoughts all day, every day. As soon as I capture these wrong thoughts, they come back. What am I supposed to do?"* As you fight the battle in your mind, you may find yourself praying the same prayer, so I want to share with you the simple answer God gave me. He said all I needed to do was to think about something else!

When you think about something good, there is no room for wrong thoughts to get into your mind. Concentrating on trying to not think wrong thoughts can actually increase them, but simply filling your mind with good things leaves no room for bad things to get in.

The Bible says that if we walk in the Spirit we will not fulfill the lusts of the flesh (see Gal. 5:16), and this simply means that if we concentrate on the things God desires, then we will not have room in our lives for what the devil desires.

This was a life-changing revelation for me. I realized I couldn't wait for something good to just fall into my mind. I had to *choose* my thoughts *on purpose*. The Bible says in Deuteronomy 30:19 that God sets before us life and death, blessings and curses. If you and I do not choose thoughts that lead to life, the enemy will make the choice for us—and he will choose thoughts that lead to death. But when we choose thoughts that lead to life, our lives will be blessed.

Take time to roll good thoughts over and over in your mind and this will help you form the habit of thinking good things. You must believe you can do something or you won't even try. So I repeat: *"You can choose your own thoughts!"* You can "overcome (master) evil with good" (Rom. 12:21).

Trust in Him Take a moment and think about something good. Concentrate on the things God desires, and trust Him to help you conquer wrong thoughts.

September 19

Invest Your Thoughts

For my thoughts are not your thoughts, neither are your ways My ways, says the Lord. ISAIAH 55:8

If we can learn to agree with God in our thoughts—to think the way He wants us to think—then we can *have* what He wants us to have, *be* who He wants us to be, and *do* what He wants us to do. But it won't just happen. We have to be intentional. We have to invest our thoughts, instead of wasting them.

I have said many times, *"We have to think about what we're thinking about,"* and I believe it now more than ever. If you're in a bad mood, ask yourself what you have been thinking about, and you'll probably find the root of your mood. If you're feeling sorry for yourself, just think about what you're thinking about; your attitude may need an adjustment. Remember, *"Where the mind goes, the man follows."* Our moods are directly linked to our thoughts, so good thoughts will produce good moods.

We need to take responsibility for our thoughts. We must stop acting as if there is nothing we can do about them. God has given us the power to resist the devil by choosing to think on things that are godly and good. It gives me tremendous hope when I realize that I can be assured of a better life by thinking good thoughts. That is exciting!

God will show us what to do to "clean up" our thinking, but He will not do the cleaning for us. He gives us His Word to teach us, and His Spirit to help us, but only we can make the decision to do what we should do. You can learn to think properly and powerfully if you want to; it will take time but it is an investment that pays great dividends. The Bible is a record of God's thoughts, ways, and deeds. As we agree with it, we are agreeing with God!

Trust in Him **Have you taken personal responsibility for your thoughts and attitudes? Are you investing them? If not, make a commitment to begin trusting God to give you the power to think responsibly.**

September 20

On-Purpose Thinking

But Jesus, knowing (seeing) their thoughts, said, Why do you think evil and harbor malice in your hearts? MATTHEW 9:4

It's amazing how quickly and completely our thoughts can change our moods. Negative thinking of any kind quickly steals my joy and causes a variety of bad moods. When we are negative and gloomy, other people don't enjoy being with us; when our thoughts are down, everything else goes down with them. Our moods, countenance, conversation, and even our body can begin to droop in a downward position. Hands hang down, shoulders slump, and we tend to look down instead of up. People who tend to be negative in their thoughts and conversations are usually unhappy and rarely content with anything for very long.

Even if something exciting does happen, they soon find something wrong with it. As soon as they see one thing wrong, they tend to fix their minds on it; any enjoyment they might have is blocked by concentrating on the one negative. They may occasionally experience momentary enthusiasm, but it quickly evaporates and gloom once again fills their entire demeanor. They probably do not realize that they could be happy if they would simply change the way they think. We must stop merely *waiting* for something good to happen and take action to ensure that something good will happen.

I am truly amazed when I consider the fact that we have the ability to make ourselves happy or sad by what we choose to think about. The Bible says we must be satisfied with the consequences of our words, whether they are good or evil (see Prov. 18:20).

Our words begin with our thoughts, so the same principle that applies to our mouths also applies to our minds. We need to be satisfied with the consequences of our thoughts because they hold the power of life and death. I would add that they hold the power of contentment and discontent, of joy and sadness.

Trust in Him God has given us the ability to make choices about so many things in life, including our thoughts, and we must be responsible to make those choices carefully. Trust Him to help you choose positive thoughts and to think on purpose.

September 21

Set Your Mind and Keep It Set

And set your minds and keep them set on what is above (the higher things), not on the things that are on the earth. COLOSSIANS 3:2

Wet concrete can be moved with ease and is very impressionable before it dries or "sets." But once it does set, it is in place for good. It cannot be easily molded or changed. The same principle applies to setting your mind.

To set your mind is to determine decisively what you will think, what you believe, and what you will or will not do—and to set it in such a way that you cannot be easily swayed or persuaded otherwise. Once you set your mind according to the truth of God's principles for a good life, you need to keep it set and not allow outside forces to reshape your thinking. To set your mind on godly things means to be firm in your decision to agree with God's ways of living no matter who may try to convince you that you are wrong.

The reason setting your mind and keeping it set is so important is that there's really not much hope of being able to resist temptation if you don't make up your mind ahead of time concerning what you will do when you are tempted. You will be tempted; that's just a fact of life. So, you need to think ahead of time about the situations that can pose problems for you. If you wait until you are in the midst of a situation to decide whether or not you will stand firm, then you are sure to give up.

Make up your mind ahead of time that you are going to go all the way through with God. Some people spend their entire lives starting and quitting. They never follow through. They may set their minds, but when temptation comes—when things get difficult—they don't keep it set. I strongly encourage you to be one of the ones who finishes what you start by keeping your mind set in the right direction all the way through to victory.

Trust in Him Whatever challenges you the most, *decide now* that you are going to set your mind for total victory. Trust God to give you the strength to follow through.

September 22

Renew Your Mind

Do not be conformed to this world (this age), [fashioned after and adapted to its external, superficial customs], but be transformed (changed) by the [entire] renewal of your mind [by its new ideals and its new attitude], so that you may prove [for yourselves] what is the good and acceptable and perfect will of God, even the thing which is good and acceptable and perfect [in His sight for you].

ROMANS 12:2

Renewing your mind is not like renewing your driver's license or library card, which can be done quickly and doesn't have to be repeated for months or years. Renewing your mind is more like undertaking the job of renewing and refurbishing an old house. It doesn't happen quickly; it takes time, energy, and effort, and there is always something that needs attention.

Don't fall into the trap of believing you can renew your mind by thinking right thoughts one time. To get the mind renewed, you will have to think right thoughts over and over again, until they become rooted in your thinking—until right thoughts come to you more easily and naturally than wrong thoughts.

You will have to discipline yourself to think properly, and you will have to guard against falling into old thought patterns, which can happen very easily. When it does, don't feel bad—just start thinking rightly again. You will eventually come to the place where wrong thoughts make you uncomfortable and they just don't fit right into your thinking processes any longer.

Let me be quick to say that you should not feel condemned if you are struggling with your thought life right now or if you face struggles in the days to come. Condemnation only weakens you; it never helps you make progress. Anytime we recognize that we are allowing wrong thoughts into our minds, we should ask God to forgive us and continue pressing on toward our goal.

Celebrate every victory because it helps you to not feel overwhelmed by what still remains to be conquered, and remember that God is very patient and long-suffering. He is understanding and will never give up on you.

Trust in Him In what areas of your life does your mind need to be renewed? Trust that God will be patient with you as you practice right thinking.

September 23

"Gird Up" Your Mind

Therefore gird up the loins of your mind, be sober, and rest your hope fully upon the grace that is to be brought to you at the revelation of Jesus Christ. 1 PETER 1:13 NKJV

You and I aren't accustomed to hearing the phrase "gird up" today. But in biblical times both men and women wore long, skirtlike outfits. If they tried to run in those clothes, there was a good chance they could get tangled up in the long fabrics and stumble. When they needed to move quickly, they gathered the material of their garments and pulled it up so they could walk or run freely. They would "gird up" their clothing.

When the Bible tells us to "gird up the loins" of our minds, I believe it means to get our minds off of everything that would cause us to stumble as we run the race God has set before us. I think it may also refer to concentrating on the thing at hand rather than allowing our thoughts to wander all over the place. God has a good plan for each of us, but we must walk the path that leads us to it.

Focus and concentration are both real challenges in our world today. We have a great deal of information coming at us all the time, and to keep our minds on what our purpose is requires great determination, and even training.

You might get up on Monday and fully intend to start your day by spending time with God in prayer and Bible study. Then you intend to get three specific projects finished that day. You need to go to the grocery store, get some maintenance done on your car, and finish cleaning out a closet that you started working on last week. Your intention is good, but if you don't focus on those projects you will surely be pulled away by other things or people. Girding up your mind is another way of saying "*stay focused on what you need to do.*"

Trust in Him Have you developed an ability to concentrate and focus on what you need to do? In order to stay on God's track for your life, you must keep focused and trust Him to be your guide.

September 24

Happiness Comes from Serving the Lord

After these events, God tested and proved Abraham and said to him, Abraham! And he said, Here I am. [God] said, Take now your son, your only son Isaac, whom you love, and go to the region of Moriah; and offer him there as a burnt offering upon one of the mountains of which I will tell you. So Abraham rose early in the morning, saddled his donkey, and took two of his young men with him and his son Isaac; and he split the wood for the burnt offering, and then began the trip to the place of which God had told him. GENESIS 22:1–3

I believe God was testing Abraham's priorities in this Scripture. Isaac had probably become very important to Abraham, so God tested Abraham to see if he would give up Isaac to Him in faith and obedience. When God saw Abraham's willingness to obey, He provided a ram for Abraham to sacrifice in place of Isaac (Gen. 22:12–13).

We all go through tests. As with Abraham, these tests are designed to try, prove, and develop our faith. One of the tests I had to face was: "*What if I never have the ministry I've dreamed about for so long? What if I never get to minister to more than fifty people at a time? Can I still love God and be happy?*"

What about you? You may want to get married. What if you never get married? Can you be happy anyway? You may want a certain person in your family to change. What if that individual never changes? Can you be happy anyway? You may want to make more money. What if you never have any more money than what you have right now? Can you be happy anyway?

If you don't get whatever it is you want, can you still love God? Will you still serve Him all the days of your life, or are you just trying to get something from Him? A fine line divides the motives of the heart between selfish and selfless; we must always make sure we understand which side of the line we are standing on.

Trust in Him What do you want? If you never get it, can you still love God and trust that He has an even better plan for your life?

September 25

Trust God with Your Life

Therefore, [inheriting] the promise is the outcome of faith and depends [entirely] on faith, in order that it might be given as an act of grace (unmerited favor)... ROMANS 4:16

Early in my Christian walk, I continually worked at trying to change things by myself. But many of the changes that have come about in my life began the day I finally realized that only God could make those changes.

That day, I simply sat in the presence of God, weeping and telling Him, *"If You don't change me, Lord, I am never going to be different, because I have done everything anybody can do to change. I have tried everything I know. I have worked every formula. I have rebuked every devil. I have fasted. I have prayed. I have cried. I have begged and pleaded. And none of it has worked. So, Lord, You will have to take me the way I am and I will have to stay this way forever. If I am ever to be different, You have to change me. I give up."*

When I finished talking, the Holy Spirit spoke in my heart: *"Good. Now I can finally do something."*

I had finally reached the point where I didn't care whether my ministry grew or not. I just wanted some peace. I had finally come to the place where I didn't care whether Dave or my children changed or not. I just wanted some peace. I had finally realized I would have to stop trying to change everything and everyone around me, including myself, and let God handle it if I was ever going to have peace.

You are never going to enjoy the promise of the new life (see Rom. 4:16) Jesus died to give you until you change the way you think. It's not about what you can do—it's about what Jesus has done for you.

Trying to face all the challenges of everyday life can cause you to focus on human works, which rob you of your peace, joy, self-respect, and confidence. Works trap you into always struggling to *be* better so you will *feel* better about yourself. But if you try to do things on your own, you will be unable to bring about the positive changes you desire.

Trust in Him If you have tried everything and are still desperate for peace, change your thinking and trust God with your life.

September 26

Stop Over-Thinking Things

O you [men, how little trust you have in Me, how] little faith!

MATTHEW 16:8

If you want to have joy, you must stop trying to figure everything out. You must stop rolling your problems around in your mind. You have to quit anxiously searching for an answer to your situation, trying to find out what you should do about it.

When Jesus saw that His disciples were trying to "figure out" what to do about the fact they had forgotten to bring bread to feed the crowd, He said to them, "O ye of little faith, why reason ye among yourselves?" (Matt. 16:8 KJV).

I spent many years attempting to solve my own problems and finally discovered that it is not God's will for me to do that. All my efforts did was make me frustrated and more selfish and self-centered. I focused on myself and expected everyone else to focus on me, too. I looked to others (and myself) to do for me what only God could do.

We reason and try to figure things out, asking, "*Why, God, why?*" and "*When, God, when?*" We want to know the answers to our situations so we won't have to trust God. We don't want any surprises; we want to be in control because we are afraid things won't turn out the way we want. This driving desire to be "in the know" will usually produce one thing—a mind riddled with excessive reasoning.

"*Why, God, why?*" and "*When, God, when?*" are two questions that can keep us frustrated and prevent us from enjoying the lives Jesus died to give us. Many times we do not understand what God is doing, but that is what trust is all about. Nobody says we have to know everything; no one has ever told us we have to understand everything. We need to be satisfied in knowing the One Who does know, and that is God. We need to learn to trust God, not ourselves.

Trust in Him Stop over-thinking things. Trust means not needing to know the whys and the whens in order to be at peace.

September 27

You Don't Need All the Answers to Stop Worrying

For God is not the author of confusion, but of peace…

1 CORINTHIANS 14:33 KJV

I was holding a meeting in Kansas City, and it came to my heart to ask the audience how many of them were confused. There were about 300 people at that meeting and, from what I could tell, 298 of them raised their hands. And my husband was one of the two who didn't.

I can tell you that Dave has never been confused in his life, because he doesn't worry. He doesn't try to figure anything out. He is not interested in having all the answers to everything, because he trusts God. When you trust God, you can relax and enjoy life. You don't have to go through life worrying and trying to figure out how to solve all your problems. Think about all the things you have worried about in your life and how they have all worked out. That should help you realize that worrying and reasoning are a waste of time and energy.

I have four grown children. It amazes me when I look back at everything I went through with them as they were growing up—when they didn't get good grades in school, when I was called to the principal's office because of them, when the neighbor complained about them, when it looked as if they would never want to work or do anything worthwhile or would never be able to handle their finances. I would think, *How are they ever going to handle life when they get away from me? They can't even handle their allowances*. I wasted a lot of time worrying over them, and in the end they all turned out fine.

I am sharing these stories with you to help you realize that where your kids, and your relationships, and your finances, and your job, and your health are right now is not where they are going to end up. And worrying about these things only helps the problem; it doesn't help the answer. Stop worrying. Stop complicating your life by trying to figure everything out. Just admit that you don't know, that you are not able, that you need God. Then go on living, and enjoy life while God is giving you the answers.

Trust in Him Pray and trust God, and He will show you what to do at the right time. He will show you because He is a God Who never fails His children (see Deut. 31:6, 8). He is a God of faithfulness, and He always comes through.

September 28

Purpose and Blessings

And Simon (Peter) answered, Master, we toiled all night [exhaustingly] and caught nothing [in our nets]. But on the ground of Your word, I will lower the nets [again]. LUKE 5:5

I love the story in Luke 5—Peter and his companions returning from an unsuccessful fishing trip. After Jesus had finished speaking to the crowds that had gathered by the shore, "He said to Simon (Peter), Put out into the deep [water], and lower your nets for a haul" (v. 4).

When I first read this years ago, it got my attention because I was looking for a *haul* of blessings in my life. I had Christian tapes, T-shirts, books, bumper stickers, a Jesus pin, and could talk "Christian-ese" as well as anyone. But I was missing out on the abundant life that the Bible says God wants me to have because I didn't understand God's purposes.

After Jesus told Peter to put out into the deep, Peter said, "Master, we toiled all night [exhaustingly] and caught nothing [in our nets]. But on the ground of Your word, I will lower the nets [again]" (Luke 5:5). Look at what happened in verses 6 and 7: "And when they had done this, they caught a great number of fish; and as their nets were [at the point of] breaking, they signaled to their partners in the other boat to come and take hold with them. And they came and filled both the boats, so that they began to sink."

Here's what I'd missed. If Peter had been living by his feelings, he would not have gone back to fish, because he and his men were exhausted. Instead, he chose to live by the Word.

God showed me that the same thing holds true for us. If we want a "haul" of provision in our lives, then we need to live on a level deeper than what we want, think, and feel. We need to live according to the Word of God and do what it says—whether we feel like it, understand it, want to, or think it's a good idea or not. We must make a decision to stop chasing after things that have no ability to make us happy. It doesn't matter what we have if we don't know and understand our purpose in life—which is to glorify God.

Trust in Him Do you desire the abundant life that the Bible promises? It is available to you. All you have to do is trust God and do what His Word says to do. Your obedience will glorify God and bring a haul of blessings into your life.

September 29

Simplicity Brings Joy

... Truly I say to you, unless you repent (change, turn about) and become like little children [trusting, lowly, loving, forgiving], you can never enter the kingdom of heaven [at all]. MATTHEW 18:3

Christians have available to them the abundant quality of life that comes from God, Who is not full of fear, stress, worry, anxiety, or depression. He is not impatient or in a hurry; He takes time to enjoy His creation. And He wants us to do the same.

Unfortunately, I don't really think that the majority of people are enjoying their lives. When you ask them how they are, their response is nearly always *"Busy! I am just so busy with work, the kids, church, and school activities."*

We live in a stressful world that seems to be getting more stressful with each passing year. People are hurrying everywhere. They are rude, short-tempered, and it is easy to see that many people are frustrated and under pressure. They are experiencing financial stress, marital stress, and the stress of raising children in today's world.

I have a thought for you to consider: *Simplicity brings joy but complication blocks it*. Matthew 18:3 says God wants us to approach life with simple, childlike faith. He wants us to grow up in our behavior, but remain childlike in our attitude toward Him concerning trust and dependence. He wants us to know that we are His precious little ones—His children. We show faith in Him when we come to Him this way, which allows Him to care for us.

We cannot have peace and enjoy life without childlike faith. When you begin to live your life with all the simplicity of a child, it will change your whole outlook in a most amazing way.

Start looking for ways that you complicate things and ask the Holy Spirit to teach you simplicity in those areas. He lives in you, and although He is extraordinarily powerful, He is also extraordinarily simple. He will teach you simplicity if you truly wish to learn.

Trust in Him Take the time to observe a child and notice how they approach things with such simplicity. Approach God with that same kind of innocence and complete dependence. Trust Him to take care of all of your needs so that you can enjoy your life.

September 30

Nudged Out of the Nest

As an eagle that stirs up her nest, that flutters over her young, He spread abroad His wings and He took them, He bore them on His pinions. DEUTERONOMY 32:11

Baby eagles spend the first three months of their lives in the comfortable nest their parents have prepared. But the eaglets get a big surprise when they are about twelve weeks old. Their mother suddenly begins to throw all of their toys out of the nest.

Next, she begins to pull out all of the comfortable material in the nest—the feathers and the animal fur—and leaves the babies sitting on thorns and sticks. This is what the Bible means when it mentions that the mother eagle "stirs up her nest." The reason she stirs the nest is that she wants her babies to get out and fly.

Before long, the mother eagle begins to nudge them out of the nest. The little eaglets, who have no idea how to fly, fall through the sky, probably very frightened. Soon, though, they hear a "*whoooooooosh*" as the mother eagle swoops up under them to catch them. At that point, the mother eagle takes the babies right back up to the nest and then nudges them out again. She keeps repeating the process, over and over again, until they finally understand that they have no choice but to fly.

The mother eagle does this because she loves them and wants them to have the best lives they can possibly have. Most eaglets won't get out of the nest without this push. Similarly, most of us will also choose comfort over challenge unless we have no choice at all.

Do you feel God is working in your life the same way the mother eagle does with her young? Has He been pulling some of the padding out of your nest so you find yourself sitting on prickly branches? Is He saying to you, *"Come on, it is time to fly"*? If so, remember the mother eagle's intentions and know that you can trust God's good intentions for you.

Trust in Him Do you feel as if God has pushed you out of your comfortable nest? Trust Him. He isn't trying to harm you—He's teaching you to fly!

October 1

Make Your Neighbor Happy

Let each one of us make it a practice to please (make happy) his neighbor for his good and for his true welfare, to edify him [to strengthen him and build him up spiritually]. ROMANS 15:2

The Bible teaches that if we are strong in faith, we ought to bear with the faults of the weak and live to please others. Each one of us should make it a practice to please and make our neighbors happy for their good, to edify, strengthen, and build them up (see Rom. 15:1–2).

This is wonderful advice, but we do the opposite far too often. We want others to live to make *us* happy and do what pleases *us*. The result is that no matter what people do, we are never happy and satisfied.

Will you be honest and ask yourself some questions that may be difficult to answer but will bring you face-to-face with where you are in regards to loving other people?

- How much do you do for others?
- Are you trying to find out what people want and need so you can help?
- Are you sincerely trying to know the people in your life in a genuine way?
- How much do you really even know the people in your own family?

As I answered these questions a few years ago, I was appalled at the level of selfishness in my life even though I had been a Christian minister for many years. The truth began to open my eyes about why I was still unhappy and unfulfilled even though I had every reason to be really happy. The bottom line was that I was selfish and self-centered, and I needed to change. These changes did not come easily or quickly, neither are they completed even now, but as I press on daily I am making progress and I am happier all the time.

Trust in Him Trust God enough to deposit yourself with Him, and trust Him to meet all of your needs while you are busy meeting the needs of others.

October 2

Give Yourself a Head Start

He wakens Me morning by morning, He wakens My ear to hear as a disciple [as one who is taught]. ISAIAH 50:4

Nothing will prepare you to face what you have to face at work, at home, in relationships, or in daily life like taking some time to commune with God before your busy day begins.

When I first understood that I needed to prepare myself for every day by spending time with God, some of my children complained. They were teenagers at that time, so I told them: *"Listen, you're old enough to put cereal in a bowl and pour milk on it. And you should be glad I go to my study every morning. You will have a much nicer day if I take this time with God!"*

Yesterday morning, I told my daughter, Sandra, I was going to spend my early morning time with the Lord, and she replied, *"Are you going to get nice?"* We both laughed because we've learned that even something as simple as being nice to others can be impossible without that daily preparation in God's presence and Word.

I know many people feel extremely pressed for time, and the very thought of adding something else to your schedule makes you shudder. All I have to say is, the more you have to do and the busier you are, the more you really need to spend time with God. I do not know how you need to adjust your schedule, but I know the time you give to God is no different from the money you give to God—if you give Him time, He will give it back to you.

God is in charge of time; He knows how much time you need to accomplish the things you really need to do, and He can protect and help you manage it if you will spend time with Him first. Stop trying to fit God into your schedule and make a decision to put Him first, then work the rest of your schedule around Him.

Trust in Him Have you spent time with God in preparation to face whatever comes your way today? Life does not have to overwhelm you or catch you off guard. Prepare yourself for the challenges you will face each day by trusting Him with your time.

October 3

God Forgets!

For I will forgive their iniquity, and I will [seriously] remember their sin no more. JEREMIAH 31:34

God not only *forgives* but also *forgets* all your sins. He does not forgive you and then say, *"Oh, boy, I remember when I had to forgive Johnny for pulling his sister's hair and making her cry. Now he wants me to forgive him for cheating on his algebra test. His list of forgiven sins is getting awfully long."*

No, if Johnny were to say to God, *"I know You've already forgiven me for pulling my sister's hair, but now I need Your forgiveness for cheating on a test,"* God would say, *"Your sister's hair? You asked me to forgive you for that? I have absolutely no recollection of that; there's no record of it anywhere."*

The passage above from Jeremiah, and many others you will find in the Bible (Heb.10:14–17, for example), is not talking about a forgiveness that happens the day we receive Christ and only takes care of all of our *previous* sins. God's forgiveness is ongoing for the duration of our lives; it is for every day.

When Jesus died on the cross 2,000 years ago, He not only forgave everything we had done in our pasts, but He also committed Himself to forgive every sin we would commit in the future. He knows every wrong decision we will ever make, and they're all covered. All we have to do is admit our sins, be willing to turn away from them, and stay in relationship with Him. When God looks at our sins, He sees our faith in Jesus, Who is our perfect sacrifice—not the sin we just committed.

Because of this, what God really wants from us is not perfect performance, perfect behavior, or perfect attitudes, because He already sees those things in Jesus on our behalf. What God wants from us are hearts that truly love Him.

Trust in Him God is not surprised by anything you do. You can trust His love and forgiveness because He knew about your mistakes long before you did, and He wants you anyway. Today, determine to stop remembering what God has forgotten and focus instead on loving Him.

October 4

You Can Pray or Worry, But Don't Do Both!

[For Abraham, human reason for] hope being gone, hoped in faith that he should become the father of many nations, as he had been promised, So [numberless] shall your descendants be.

ROMANS 4:18

When God promised Abraham and his wife, Sarah, a child, they were both very old and long past their childbearing years. They had a rather impossible situation. Romans 4:19 says Abraham did not weaken in faith even when he looked at himself and saw it was impossible. Both his body and Sarah's womb were as good as dead. Yet verse 20 says, "No unbelief or distrust made him waver (doubtingly question) concerning the promise of God, but he grew strong and was empowered by faith as he gave praise and glory to God." Abraham waited twenty long years for God to fulfill His promise, and he never gave up!

I like to use this story about Abraham as an example because it amazes me that he had such a huge task—really an impossible situation—and yet he saw beyond the problem-filled task as he hung on to the promise of God. That's what we have to do.

In whatever situation you are in right now in your life—whether it is something with your kids, or your marriage, or your finances, or you think you're never going to recover from your past, or you're fighting with an addiction, or sin that keeps trying to cling to you—know that God is greater than any problem you have. Don't worry, because when you pray and then you worry, the worry nullifies your prayer. Prayer is something you do *instead of* worry. It's not something you do *with* worry. Worry says we don't really think God is going to come through so we are going to have a backup plan in case He doesn't. Prayer says we trust God to work it out.

We don't need to know what God is going to do or when He is going to do it; we just need to know that He is with us. God is working in your life right now in ways you don't see, don't feel, and don't understand. Just because what is going on in your life right now doesn't feel good doesn't mean God is not working. He is!

Trust in Him No matter what you are going through, lift it up to God and say, *"God, I trust that You are working in my life right now, and I'm expecting something good."*

October 5

Double for Your Trouble

Instead of your [former] shame you shall have a twofold recompense; instead of dishonor and reproach [your people] shall rejoice in their portion. Therefore in their land they shall possess double [what they had forfeited]; everlasting joy shall be theirs. ISAIAH 61:7

Look with me at the first part of the passage: "Instead of your [former] shame you shall have a twofold recompense." The word *recompense* means "reward," or "payment for past hurts."

Recompense reminds me of the word *compensation*. When I think of workman's compensation, I think of payment made to a person who has been injured on a job. Likewise, if we get hurt while working for God, He takes care of us. If someone comes against us, hurts us, rejects us, or wounds us, we need to keep serving God and doing right, and He will make sure we get due compensation in the end.

Realizing that I did not have to collect from people who hurt me was life-changing for me. The truth is, they couldn't pay me. They could not give me back what they took from me, but God can always give you more than people take from you. We find another promise of reward in Joel: "And I will restore or replace for you the years that the locust has eaten... And *you shall eat in plenty and be satisfied* and praise the name of the Lord, your God, Who has dealt wondrously with you.

And My people shall never be put to shame" (Joel 2:25–26, emphasis added).

Note the words *you shall eat in plenty and be satisfied*. This part of the promise means so much to me because I spent many years dissatisfied and discontent. No matter what I had, I wasn't satisfied. No matter what anybody did for me, I wasn't satisfied. No matter what I accomplished, I was not satisfied. Why? Because I was looking for people to satisfy me, but only God can satisfy.

Whatever you have lost in your life, He will restore. That's a promise. As you trust Him, He will make sure you "shall eat in plenty and be satisfied."

Trust in Him You are not on the world's payroll; you are on God's payroll. Trust Him and He will pay you double for your trouble.

October 6

Be a Blessing to Others

And let us consider and give attentive, continuous care to watching over one another, studying how we may stir up (stimulate and incite) to love and helpful deeds and noble activities... HEBREWS 10:24

I have asked hundreds of people to share with me some practical ways they believe we can show love. I have read books, searched the Internet, and been very aggressive on my own journey to find creative ways to incorporate this concept of loving people into my everyday life. I would like to share with you some of the things I have learned.

Here are some ideas I have collected:

- When it is obvious that you and someone else want the same parking place, let the other person have it and do so with a smile on your face.

- Mow an elderly neighbor's lawn or shovel their snow in the winter.
- Go grocery shopping for a family with a newborn baby.
- Give someone without transportation a ride to church or another event, even if it is out of your way to do so.
- Truly listen to someone without interrupting.
- Hold a door open for a stranger and let him or her go ahead of you.
- Let someone with just a few items go in front of you when you're in a checkout line.
- Babysit for a single parent to give that person a bit of alone time or time to get a project done peacefully.
- Invite a person who has no family in town to your house for the holidays.
- Send cards and/or flowers to show appreciation.

Start with this simple list, but let the Holy Spirit show you more ideas. Doing random things for people just to be a blessing is an amazing way to show God's love.

Trust in Him If you trust that God's love for you is limitless, you will have no problem showing love to others and even going out of your way to be a blessing to them. We love because He first loved us (see 1 John 4:19)!

October 7

Ask God Boldly!

Up to this time you have not asked a [single] thing in My Name [as presenting all that I AM]; but now ask and keep on asking and you will receive, so that your joy (gladness, delight) may be full and complete. JOHN 16:24

I believe there are people who are not receiving from God what He wants them to have because they won't ask Him boldly. They make weak, faithless requests. I've had people ask for prayer and say: *"Is it okay if I ask for two things?"* Their uncertainty is sad to me because Jesus clearly told us to ask so that our joy would be complete.

I want whatever God wants to give me spiritually, emotionally, financially, physically, socially, and mentally. I pray boldly, but I don't do it because I think *I'm* worthy. I know that I have faults, but I also know that God loves me, and, my confidence is not in myself—it's in Him. My joy isn't from having things that God gives to me, but from loving God intimately and knowing that He wants me to be totally dependent on Him for everything I need. I get up every day and do the best I can, and by faith I want to receive all that God wants me to have.

A few years ago, I stepped out in faith and prayed a bold prayer that even sounded crazy to me. I said, *"God, I'm asking You to let me help every single person on the face of the earth."* My mind said: *"Now that is stupid."* But I kept praying that prayer anyway, and our television ministry has expanded greatly since that time. God has caused tremendous growth; one station that we added after that prayer increased our coverage to 600 million people in India alone.

I don't know *how* God is going to let me help every person on the face of the earth, but I am going to continue trusting Him. I would rather ask for a lot and get part of it than ask for a little and get all of it.

Trust in Him What are you asking God for? God wants you to trust Him for everything you need and everything He wants to give you. Come boldly before the throne and ask so that He can meet your needs and your joy can be complete.

October 8

Receive His Forgiveness

What shall we say then? Shall we continue in sin, that grace may abound?

ROMANS 6:1 KJV

We often have very strong feelings and emotions that we don't seem to be able to control! The truth is, you don't have to make decisions based on your feelings! You have a free will, and you can choose to believe God's Word more than you believe how you feel at the time. When you begin to live by the Word of God and what you know through Him instead of how you feel, your feelings will eventually change and line up with the Word.

Satan used guilt to steal from me for years, which was often false guilt because much of the time I had nothing to be guilty for. I had repented, asked God to forgive me, and even believed that He had forgiven me. And yet I would still live my life feeling guilty and badly. I carried the burden of guilt everywhere that I went. I often said, *"I did not feel right if I did not feel wrong."* At times I even felt very spiritual because I always felt bad about my behavior; now I understand God doesn't want me to feel that way.

Every morning when I went to have my prayer and time with God I would go over one of two things: all of my problems or all of my mistakes. The Bible says ask and *receive* that your joy may be full. I was asking for forgiveness, but I never took the time to receive. I'd like to encourage you from now on when you ask God to forgive your sins for anything you've done wrong, take a moment and say, *"I receive your forgiveness right now."* Don't just ask, ask and *receive* so that you can take the next step and be filled with joy.

One morning as I was attempting to spend time with God, He spoke to my heart and said, *"Are you going to fellowship with Me this morning or with your problems and your sins?"* Do you spend more time with your sins than you do with God? Do you spend more time thinking about what you've done wrong than about what He's done right? Remember, where sin does abound, grace and forgiveness and mercy does much more abound.

Trust in Him When you go to God in prayer today, ask Him to forgive you for whatever it is you need forgiveness for, *receive* His forgiveness, and trust His grace as you press on with joy to what He has for you.

October 9

Cast Your Care

All the days of the desponding and afflicted are made evil [by anxious thoughts and forebodings], but he who has a glad heart has a continual feast [regardless of circumstances]. PROVERBS 15:15

Do you have something in your life that you could be very worried about and very anxious about if you didn't decide not to be? Most people do, and if you don't have something today you might have something tomorrow or the next day. That's not being negative, it's just saying that life is real and you never know exactly what is going to come your way. But we do know God and we don't have to live in fear. He is with us and He's on our side.

I had a lot of bad things happen to me in the early years of my life, and I got to the point where I was afraid that bad things would happen. Proverb 15:15 calls that "evil forebodings," which means you have this sense that you are waiting for the next disaster. I've learned instead of doing that to expect something good to happen in my life and to expect it on purpose.

You can choose your own thoughts. You don't have to just think whatever falls in your head. You can cast out wrong things and choose right thoughts. Faith starts in our hearts, a gift from God, but it is released through our thinking and speaking right things. When we have a problem, we can either do what the devil wants us to do and worry about it and get anxious and try to figure things out on our own, or we can do what God wants us to do and think about the promises in His Word.

The Bible teaches us to cast all of our care on God because He cares for us (1 Pet. 5:7).

Throughout our married life, every time we've had a problem in our house Dave has had one answer: "*Cast your care.*" It's not wrong to see our problems, but we need to tell them where they stand in relation to God. Worry sees the problem, but faith sees the God Who can handle the problem.

Trust in Him Will you worry and have anxiety today, or will you cast your care and choose to trust God instead?

October 10

Leave the Choice to God

But instantly He spoke to them, saying, Take courage! I AM! Stop being afraid! MATTHEW 14:27

God will do one of two things if you have a problem: He will either remove the problem (which is always our first choice!) or He will give you the strength, the grace, the ability to go through the problem. I know we don't like the going through part, but if that is what God chooses, we need to trust Him.

If God lets us go through something, then He's got a purpose in mind; there's something we are going to get out of it that we need. If we don't trust God, we're going to be miserable. The only choices we have are—trust and be happy, or don't trust and be miserable!

Trusting God is very peaceful. It is so wonderful to be able to say, "*I don't understand this, but I believe God's going to work it out.*" When you are in a difficult situation, believe God is with you and that He will give you direction at the right time. Believe you are growing spiritually even though you might be hurting right now.

I went through many years when I tried to have enough faith to prevent myself from having problems, or when I did have problems,

I wanted enough faith to resist the devil and believe God would make my problem go away. To be honest, I was under so much pressure and stress that it began to adversely affect my health. Finally I decided, *"Oh! I'm supposed to trust God. And if God doesn't get rid of my problem, then I trust God to take me through it."* By believing in God, I entered His rest!

We trust God's timing, we trust His wisdom, we trust His ways, and by doing that, we can enjoy every single day of the journey. We don't have to just be happy when we have no problems; we can also enjoy life while we are "going through."

> Trust in Him If you can say, *"God, I know You'll do one of two things—You'll either remove this or You're going to give me the grace to deal with it,"* and trust God enough to leave that choice up to Him, you'll reap the reward.

October 11

Do What You Can Do

> *And there was a man called Zacchaeus, a chief tax collector, and [he was] rich. And he was trying to see Jesus, which One He was, but he could not on account of the crowd, because he was small in stature.*
>
> LUKE 19:2–3

You can't add anything to your life by worrying. I enjoy people who don't worry but are confident and really know who they are in Christ. That is why Zacchaeus is one of my favorite people in the Bible (see Luke 19).

Jesus was coming to town, and Zacchaeus wanted to see Jesus, but he was so short he couldn't see over all the people in the huge crowd. I love what he did. He didn't go sit down and have a pity party. Instead, he ran up ahead and climbed up in a sycamore tree. When Jesus came by He said, *"Zacchaeus, come on down here. I'm going to your house for dinner!"*

Instead of whining about what he thought was a problem in his life,

Zacchaeus had a positive attitude about it. Instead of worrying about what he couldn't do, he found something he could do. And God so loved that spirit of determination that He said, "Of all these people, I am going to go home with you!"

Stop worrying about what you can't do. Stop comparing yourself to everybody else and wishing you were them and being jealous and envious of them. Whatever your inabilities are, say to them, "*It is what it is. And I'm going to deal with it. Whatever I don't have, God is going to make it up to me in another way.*"

I like to talk; I am a good communicator and it is working out really well. I've got a lot of good common sense and some business sense and I'm good at managing people, but mainly I talk. I encourage you to start using the abilities that you do have, and don't be concerned about the ones you don't have.

Trust in Him If you've already wasted much of your life worrying or comparing or complaining, make a decision today that you are going to trust God instead. Do what you can do and trust Him to do the rest.

October 12

Waiting on God Means Being One with Him

But those who wait for the Lord [who expect, look for, and hope in Him] shall change and renew their strength and power; they shall lift their wings and mount up [close to God] as eagles [mount up to the sun]; they shall run and not be weary, they shall walk and not faint or become tired. ISAIAH 40:31

I believe God chose to liken us to eagles in order to motivate us so we can rise to our potential in life and so He can encourage us to wait on Him. When success does not come easily, when we find ourselves frustrated and weary in our efforts, we can be refreshed by waiting on the Lord.

What does it really mean to wait for the Lord? It simply means spending time with Him, being in His presence, talking to Him, listening, meditating on His Word, worshipping Him, keeping Him at the center of our lives, all the while expecting Him to do something amazing. One meaning of the word *wait* is "to be twisted or braided together." If we think about a braid in someone's hair, we realize that the hair is woven together so that we cannot tell where one strand ends and another begins. That is the way God wants us to be in our union with Him—so intimately intertwined and tightly woven together with Him that we are truly one with Him. As we wait on Him, we become more and more like Him.

An intimate relationship with God will strengthen you in the innermost part of your being. It will strengthen your heart; it will carry you through the hard times in your life with a sense of peace and confidence that all is well, no matter what is happening. It will give you the strength to endure tough situations in such a way that many of the people around you may not be able to detect even the slightest stress in your life.

When you wait on the Lord by faith, you draw everything you need from Him. He is your refuge, your enabler, your joy, your peace, your righteousness, your hope. He gives you everything you need to live in victory over any circumstance.

Trust in Him Are you ready to rise to your potential? You will do so when you can wait on God. When you wait on Him, your strength is made new again; you can fly as eagles do, over the storms of life; you can walk and run and not faint, because your trust is in Him.

October 13

Resist the Devil at His Onset

Pray that you may not [at all] enter into temptation. LUKE 22:40

The temptation to quit is part of being human, but we must resist that temptation and never give up. It is important that we recognize the lies of Satan, and that we resist him at the onset of his attack. Temptation is one of the realities of the Christian life and a hindrance to success we must work to overcome. Jesus said, "Temptation must come," so be on your guard against it.

There are many types of temptation, so we don't always recognize discouragement and thoughts of giving up as being a temptation from the devil. Some thoughts the enemy may plant in your mind to tempt you to give up might sound like this:

- This is too difficult.
- I really am not qualified to do this.
- I am facing too many problems and can't possibly solve them all.
- I have no one to help me.
- My friends and family think I'm crazy for pursuing this.
- I don't have the money to do this.
- This is taking too long.

I encourage you to begin to recognize temptations as works of the enemy; and I want you to start resisting each temptation with everything in you. Don't consider any temptation insignificant. Don't let the devil lure you into passivity or wait until you've been in a depressed, hopeless slump for three days, listening to the enemy list reasons to abandon your cause. Resist the devil at his onset! Declare war against all forms of temptation. Show the enemy no mercy.

Trust in Him The *instant* you feel tempted to give up, you need to say aloud, *"I will not quit. I refuse to give up. I trust God and I will finish what He has called me to do."*

October 14

"You Could Use a Blessing"

See that none of you repays another with evil for evil, but always aim to show kindness and seek to do good to one another and to everybody. 1 THESSALONIANS 5:15

This Scripture in 1 Thessalonians tells us to *always* show kindness. Living in this generous kind of way is pleasing to God. There are many other Scriptures that also tell us to be good to everybody, not just those we consider to be like-minded with or who are in our church, but to *everybody*.

Even if someone is your employee and they serve you, you should think of ways that you can serve them also. When you get your morning coffee, bring one for them. Pick up after yourself and don't make extra work for them. The people who help us in our lives should always be shown appreciation.

My daughter once wrote a note of appreciation to her garbage collectors and gave them a gift card to get lunch. I think these things not only bless people, but can often be shocking because they almost never happen. The world is filled with people who work hard doing jobs that are not very pleasant, and yet nobody notices.

I once saw a woman cleaning the bathroom at a department store where I shop, and I gave her some money and said, "*You look like you work hard and I thought you could use a blessing.*" I smiled and quickly left. A few minutes later, she found me in the shoe department and expressed her gratitude and told me how this act of kindness lifted her up. She told me that she did indeed work hard and felt nobody paid much attention to that fact.

You'll be amazed at how your joy will increase if you make a habit of noticing those who usually aren't noticed. God watches out for them, and He will be delighted to have you make yourself available as His partner in this endeavor.

Trust in Him Partner with God to be a blessing to everyone you come in contact with, especially the people often overlooked. Trust the nudges He places in your heart to do good for others.

October 15

Seek God First and He Will Add Things

But seek (aim at and strive after) first of all His kingdom and His righteousness (His way of doing and being right), and then all these things taken together will be given you besides.

MATTHEW 6:33

Matthew 6:33 tells us that when we seek *first* the kingdom of God and His righteousness, He will give us everything we need. It is a matter of putting God first in our lives. Simple? Yes. Easy? Not necessarily!

Even though we want God to help us, it is sometimes difficult to consistently put Him first. It may seem easy to trust Him with your life when you're in church on Sunday morning, but on Monday you may be tempted to take control again. Seeking God and putting Him first requires building an intimate relationship with Him that will sustain you every day of the week. God knows what we need better than we do, and He longs to provide it, but He requires that we make Him top priority in our lives.

Many years ago, when I began my relationship with God, I wasn't really serious about it. Like many other Christians, I put in my church time on Sunday. I was even on the church board, and my husband, Dave, was an elder. The problem was, when I was at home or at work, it was hard to tell the difference between an unbeliever and me. I had accepted Christ, I was on my way to heaven, and I loved God. But I didn't love Him with my *whole* heart—there were many areas of my life that I had not yet surrendered to Him. As a result, I was frustrated, and my life lacked victory and joy.

Finally I cried out to God for help, and thankfully, He heard and answered my prayer. He began to show me that I needed to let Him out of my "Sunday Morning Box" and allow Him to be first in every area of my life. Since I did that, I am continually amazed at the ways that God provides for everything else I need.

Trust in Him Do you seek God first? Give Him first place in every area of your life through trust and fellowship, and experience the happiness and stability that come from a changed life—a life with proper priorities!

October 16

Testimony Begins with "Test"

Consider it wholly joyful, my brethren, whenever you are enveloped in or encounter trials of any sort or fall into various temptations. JAMES 1:2

I'm sure you know people with amazing stories of the way God has worked in their lives. I always love to hear a great testimony, but I also know that behind every extraordinary account of someone's life lies some kind of challenge or difficulty. No one ever has a testimony without a test.

We must pass all kinds of tests as we go through our lives, and passing them is part of never giving up. It's vital for us to understand the important role that tests and trials play in our lives, because understanding them helps us endure them and actually be strengthened by them.

Everything God permits us to go through will ultimately be good for us—no matter how much it hurts, how unfair it is, or how difficult it is. When we encounter tests and trials, if we will embrace them and refuse to run from them, we will learn some lessons that will help us in the future and make us stronger.

One reason we must go through trials is to test our quality (1 Pet. 4:12). Often, we find ourselves wishing we had the faith of Sister so-and-so or Brother so-and-so. I can assure you, if they have a strong and vibrant faith, they did not develop it easily. Just as muscles are strengthened through exercise, firm faith comes from the furnace of affliction.

Sometimes people say to me, *"Oh, I wish I had the kind of ministry you have, Joyce."* Well, I did not get it by wishing. These people didn't see when I was feeling I couldn't hold on one more second, begging God to help me to not quit or give up. They don't know the tests and trials I've faced along the way.

No one who does anything worthwhile for God has traveled an easy road. Doing great things for God requires character, and character is developed by passing life's tests and staying faithful to Him through the trials.

Trust in Him God has a unique plan for your life. Trust Him when you go through tests, knowing that they are strengthening and preparing you for the great things He has planned specifically for you.

October 17

The Why Behind the What

The Lord's light penetrates the human spirit, exposing every hidden motive. PROVERBS 20:27 NLT

I like to define a motive as "the *why* behind the *what*." A motive is the reason we do what we do. We often say we are doing things for God, but sometimes we do not understand why we do them. We only know *what* we are doing, but we have not taken the time to truly understand *why*.

Impure motives can cause many problems, one of which is being overcommitted, which results in unnecessary stress in our lives. Surely we won't live with extreme stress if we are obeying God and doing only what He wants us to do. Never agree to do something in order to impress people or because you fear what they may think or say about you if you don't. God wants us to help and bless people, but a "good work" done with a wrong motive is no longer a good work. Don't say yes with your mouth if your heart is screaming no.

Take the motive test as often as you can. Begin to ask yourself questions that will help you assess your motives, such as:

- Why did I agree to serve on that committee?
- Why did I say I would lead the missions group at church? Do I really have a heart for evangelism and a longing to serve God, or do I want people to talk about what a good church member I am, or am I afraid of what they will say if I do not agree to help?
- Why do I really want that promotion at work so much? Is it motivated by God or worldly ambition?

As you evaluate your motives, you will begin to see what is in your heart. Pass the test by making sure your motives are pure and right before God—even if that means changing the "what." The motive test is a lifelong test. I frequently reevaluate my motives and discontinue things I find I am doing for the wrong reason, and that helps me keep my priorities in order.

Trust in Him Take a look at *why* you are doing what you are doing. Trusting God will help you keep your priorities in order and give you the freedom to do only what He wants you to do, which is essential to living a stress-free life.

October 18

Use Your Talents to Show Love

And he who had received the five talents came and brought him five more, saying, Master, you entrusted to me five talents; see, here I have gained five talents more. MATTHEW 25:20

God has given each of us abilities, and we should use them to benefit one another. Whatever your particular talent is, offer it as a free gift occasionally rather than always wanting or expecting to be paid for it.

For example, if you are a photographer, offer to take free wedding pictures for a friend or someone on a tight budget. If you are a hairdresser, offer to go to a homeless shelter or nursing home and cut hair once a month or more if you're willing. A friend of mine is a decorative painter, and she recently donated three days of her time painting at a home for troubled young women.

I met a woman once who had little money but wanted to support missions financially. She did so by selling her baked goods to raise money for missions. Her story emphasizes the point that if we refuse to do nothing, we will be able to find the something that we can do, and when everyone gets involved it won't be long until the good in our world will overcome the evil.

To say we can't do anything is just not true. We may make excuses, but excuses are nothing more than a way to deceive ourselves and justify doing nothing. You will come alive like never before if you will aggressively reach out to others.

Let us not forget the words of Jesus: "I give you a new commandment: that you should love one another. Just as I have loved you, so you too should love one another" (John 13:34). Without a doubt, this is our purpose and the will of God for our lives.

Trust in Him What is your talent? God gifted you with talents so that you would use them for His purposes—to show love to the world. If you trust Him and refuse to do nothing, you can make a difference.

October 19

Help People Feel Good About Themselves

Let this same attitude and purpose and [humble] mind be in you which was in Christ Jesus: [Let Him be your example in humility]... PHILIPPIANS 2:5

I am fairly disciplined in my eating habits, and recently I spent a week with someone who really struggles in that area. The person mentioned several times how disciplined I am and how undisciplined she is. Each time she did so, I downplayed my ability to discipline myself by saying, *"I have areas of weakness also, and you will overcome this as you continue to pray and make an effort."*

There was a time in my life when I would not have been so sensitive to my friend's feelings. I would have probably given her a sermon about the benefits of discipline and the dangers of overeating and poor nutrition. However, I would not have succeeded in doing anything but making my friend feel guilty and condemned. When she asked me to share ideas that might help her I did so, but with an attitude that did not make her feel that I had it all together and she was a mess. I have discovered that one way to love people is to help them not to feel worse about the things they already feel bad about.

Meekness and humility are two of the most beautiful aspects of love. Paul said love is not boastful and does not display itself haughtily (see 1 Cor. 13:4). Humility serves and always does things to lift others up. The Bible teaches us to have the same attitude and humble mind that Jesus had (see Phil. 2:5). He was one with God, but stripped Himself of all privileges and humbled Himself to become like a human being so He could die in our places and take the punishment we deserved as sinners (see Phil. 2:6–9). He never made people feel badly because they were not on His level, but instead He stooped to their level. Paul did the same, and we need to follow these biblical examples.

Trust in Him If you believe God's Word that says Jesus was exalted because He humbled Himself, you can trust that God will bless you when you lift others up, even if you have to get below them to do so.

October 20

We All Need Different Things

To the weak (wanting in discernment) I have become weak (wanting in discernment) that I might win the weak and overscrupulous. I have [in short] become all things to all men, that I might by all means (at all costs and in any and every way) save some [by winning them to faith in Jesus Christ]. 1 CORINTHIANS 9:22

We are all different, and we each have different needs. I urge you to go the extra mile and find out what people really need instead of merely giving them what you want to give them, or what you think they need.

I like to give gifts, so I usually do that to show love. I once had an assistant who did not seem to appreciate my gifts very much. This really bothered me because she seemed ungrateful, but when I got to know her better, she told me that the most important thing to her was hearing words that conveyed love.

I wanted to give her gifts because that was easier for me than saying the words she wanted to hear. I often show appreciation for someone's hard work by giving them things, but she needed me to *tell* her what a good job she was doing and how much I appreciated her.

Through gift-giving, I was trying really hard to show her love, but amazingly she did not feel loved. Because I enjoyed giving and receiving gifts, I assumed she did as well. I think that happens more often than we realize simply because we don't learn enough about people to be able to give them what they truly need; we simply want to give them what we want to give them because that is easier for us. We cannot expect everyone to like what we like. We need to take the time to get to know them and then minister to them according to their need. When we expect everyone to be like us, we end up pressuring them to be something they don't know how to be. God graciously places many different types of people in our lives because we need them all. Each of us has a gift that we can learn to use for the benefit of the others around us. Appreciate people for who they are, and help them to become all they can be.

Trust in Him Ask God to put people in your life you need, as well as those who need you. Take the time to truly get to know what they want and need, and humbly provide it.

October 21

Love—Even When They Don't Deserve It!

But God shows and clearly proves His [own] love for us by the fact that while we were still sinners, Christ (the Messiah, the Anointed One) died for us. ROMANS 5:8

One of the most beautiful things the Bible says is that while we were still sinners, Christ died for us. He did not wait for us to deserve His love; He loves us unconditionally. To be honest, that's hard for many of us to comprehend because we are so accustomed to having to earn and deserve everything in life.

God is rich in mercy, and in order to satisfy the great, wonderful, and intense love with which He loves us, He poured His life out for us freely (see Eph. 2:4). *That* is revolutionary love! Real, revolutionary love must give itself, for it can never be satisfied to do anything less.

It is God's unconditional love that draws us to Him, and it is our unconditional love toward others in His name that will draw others to Him. He wants us to love people in His place, and do it the same way He would if He were here in bodily form.

Human love finds it impossible to love unconditionally, but we have the love of God in us as believers in Jesus Christ, and we can let that love flow freely, without conditions. Man's love fails, but God's does not. Man's love comes to an end, but God's does not. Sometimes I find that although I cannot love a person in my own human strength, I am able to love them with God's love.

The true love of God doesn't depend on feelings; it is based on decision. I will help anyone who needs help, unless helping them would ultimately hurt them. They don't have to deserve it. As a matter of fact, sometimes I think the less they deserve it, the more beautiful and impacting it is. It is absolutely freeing to be able to love people without stopping to ask if they deserve it.

Trust in Him Do you love others unconditionally? God wants you to love everyone, but you don't have to do so in your own strength. Trust in His strength and love others with His love.

October 22

Believe the Best

Love (God's love in us) does not insist on its own rights or its own way, for it is not self-seeking; it is not touchy or fretful or resentful; it takes no account of the evil done to it [it pays no attention to a suffered wrong]. 1 CORINTHIANS 13:5

If we want to love people, we must let God transform the way we think about people and the things they do. We can believe the worst and be suspicious of everything others do and say, or we can believe the best. Real love always believes the best.

What we think and believe is a choice. The root of much of our trouble in life is that we don't control or discipline our thoughts. If we don't discipline our thoughts, we will probably end up being suspicious and believing bad things that don't glorify God.

The prophet Jeremiah asked the people this: "How long will you allow your...grossly offensive thoughts to lodge within you?" (Jer. 4:14). The thoughts the people chose to think were offensive to God. When we choose to believe the best, we are able to let go of everything that could be harmful to good relationships.

When people do something that hurts you, you can believe they didn't realize what they were doing. If you do, you will save a lot of energy that you might otherwise waste on anger. When your feelings get hurt you will feel angry, but you can say to yourself, *"Even though what they said or did hurt me, I choose to believe their heart was right."* Keep talking to yourself until your feelings of anger start to dissipate. Say things like, *"I don't believe they really understood how their actions affected me. I don't believe they would try to hurt me on purpose. Maybe they are just having a bad day today."*

I know from experience that keeping mental records of offenses poisons our own lives and does not really change the other person. Many times we waste a day being angry at someone who doesn't even realize they did anything that bothered us. If we are going to keep records, then why not keep records of the good things people do rather than the mistakes they make?

Trust in Him **Choose to believe the best in all people and trust God to deal with any offense. Doing so will help you enjoy everyday life.**

October 23

God Even Cares About Remotes and Car Keys

But the Counselor, the Holy Spirit, whom the Father will send in my name, will teach you all things and will remind you of everything I have said to you.

JOHN 14:26 NIV 1984

Countless times over the years the Holy Spirit has reminded me where things are that I have misplaced and to do things I have forgotten to do. He has also kept me on the right track by reminding me of what God's Word says about certain issues at key times of decision in my life.

I learned I could trust God to help with big decisions by taking small needs to Him, too. One time we had some family members over and wanted to watch a movie, but we couldn't find the remote control. We searched everywhere for it, but nothing was producing the remote control. I decided to pray. So silently in my heart I said, "*Holy Spirit, show me where the remote control is, please.*" Immediately in my spirit I thought of the bathroom and, sure enough, that's where it was.

The same thing happened to me concerning my car keys one day when I needed to leave. I was in a time crunch and couldn't find my keys. I searched frantically to no avail and then decided to pray. In my spirit I saw the keys on the front seat of my car, and that is exactly where they were.

One of the gifts of the Holy Spirit discussed in 1 Corinthians 12 is the word of knowledge. God gave me a word of knowledge about the remote control as well as the misplaced keys. We can count on the Holy Spirit to remind us of things we need to be reminded of. If we needed no help, we would always perfectly remember everything and never need to be reminded; but if we are honest, we all know that is not the case.

If the Lord cares enough to speak to us about remote controls and lost keys, think how eager He must be to talk to us about more intimate things.

Trust in Him If you need help learning to trust God with the big decisions in your life, as I did, start by taking your small needs to Him. He cares about all your needs, no matter how insignificant they may seem!

October 24

Receive Jesus into Your Daily Life

If we live by the [Holy] Spirit, let us also walk by the Spirit. [If by the Holy Spirit we have our life in God, let us go forward walking in line, our conduct controlled by the Spirit.] GALATIANS 5:25

We ask people all the time if they have received Jesus, without ever really thinking about what that means. If we receive Him, then what do we do with Him? We certainly don't put Him in a little box marked "Sunday morning," go get Him out on that day, sing a few songs to Him, talk to Him a little, then put Him back in the box until the next Sunday. If we receive Him, then we have Him with us always.

It is not pleasing to God for people to leave Him out of their daily lives, while going through religious formulas to try to get what they need. Don't just go through the motions. Either have a real relationship with God that is alive and meaningful, or face the fact that you don't have one at all and do whatever is needed to get one.

Ask yourself these questions, and you will discover where you are spiritually:

- Are you growing daily in your knowledge of God and His ways?
- Do you look forward to going to church, or is it something you do out of obligation? Are you waiting for it to end so you can finally go to lunch?
- Do you feel close to God?
- In your life are you manifesting the fruit of the Spirit—love, joy, peace, patience, kindness, goodness, faithfulness, gentleness (meekness, humility), and self-control (see Gal. 5:22–23)?
- Do you have areas of your life that you have not let God into?

If you are not satisfied with your answers to these questions, throw your life entirely open to God and ask the Holy Spirit to get involved in every aspect of it. If you will do that in honesty and sincerity, He will begin to work in you in a powerful and exciting way.

Trust in Him Are you just going through the motions, or have you fully committed your life to Christ, trusting Him with everything so that He can do a powerful work in you?

October 25

"If You Miss Me, I'll Find You"

The Lord says this to you: Be not afraid or dismayed at this great multitude; for the battle is not yours, but God's.

2 CHRONICLES 20:15

God wants us to lean entirely on Him; that is what faith really is. It is too complicated to try to stay in His will under our own power. Which one of us can even say that we know 100 percent, for sure, what we're supposed to do every single day?

You can do everything that you know to do to make a right decision. You may be right, but there is a possibility you could be wrong. How can you know if you're right or not? You can't. You have to trust God to keep you in His will, straighten out any crooked paths in front of you, keep you on the narrow path that leads to life, and off the broad path that leads to destruction (see Matt. 7:13 KJV).

I know some things about God's will for my life, but I don't know everything, so I have learned to stay in rest and peace by leaning on God, praying for His will to be done, and trusting Him to keep me. I learned this when God was dealing with me to make a certain decision. I agonized, *"But, oh, God, what if I'm wrong? What if I make a mistake? What if I miss You, God!"*

He said, *"Joyce, if you miss Me, I'll find you."*

Leaning is a good thing, as long as we are leaning on something or someone that won't cave in when we least expect it! God is a good choice to lean on. He has a proven record of faithfulness to those who commit their lives to Him.

Trust in Him Faith in Jesus is "the leaning of your entire personality on Him in absolute trust and confidence in His power, wisdom, and goodness" (Col. 1:4). Are you leaning on Him?

October 26

Step Out to Find Out

The plans of the mind and orderly thinking belong to man, but from the Lord comes the [wise] answer of the tongue.

PROVERBS 16:1

We often find it difficult to trust what we believe may be direction from the Lord. It is not that we distrust Him, but we distrust our ability to hear from Him.

I eventually found that I had to take a step of faith, and then I would find out by experience how to recognize the leadership of the Holy Spirit. "*Step out and find out*" is what I always say. As we are learning to be led by the Holy Spirit, we are bound to make a few mistakes, but God always helps us get back on the right track, and we learn from our mistakes.

The process of learning to be led by God is no different from the process that babies go through when learning to walk. They all fall down in the process, but as long as they get up and try again, eventually they will end up not only walking, but also running at full speed.

James, chapter 1, begins by telling us how to handle the trials of life. There is a natural way of handling problems, but there is also a spiritual way to handle them:

> If any of you is deficient in wisdom, let him ask of the giving God [Who gives] to everyone liberally and ungrudgingly,

without reproaching or faultfinding, and it will be given him. Only it must be in faith that he asks with no wavering (no hesitating, no doubting). For the one who wavers (hesitates, doubts) is like the billowing surge out at sea that is blown hither and thither and tossed by the wind. (James 1:5–6)

Jesus is saying here, *"If you are having trouble, ask God what you should do."* You may not receive an answer immediately upon making your request, but you will find as you go about your business that God's wisdom is operating through you and His wisdom is divine and beyond your natural knowing.

Trust in Him If you are having trouble trusting your ability to hear from God, "step out and find out!" Learning to discern God's voice is a process. Even if you fall down, you can trust Him to help you find your way again.

October 27

The Holy Spirit Gives You Strength

So for the sake of Christ, I am well pleased and take pleasure in infirmities, insults, hardships, persecutions, perplexities and distresses; for when I am weak [in human strength], then am I [truly] strong (able, powerful in divine strength).

2 CORINTHIANS 12:10

When I had to have an operation, I went through all the moments of doubt and fear that often occur before a serious surgery. Naturally, all my family members and everybody around me were telling me to trust God. I wanted to trust, but sometimes I found it more difficult than others. At times I would be feeling secure, and then suddenly a spirit of fear would attack me, and I would once again feel frightened about the surgery.

This continued until one morning at about 5:00, during a time when I could not sleep. The voice of the Lord spoke in my heart saying, *"Joyce, trust Me; I'm going to take care of you."* From that moment forward I did not have fear, because when God speaks to us in a personal way, faith comes with what He says (see Rom. 10:17).

If we knew we could go to the doctor and get a prescription for pills that would give us instant strength anytime we feel weak, we probably would not hesitate to do so. I am telling you from Scripture that this strength is available to you through the power of the Holy Spirit.

The apostle Paul found the strength of God so wonderful that in 2 Corinthians 12:9–10 he actually said he would glory in his weaknesses. To put it in our language today, Paul was saying that he was glad when he was weak because then he got to experience the strength of God. This particular Scripture has truly ministered to me over the years.

I thank God I don't have to give up just because I feel weak or tired mentally, emotionally, physically, or even spiritually. I can ask God to strengthen me by the power of the Holy Spirit Who dwells in me (Eph. 3:16)—and you can do the same thing!

Trust in Him You can trust God to be your strength, and you can even delight in your weaknesses because they allow you to see Him at work in you!

October 28

Stay Sensitive to the Spirit

And I will pour out upon the house of David and upon the inhabitants of Jerusalem the Spirit of grace or unmerited favor and supplication.
ZECHARIAH 12:10

According to this verse, the Holy Spirit is the Spirit of Supplication. That means He is the Spirit of Prayer. Each time we sense a desire to pray, it is the Holy Spirit giving us that desire.

Recognize that when we are being led by the Holy Spirit to pray, it is often a lesson that takes a long time to learn. We often attribute far too many things to coincidence or chance rather than realizing that God is attempting to lead us by His Spirit.

One Monday, I began thinking about a friend whom I respect and appreciate so much that thinking about him is not that unusual. But during a three-day period, he kept coming to my mind. I consistently put off calling him because I was busy. (Does that sound familiar?)

On Wednesday, I was on my way to an appointment when I ran into my friend's assistant. I immediately asked her how he was doing. I learned he had been sick, and that while returning from his own doctor's appointment, he had received a phone call telling him his father had just been diagnosed with cancer that was spreading throughout his entire body.

I quickly realized why my friend had been in my heart so much that week. I must admit that I had not taken the time to pray for him. I *thought* about him, but I had never taken any action to call him or to pray for him. I am sure God worked through someone else to prepare my friend for the week he was facing, since I was missing the call from the Spirit. But had I immediately prayed on Monday, and perhaps made a phone call that day, I would have had the pleasure of knowing God used me to minister encouragement to someone who was about to face a difficult ordeal.

God wants to use us as His ministers and representatives, but we must learn to be more sensitive to the Spirit of Supplication.

Trust in Him Are you tuned in to the Spirit Who leads you to pray? Welcome the Spirit of Supplication into your life and trust God to speak to and through you. It is quite wonderful to watch the miraculous things that take place in response to prayer.

October 29

You Look Just Like Your Father

Although my father and my mother have forsaken me, yet the Lord will take me up [adopt me as His child]. PSALM 27:10

When I met my husband, Dave, I was twenty-three years old and had a nine-month-old baby from a marriage I had entered into at the age of eighteen. When Dave asked me to marry him, I responded with these words, *"Well, you know I have a son, and if you get me, you get him."*

Dave said a wonderful thing to me: *"I don't know your son that well, but I do know that I love you, and I will also love anything or anyone that is a part of you."*

This story closely corresponds to the reason God adopts us. As believers in Christ, we are part of Him—God the Father decided before the foundation of the world that anyone who loved Christ would be loved and accepted by Him. He decided He would adopt all those who accepted Jesus as their Savior (see Eph. 1:3–6 KJV).

Through the new birth, we have been brought into the family of God. He has become our Father. Just as our children inherit our traits, we are to have ways and traits like God. His character is to be duplicated in us—His sons and daughters. In John 14:9 Jesus said, "If you have seen Me, you have seen the Father" (paraphrase).

An adopted child may not look like the adoptive parent initially, just as we don't resemble God in any way prior to our adoption by Him. But even an adopted child begins to take on the traits of the adoptive parents. People are absolutely amazed when they discover that our older son, David, is adopted by Dave. People continually tell him how much he looks like his dad, which, of course, is quite impossible because he has none of Dave's genes or blood.

When I was adopted into the family of God, I acted nothing like my heavenly Father, but over the years I have changed, and hopefully, people can now see Him in me.

Trust in Him Do you look like God? If you need convincing that you are a child of God, a legal joint-heir with Christ, trust the Spirit of Adoption, the wonderful Holy Spirit, to work in your heart. Rejoice as you begin to look more and more like Him every day.

October 30

Invite Him into Every Room in Your House

Jesus, full of the Holy Spirit, returned from the Jordan and was led by the Spirit in the desert... LUKE 4:1 NIV 1984

After I was filled with the Holy Spirit, I found God in areas of my life in which I had not previously invited Him. He dealt with me about every area; there was nothing He was not involved in. I liked it, but I didn't like it, if you know what I mean. It was exciting, but frightening.

God got involved in how I talked to people and how I talked about them. He got involved in how I spent my money, how I dressed, who I had for friends, and what I did for entertainment. He got involved in my thought life and my attitudes. I realized He knew the deepest secrets of my heart and that nothing was hidden from Him. He had the keys to every room in my house (my heart), and He entered without notice—without even knocking or ringing the bell. In other words, I never knew when He might show up and voice an opinion about an issue, but it seemed to be happening more and more frequently. As I said, it was exciting, but I quickly realized that a lot of things were going to change.

We all want change, but when it comes, it is frightening. We want our lives to change, but not our lifestyle. We don't like what we have, but we think, *What if I like it more than what I get next?* It frightens us when we seem to be out of control and in the hands of another.

To be filled with the Holy Spirit means to live our lives for God's glory and pleasure, not for our own. It means laying down the life we had planned and discovering and following His plan for us. When we give God the driver's seat in our lives, things can change fast. Even though the changes God makes may seem frightening at first, we will ultimately understand that they were for our good.

Trust in Him Inviting God to dwell in every area of your life can be frightening, but if you truly want to grow into the person He created you to be, you must trust that He knows best and will work everything out for your benefit.

October 31

Change—The Most Visible Evidence

Then the Spirit of the Lord will come upon you mightily, and you will show yourself to be a prophet with them; and you will be turned into another man. 1 SAMUEL 10:6

The most important evidences that the Holy Spirit has filled your life are a change of character and the development of the fruit of the Holy Spirit described in Galatians 5:22–23 (patience, kindness, self-control, etc.).

God baptizes people in the Holy Spirit to enable them to live boldly for Him. And when you walk in the power of His Spirit, there will be the right evidence of Holy Spirit baptism. Speaking in tongues was one of the evidences of the outpouring of the Holy Spirit at Pentecost, but the most important evidence was then, and always will be, changed men and women.

At the trial of Jesus, Peter denied Christ three times for fear of the Jews (see Luke 22:56–62), but after being filled with the Holy Spirit on the Day of Pentecost, he stood and preached an extremely bold message. The result of Peter's preaching that day was 3,000 souls added to the kingdom of God (see Acts 2:14–41). The baptism in the Holy Spirit changed Peter; it turned him into another man. His fear suddenly disappeared, and he became bold.

As a matter of fact, it was not just Peter who took a bold stand that day. All of the remaining apostles did the same. They had all been hiding behind closed doors for fear of the Jews when Jesus came to them after His resurrection (see John 20:19–22). Suddenly, after being filled with the Holy Spirit, they all became fearless and bold.

The world is full of people who live with the torment of fear daily. Sadly, most of them don't even realize there is help available to them through the infilling of the Holy Spirit. The baptism in the Holy Spirit changed Saul; it changed Peter and the disciples; it changed me, and it continues to change earnest seekers the world over.

Trust in Him If you have a desire to live for God and want to glorify Him, let your life be the evidence. Trust the Holy Spirit within you to change you into a fearless and bold follower of Christ.

November 1

Open the Door to Christ

Behold, I stand at the door and knock; if anyone hears and listens to and heeds My voice and opens the door, I will come in to him and will eat with him, and he [will eat] with Me. REVELATION 3:20

Jesus is knocking at the door of many hearts right now, but we must remember that the doorknob is on our side. The Holy Spirit is a Gentleman; He will not force His way into our lives. We must welcome Him.

Open the door of your heart to Him by stretching your faith a little. Be like Peter—the one person in the group who got out of the boat and walked on the water. Peter probably had butterflies in his stomach when he got out of that boat, but as long as he kept his eyes on Jesus, he did all right (see Matt.14:23–30).

God has a great, big, wonderful life planned for you and me, but if we are stiff-necked, as God called the Israelites (see Exod. 33:3), or hardheaded (as we say today), then we will miss what God has for us. Stubbornness sets us in our ways, and we never stop to ask ourselves if our ways are really God's ways or not.

In the Old Testament book of Haggai, the people were living in lack and experiencing many problems, so God told them to consider their ways (see Hag. 1:5). Many times when people are not fulfilled in life, they look for the reason in everything and everyone except themselves. If you are not satisfied with your life, do as God told the people of Judah: "Consider your ways." Like me, you may find that you need to make some changes.

I was stubborn, opinionated, hardheaded, proud, and everything else that kept me from making progress. But, thank God, He has changed me! I pray that He continues to change me until I am just like Him—and that will be a lifelong journey.

Answer that knock at your heart's door and allow the Holy Spirit to come into your life in all His fullness.

Trust in Him God will not force His way into your life—you must open the door for Him. Step out in faith and put your trust in Him, so that He can do great things through you and for you.

November 2

Let the Holy Spirit Guide You

For this God is our God forever and ever; He will be our guide [even] until death. PSALM 48:14

Often when my husband, Dave, and I travel, we hire a guide to show us the best and most important sites to see. Once, however, we decided to explore by ourselves; that way we could do what we wanted to, when we wanted to.

We quickly found that our independent trips were nearly wasted. We often spent a large part of the day getting lost and then trying to find our way again. We have found it to be the best use of our time to follow a guide rather than wandering aimlessly to find places ourselves.

I believe this example relates to how we are in life. We want to go our own way so we can do what we want to do, when we want to do it, but we end up getting lost and wasting our lives. We need the Holy Spirit guiding us through every day of our time on this earth. God is committed to guide us even until we leave this life, so it seems important to learn how to hear what He is telling us.

The Holy Spirit knows both the mind of God and God's individual plan for you. His road map for you is not necessarily like anybody else's, so it doesn't work to try to pattern your life after someone else or what he or she has heard from God. God has a unique plan for you, and the Holy Spirit knows what it is and will reveal it to you.

Perhaps you are like I was and have wasted many years walking your own way without seeking God's guidance. The good news is that it's not too late to turn and go in a new direction—toward God's plan and purpose for your life. It is not too late to learn how to hear from God. If you are sincerely willing to obey God, He will guide you on an exciting journey of learning to hear from Him every day of your life.

Trust in Him Following a guide requires trusting someone or something other than yourself to lead the way. God will never fail you, so you can trust Him to be your Guide in life.

November 3

God's Preparing You for the Future

When the Spirit of truth comes, he will guide you into all truth. He will not speak on his own but will tell you what he has heard. He will tell you about the future. JOHN 16:13 NLT

We see many instances in the Bible where God gave people information about the future. Noah was told to prepare for a flood that would come to destroy the people of the earth (see Gen. 6:13–17). Moses was told to go to Pharaoh and ask for the release of the Israelites, but he was also told that Pharaoh would not let them go (see Exod. 7). Obviously, God does not tell us everything that will happen in the future, but the Bible says He will tell us of things to come.

There are times when I can sense inside my spirit that something good or something challenging is going to happen. Of course, when I sense something challenging is about to happen, I always hope it is just my imagination. But if I am right, then having the knowledge ahead of time acts as a shock-absorber in my life. If an automobile with good shock-absorbers hits a hole in the road, the absorbers cushion the impact for the passengers so no one gets hurt. God giving us information ahead of time works the same way.

I remember many times when God informed me of things coming in the future. One time in particular was when I felt strongly inside my heart that one of my children was really struggling with something major. When I asked my child about it, I was told that everything was just fine, but by the Spirit I knew something was wrong. Several days later I received some painful and discouraging news—but it would have been a lot more difficult if I hadn't had a previous warning.

Trust in Him God cares about you so much that He prepares you for the things to come. The next time you have a sense in your spirit about things to come, thank God for preparing you and trust His promise that He will never give you more than you can bear.

November 4

No More "Selective Hearing"

But the house of Israel will not listen to you and obey you since they will not listen to Me and obey Me, for all the house of Israel are impudent and stubborn of heart. EZEKIEL 3:7

God has taught me that when we are *unwilling* to hear in one area, it may render us *unable* to hear in other areas. Sometimes we choose to turn a deaf ear to what we know the Lord is clearly saying to us. We only hear what we want to hear; it's called "selective hearing."

A woman once shared with me that she asked God to give her direction concerning what He wanted her to do. He clearly put in her heart that He wanted her to forgive her sister for an offense that had happened between them months earlier.

Because this woman wasn't willing to do so, she pulled away from her prayer time. When she did seek the Lord again for something, He responded, *"Forgive your sister first."*

Over a period of *two years*, every time she asked the Lord for guidance about something new, He gently reminded her, *"I want you to forgive your sister."* Finally, she realized that she would never grow spiritually if she didn't do the thing God had told her to do.

She got on her knees and prayed, *"Lord, give me the power to forgive my sister."* Instantly she understood many things from her sibling's perspective she hadn't considered before, and within a short time their relationship was healed and made stronger than it had ever been before.

If we really want to hear from God, we can't approach Him with selective hearing, hoping to narrow the topics down to only what we want to hear. People want God's direction when they have issues *they* want solved. But, don't just go to God and talk to Him when you want or need something; spend time with Him just listening. He will open up many issues if you will be still before Him and simply listen.

Trust in Him Is there anything God has spoken to you that you have not yet obeyed? Why are you hesitating? Trust God to give you the strength to do whatever He has asked of you, knowing that He always has your best interest in mind. Your obedience will lead to your blessing.

November 5

Know God's Character

For My yoke is wholesome (useful, good—not harsh, hard, sharp, or pressing, but comfortable, gracious, and pleasant), and My burden is light and easy to be borne. MATTHEW 11:30

I sat down at my computer today and was ready to begin working when I sensed that the Lord wanted me to "*take a few minutes and just wait on Him.*" I waited very briefly, then started to make a phone call.

The Lord gently prompted me not to make a phone call, but to wait on Him as He had directed me to. Our flesh is so full of energy it is difficult for us to just be still, but it is very important to learn to be promptly obedient to God, even when He is asking us to be still.

You might ask, "*Joyce, how do you know for sure God was leading you—that your mind was not just making it up?*" The answer is that I had peace about what I was receiving. It felt right inside me. My spirit confirmed it as being truly from the Lord. We know things about God by the Spirit, not necessarily by the head. In my mind I wanted to get to work, but in my spirit I knew I was to wait. Are you following your own mind most of the time, or discerning what God is leading you spiritually to do?

Satan will try to deceive us and lead us in the wrong direction, but if we know God's character, we will recognize any voice or leading that is not from God. When I sensed I was not to make the phone call, I didn't feel guilt or condemnation because that is not God's nature. I sensed a gentle reminder from God that I was not following His instructions. He is not harsh, hard, sharp, or pressing, but He is gentle and loving.

There are many facets of God's character, and each one of them seems to be more wonderful than the next. He is faithful, true, loving, kind, long-suffering, just, and honest—among many other wonderful attributes. Know God, know His character, and you will not be led astray, for God's Word says that His sheep know His voice, and they will not follow the voice of a stranger.

Trust in Him As you grow in the Word and study the character of God, you will come to intuitively know His voice. Trust the voice that you know is His.

November 6

Honor God's Voice Above Everyone Else

But as for you, the anointing (the sacred appointment, the unction) which you received from Him abides [permanently] in you; [so] then you have no need that anyone should instruct you. But just as His anointing teaches you concerning everything and is true and is no falsehood, so you must abide in (live in, never depart from) Him [being rooted in Him, knit to Him], just as [His anointing] has taught you [to do]. 1 JOHN 2:27

This Scripture isn't saying that we don't need anybody to teach us the Word. Otherwise, God wouldn't appoint some to teach in the body of Christ. But it does say that if we are in Christ, we have an anointing that abides inside of us to guide and direct our lives. We might occasionally ask somebody for their wisdom, but we need not go constantly to other people to ask them about decisions we need to make for our lives.

Sometimes we give more consideration to what people tell us than to what God has said to us. If we pray diligently, get direction from God, but then start asking everybody else what they think, we are honoring people's opinions above the Word of God. This attitude will prevent us from developing a relationship in which we are consistently led by the Holy Spirit.

We need to have an attitude that says, *"God, no matter what anybody else is telling me, no matter what I think myself, no matter what my own plan is, if I clearly hear You say something to me, and I know it's You, I am going to honor You and what You say above anything else."*

When people ask me for advice I am willing to help them, but I also want them to have confidence that they can be led by God's Spirit themselves. If we are ever going to develop an ability to hear from God and be led by His Spirit, we have to start making our own decisions and trust the wisdom God has deposited in our hearts.

Trust in Him Jeremiah 17:7 says, "Blessed is the man who believes in, trusts in, and relies on the Lord."

November 7

The God Kind of Love

Love never fails [never fades out or becomes obsolete or comes to an end]. 1 CORINTHIANS 13:8

Human love depends on feelings. We love people because they have been good to us, they helped us, or they loved us first. They make us feel good about ourselves, or they make our lives easier, so we say we love them. Or we love them because we want them to love us. But that type of love is based on what they are doing, and if they stop doing it we will probably stop loving them.

That kind of love comes and goes; it is hot and then cold. That is the kind of love we experience in the world. Many marriages and other personal relationships are based on that kind of love. We love ice cream because it tastes good, and we love people because they give us nice Christmas gifts.

God's love is totally different—it is not based on anything except God Himself. And when we receive Christ as our Savior, the love of God is poured into our hearts by the Holy Spirit (see Rom. 5:5). As God's partners on the earth, He expects us to be His representatives. And He equips us with the love that we need to do the job He asks us to do. When human love ends, which it often does, God's love is in us and available to finish what needs to be done.

The God-kind of love cannot be grasped with the mind; it is a matter of the heart. Human love always comes to an end, but thankfully the love of God does not. God promises us that His love never fails!

Trust in Him If you trust the love that God has poured into your heart, you can love with the God-kind of love—unconditionally and without end.

November 8

God Is Talking to You

For God [does reveal His will; He] speaks not only once, but more than once. JOB 33:14

God speaks to us in many ways, including through an audible voice. Hearing the audible voice of God is rare for most people and nonexistent for many. I have heard the audible voice of God three or four times in my life.

Two of those times were at night when I was awakened by His voice simply calling my name. All I heard was, *"Joyce,"* but I knew it was God calling me. He did not say what He wanted, but I knew instinctively it had something to do with a ministry call on my life, although clarity did not come in that area for several more years.

I heard the audible voice of God the day I was filled with the Holy Spirit in February 1976. That morning I cried out to God about how awful my life was, telling Him something was missing in my relationship with Him. I felt I was at the end of my rope, so to speak. His voice seemed to fill my entire car, and He simply said, *"Joyce, I have been teaching you patience."* Since that was my first time to hear anything of that magnitude, it both thrilled and shocked me.

I instinctively knew what He meant. Several months prior to that time I had asked God to teach me patience, not realizing the lesson would include a lengthy period of feeling my life was on hold. The frustration of that feeling peaked that morning in February when I cried out to God in desperation, asking Him to do something and give me whatever it was I was missing.

When I heard God's voice, I was suddenly filled with faith that He was going to do something wonderful in my life. That event was the beginning of a new level in my relationship with God. I think it is safe to say that every new level in God is preceded by Him speaking to us in some way. He may not speak audibly; it may be through revelation in His Word or a divine circumstance that only God could arrange. His voice may be simply a whisper in your soul, but I urge you to believe that God does speak to His people still today.

Trust in Him Ask God to help you be sensitive to His voice. He wants to talk to you. It is your privilege and right as a born-again believer in Jesus Christ to fellowship daily with God the Father, Jesus Christ His Son, and the Holy Spirit.

November 9

Trials Reveal Your Character

Be assured and understand that the trial and proving of your faith bring out endurance and steadfastness and patience.

JAMES 1:3

Trials "try" us, and tests "test" us. Most of the time, the purpose of them is to show us who we really are, to reveal character in us.

We can think all kinds of good thoughts about ourselves, but until we are put to the test, we don't know whether those things have become realities in us or not. We may consider ourselves generous, honest, or deeply committed to a particular truth or ideal, but the depth of these dynamics only reveals itself when we're under pressure. When we go through trials, we learn whether or not we really have the character and commitment we think we have.

I believe it's very important for us to really know ourselves; tests are good for us because they affirm strengths and reveal weaknesses. Don't be afraid to face your weaknesses. God's strength is available to you specifically for them.

I must say that before my trials worked steadfastness and patience into my life, they brought out many other negative qualities, mind-sets, and attitudes I didn't know I had. One reason God allows us to go through tests and trials is so the hidden things in our hearts can be exposed. Until they are exposed, we cannot do anything about them. But once we see them, we can begin to face them and ask God to help us.

God does not allow us to go through difficult times because He likes to see us suffer; He uses them for us to recognize our need for Him. Everything you go through ultimately does work out for your good because it makes you stronger and builds your endurance; it develops godly character; it helps you to know yourself and to be able to deal with things at an honest level with God and take care of those things so you can reach spiritual maturity.

Trust in Him How do you behave under pressure? The next time you encounter some sort of trial or test, decide to believe it is for your good. Placing your trust in God opens the door for Him to work miracles out of messes—transforming your weaknesses into godly character.

November 10

The Simplest Recipe

Sacrifice and offering You do not desire, nor have You delight in them; You have given me the capacity to hear and obey [Your law, a more valuable service than] burnt offerings and sin offerings [which] You do not require. PSALM 40:6

God delights in our obedience. Naturally, it doesn't do God any good to instruct us if we aren't going to listen and obey.

I was moved by a story from a pastor of a very large church who spoke at a pastors' conference in Tulsa, Oklahoma. Hundreds of pastors came from all over the nation to hear this man tell what he did to build his church. He told them simply, *"I pray, and I obey. I pray, and I obey."*

One of the ministers who attended this meeting expressed to me his disappointment in the pastor's message. He said, *"I spent all that money and went all that distance to hear this world-renowned leader tell me how his ministry grew to the point it is. For three hours, in various ways, he said the same thing, 'I pray; I obey. I pray; I obey. I pray; I obey. I pray; I obey.' I kept thinking, Surely there's something else."*

Looking back over more than three decades of walking with God, I would have to agree that if I put into words the simplest explanation for the success I have enjoyed, I, too, have learned to pray, hear from God, and then do what God tells me to do to the best of my ability.

Over the years, I have been seeking God about the call on my life and pressing forward in what I feel He has told me to do. The essence of it all is that I tried doing things my way and experienced only defeat and frustration. It took a few years, but I finally learned to pray, and obey. It has not always been popular with everyone else, but I have prayed, I have obeyed—and it has worked. God's plan is not hard; we make it hard.

If you want God's will for your life, I can tell you the recipe for this in its simplest form: *pray and obey*. God has given you the capacity to do both.

Trust in Him Trusting God is simple—just pray and obey. If you do that, before you know it, you will have stepped right into His perfect plan for your life.

November 11

You Are God's Friend

Let us then fearlessly and confidently and boldly draw near to the throne of grace (the throne of God's unmerited favor to us sinners), that we may receive mercy [for our failures] and find grace to help in good time for every need [appropriate help and well-timed help, coming just when we need it]. HEBREWS 4:16

When you take God as your partner in life and you're not interested in doing anything without Him, then you are a true friend of God. Some people are not getting their needs met because they are insecure about their relationship with God and won't pray boldly and with confidence.

But when you know that you are God's friend, it gives you the boldness to approach Him at any time, for anything. This friendship causes you to press in to receive things that you know are yours according to God's Word. Possessing the knowledge that you are a friend of God causes you to be shamelessly persistent until you feel victory in your spirit. When that happens, you will feel a release that allows you to go ahead and enjoy your life, knowing that God is answering your prayer.

Unfortunately, many people are afraid to expect anything from God. But there is nothing wrong with asking God for big things and being expectant. Friendship with the Lord involves prayer, and prayer is all about moving in faith and getting situations changed. It is intimate conversation between you and Father God. It is in our prayer lives—those private conversational times alone with Him—that we develop our friendship.

If you try to wait until you are perfect to develop this divine friendship, it will never happen because we will always be growing spiritually; we will never be perfect. All God is asking is that we do our best every day to follow Him. The apostle James said, "You have not because you ask not" (see Jas. 4:2). Start asking!

Trust in Him Let Jesus be your best friend. He wants to help you in every area of your life. Trust that He hears your prayers and will answer in the best way at the right time.

November 12

God Lives in You

May Christ through your faith [actually] dwell (settle down, abide, make His permanent home) in your hearts! EPHESIANS 3:17

For many years I believed in Jesus Christ as my Savior but did not enjoy close fellowship with God. I felt that I was always reaching for Him and coming short of my goal. One day, as I stood before a mirror combing my hair, I asked Him a simple question: *"God, why do I consistently feel as though I am reaching for You and coming a little bit short of finding You?"*

Immediately I heard these words inside my spirit: *"Joyce, you are reaching out, and you need to be reaching in."* God's Word says that He lives *in* us, but many people find this truth difficult to understand. I did, too, for a long time.

I recall a day when I was walking around my house with my head hanging down—I was downcast! I was murmuring and complaining, saying, *"God, I'm so tired of all the struggles I have. When are You going to do something? When am I going to get a breakthrough?"*

Just then God reminded me that He lived inside me, and that fact alone should keep me joyful.

If you are born again, then Jesus is dwelling in you through the power of the Holy Spirit. But is God comfortable in you, and does He feel at home there within you? It took me a long time to understand that God lives in me along with all the other stuff that's going on in my inner life. Because many Christians are not willing to submit to the inner promptings of the Holy Spirit, they are not full of peace. Their inner lives are constantly in turmoil. If we want to be a comfortable home for the Lord, let's learn to dwell in peace and joy, trusting Him to take care of us.

Trust in Him Is God comfortable in you? If you want to be a comfortable home for the Lord, let go of everything you believe makes Him uncomfortable and fill yourself instead with gratitude, joy, and peace—and simply trust in Him.

November 13

Love Frees Us to Forgive

Above all things have intense and unfailing love for one another, for love covers a multitude of sins [forgives and disregards the offenses of others]. 1 PETER 4:8

The apostle Peter said love covers a multitude of sins. Love doesn't just cover one mistake, it covers a multitude. God's love for us not only covered our sins, it actually paid the price to completely remove them. Love is a powerful cleansing agent. I want you to notice that Peter said we should love "above all things."

When Peter asked Jesus how many times he would be expected to forgive a brother for the same offense, Jesus told him to keep on doing it as many times as it took (see Matt. 18:21–22). Peter suggested seven times, and I have often wondered if he was already at six and thought he had only one more effort in him.

We must understand that a lot of forgiveness is required of us. In fact, it will probably be part of our daily experience. Some of the things we need to forgive may be minor and fairly easy, but occasionally that big thing comes along and we start wondering if we can ever get over it. Just remember, God never tells us to do anything unless He gives us the ability to do it. We can forgive anyone for anything if we let God's love flow through us.

The Bible tells the story of a man named Joseph, who was sold into slavery by his brothers. When Joseph's brothers discovered years later that he was alive and in charge of the food supply they desperately relied on, they were afraid. They remembered how badly they had treated Joseph, and so did he, but he chose not to reveal it to anyone else. He spoke with them privately and simply told them he was not God—and vengeance belonged to God, not to him. He freely forgave them, urged them not to be afraid, and proceeded to provide for them and their families. No wonder Joseph was a powerful leader who found favor everywhere he went. He knew the power of love and the importance of total forgiveness!

Trust in Him The Bible tells us to love, and in order to do so we must forgive a multitude of sins. Trust God to give you the ability to forgive all things, and thank Him for forgiving you.

November 14

Everything You Need

As the deer pants for streams of water, so my soul pants for you, O God. PSALM 42:1 NIV 1984

Like a deer that has been running through fields all day, or a dog in the hot summer sun, or a man in the desert, we also thirst. What we thirst for is more of God, but if we don't know He is what we are craving, we can be easily misled.

We might think food is what we crave, or people's approval, or material things. But those things won't satisfy us. If we set our minds on seeking God—if we give Him first place in our desires, thoughts, conversation, and choices—our thirst will truly be quenched and we will not be led astray.

David expressed his longing for the Lord in Psalm 42. Verse 2 says, "My inner self thirsts for God, for the living God. When shall I come and behold the face of God?" We have needs, but God says, *"Here I am. I have everything you need."* We are to search after God like a thirsty man in the desert. What does a thirsty man think about? Nothing but water! He isn't concerned about anything else but finding what it takes to quench his thirst. Likewise, we should seek God above all else in order to quench our thirst.

If we are looking for only material things or improved circumstances instead of looking for God, Satan can set up a mirage (false image) to put us on the wrong track. But if we are seeking God, the devil can't mislead us, because God has promised that those who seek Him with their whole hearts will find Him. God essentially says, "My people shall no longer be led by a mirage, but they will know to seek Me, the Living Water. Those who come to Me will never thirst again" (see John 4:10, 14).

Until our desire for God is greater than all other things, Satan has an advantage over our lives. But we can turn that advantage into disadvantage by resetting our priorities. Seek first God's Kingdom, and all other things will be added (see Matt. 6:33).

Trust in Him God designed you to long for Him, and only He can satisfy that longing. Trust Him to quench your thirst as you continue to study, read, and listen to the Word of God, and you will never be thirsty again.

November 15

Ready for Anything

I have glorified You down here on the earth by completing the work that You gave Me to do. And now, Father, glorify Me along with Yourself and restore Me to such majesty and honor in Your presence as I had with You before the world existed. JOHN 17:4–5

This passage gripped my heart one day, and I broke into tears. I thought, *Oh, God, if only I can stand before You on the Last Day, look You in the eye, and not have to be ashamed, but be able to say, "Lord, I did it. With Your help I came through to the finish. I completed what You gave me to do."*

I realized that real joy comes from being a vessel for God to use for His glory: letting Him choose where He's going to take me, what He's going to do with me, when He's going to do it—and always submitting to Him. It is one thing to be willing to do some things for the Lord, but it's another thing entirely to be willing to do *anything* for the glory of God.

We may mistakenly think that some things would just be too difficult, but God will give us the strength through Christ to do all things He asks. When you sense that God is leading you to do something that frightens or overwhelms you, just take that first step in faith and you will find the power of God available when you take the next one.

I often feel incapable, but I have learned to trust God more than I trust my feelings. If He asks us to do something, He will definitely give us the grace to do it one day at a time. Don't stop short of finishing the work God has given you to do; glorify Him by pressing through to the end.

Trust in Him Make a decision today to glorify God by completing each task He gives you. Trust Him to give you all that you need to do so. He will never fail you!

November 16

Stop and Smell the Roses

Come to Me, all you who labor and are heavy-laden and overburdened, and I will cause you to rest...

MATTHEW 11:28

Much of the world is in a hurry, always rushing; yet very few people even know where they are going in life. People rush to get to yet another event that has no real meaning for them, or that they really don't even want to attend. We hurry so much we finally come to the place where we cannot slow down.

I can remember the days when I worked so hard and hurried so much that even if I took a vacation, it was almost over by the time I geared down enough to actually rest. Constantly hurrying definitely inhibited me from having peace in my life, and it still can if I do not stay alert to its pressure. Life is too precious to rush through it.

I find at times that a day has gone by in a blur; at the conclusion of it, I know I was very busy all day yet cannot really remember enjoying much, if any, of it. I have committed to learn to do things in God's rhythm, not the world's pace.

Jesus was never in a hurry when He was here on earth, and God is absolutely not in a hurry now. Ecclesiastes 3:1 states, "To everything there is a season, and a time for every matter or purpose under heaven..." We should let each thing in our lives have its season, and realize we can enjoy that season without rushing into the next one.

Our pace of living affects the quality of our lives. When we eat too fast, we don't properly digest our food; when we rush through life, we don't properly digest it, either. God has given life to us as a gift, and what a pitiful shame to do nothing but rush through each day and never, as they say, *"stop and smell the roses."* Each thing we do in life has a sweet fragrance, and we should learn to take it in and enjoy the aroma.

Trust in Him **Are you in a hurry? If you want to be at peace with yourself and enjoy life, you must stop rushing all the time. Trust God to give you the grace, the energy, and the time to do everything you need to do at a pace that allows you to enjoy the journey.**

November 17

You Can Be Content in All Circumstances

I have learned how to be content (satisfied to the point where I am not disturbed or disquieted) in whatever state I am.

PHILIPPIANS 4:11

People of God should be peaceful, joyful, thankful, and content. In Philippians 4:11, Paul said he "learned how to be content." Well, I don't know about you, but I spent many years, even as a believer, before I *learned* contentment, and I believe there are many others who struggle as I did trying to find it. You may be one of them.

I knew how to be satisfied if I was getting my own way—if everything was working exactly as I had planned—but how often does that happen? Very rarely, in my experience.

I knew absolutely nothing about how to handle even the ordinary trials that come along in most every person's life. I didn't know how to adapt to other people and things. I found out that a person who can only be satisfied when there are no disturbances in life will spend a great deal of time being discontented.

I finally desired stability enough that I was willing to learn whatever it took to have it. I wanted to be *satisfied* no matter what was going on around me.

The Amplified Bible defines the word *content* as "satisfied to the point where I am not disturbed or disquieted in whatever state I am in." I appreciate this definition, because it does not say that I must be satisfied to the point where I don't ever want change, but I can be satisfied to the point that I am not anxious or disturbed. I desperately wanted, and now enjoy, that kind of peace. How about you?

Trusting God and refusing to complain during hard times greatly honors Him. It is of no value to talk of how much we trust God only when all is well. But when difficulty comes, then we should say and sincerely mean, "*I trust You, Lord.*" He delights in a contented child. I have come to believe being content is one of the greatest ways we can glorify Him. Be content where you are while you are waiting for what you want or need.

Trust in Him Don't wait until everything is perfect before you decide to enjoy your everyday life. Trust God and be content regardless of your circumstances.

November 18

You Are Perfect in Christ

You, therefore, must be perfect [growing into complete maturity of godliness in mind and character, having reached the proper height of virtue and integrity], as your heavenly Father is perfect.

MATTHEW 5:48

We have a command (or perhaps it is a promise) in Matthew 5:48: "Be perfect, therefore, as your heavenly Father is perfect" (NIV). Because God is perfect and is working in us, we can also look forward to sharing in His perfection.

The apostle Paul said although he had not already been made perfect, he pressed on toward the goal. He then said those of us who are imperfect should be thus minded, to let go of what was behind us (mistakes) and press on. In essence, he was saying that in God's eyes, by faith in Jesus Christ, he was *perfect*, yet he was not totally *perfected* (see Phil. 3:12–15).

We must learn to see ourselves in Christ, not in ourselves. Corrie ten Boom taught that if you look at the world, you will be oppressed; if you look at yourself, you will be depressed; but if you look at Jesus, you will be at rest. How true it is that if we look at ourselves—at what we are in our own abilities—we cannot be anything except depressed and totally discouraged. But when we look to Christ, the Author and Finisher (perfecter) of our faith, we can enter His rest and believe He is continually working in us (Heb. 12:2 NIV).

We always say, "*Nobody is perfect.*" What we mean is that nobody manifests perfect behavior, and that is a correct statement. Our behavior, however, is quite different from our identities.

The Bible says that faith in Jesus makes us righteous, but in our actions, we don't always do the right thing. I have said for years, "*Our who is different than our do.*" We don't do everything right, but God always loves us. He always sees us "in Christ," through our faith in Him, and He views us as perfect in Christ while we are still being changed by His power.

Trust in Him You are, this very moment, perfect in God's eyes and on your way to perfection, not because of anything you have done but because of who you are in Christ. Trust God to continually work in you to help you mature, grow, and change.

November 19

The Best Thing for You

Having gifts (faculties, talents, qualities) that differ according to the grace given us, let us use them... ROMANS 12:6

We all have different gifts, but we shouldn't compare or be jealous of the gifts of others.

I remember hearing one preacher talk of how often he saw Jesus. I had never seen Jesus, so I wondered what was wrong with me. Another person I knew prayed four hours every morning. I could not find enough to pray about to keep praying for four hours and always ended up bored and sleepy, so I wondered what was wrong with me. I had no gift to remember large portions of Scripture like someone I knew, who memorized all the Psalms and Proverbs as well as other entire books of the Bible, so I wondered what was wrong with me.

I finally realized that nothing was wrong with me.

Whatever we cannot do, there are many other things we can. Whatever someone else can do, there are also things they cannot. Don't let the devil deceive you any longer. Don't compare yourself with anyone in any way, especially not spiritually. We can see other people's good examples and be encouraged by them, but they must never become our standard. Even if we learn how to do something from them, we still will not do it exactly the same way.

At some time or another, I think we all fall into the trap of wondering why we are not like others we know or why we don't have the same experiences they do, but it is a trap—and a dangerous one. We are caught in a snare set by Satan when we enter into spiritual competition and comparison, and we become dissatisfied with what God is giving to us.

We should trust that God will do the best thing for each of us and let Him choose what that is. If we trust God in this way, we can lay aside our fears and insecurities about ourselves. I am sure we would all like to see into the spiritual realm and have an abundance of supernatural experiences, but getting frustrated if we don't only steals our peace, and certainly does not produce visions of Jesus.

Trust in Him **What spiritual gifts has God given you? Remember what Romans 12:6 says: "use them." Be yourself. You are unique; trust that God has a plan just for you and the gifts He has given you.**

November 20

God Gives You Grace for Today

Give us this day our daily bread. MATTHEW 6:11

God wants us to pray *every day* for whatever provision we need for that day. God will give you all the grace you need for today, and He will also give you grace for tomorrow; but tomorrow's grace won't show up until tomorrow. We are to learn to live our lives one day at a time.

I used to be frustrated as soon as I got up in the mornings. I was always in such a hurry. No matter what I was doing, I had my mind on the next thing I needed to do. I'd rush to make my bed, but because I never kept my mind on what I was doing, I was already anxious about the next thing I needed to do.

As I started making the bed, I'd think, *I better lay out some meat to thaw for dinner.* So, I'd leave the bed half-made and rush downstairs to get meat out of the freezer, but on the way there I'd see a pile of dirty clothes and think, *I better put those clothes in the washer and get the laundry started.*

Just as I put soap in the washer, the phone would ring, so I would run back upstairs to the kitchen to answer the phone. While I talked on the phone, I'd realize I needed to load the dishwasher, so I'd put a few dishes in the dishwasher as I talked. But then whoever was on the phone would say, *"Would you like to go to town with me?"* and I'd think, *Well, I do need to get some stamps to mail some letters,* so I'd hurry to get dressed to go to town.

I'd carry on like that all day, never finishing anything I started because my mind kept moving to other tasks I needed to do. That is not the way to enjoy your life. It is a challenge to thoroughly enjoy every moment that God gives us, but when we learn to do this, we will enjoy our days. If we don't enjoy every part of our day, we will miss the life God intended for us to enjoy.

Trust in Him Have you enjoyed your day? Every moment? God wants you to! I challenge you to examine your life and ask yourself: *"How much of my life am I wasting on anxiety or simply not paying attention?"* Make trusting God your first priority in life and He will give you peace to enjoy every moment of every day.

November 21

Practice Common Courtesy

[Love] is not rude (unmannerly) and does not act unbecomingly.
1 CORINTHIANS 13:5

Being courteous is a way to show kindness and respect for others. One way to be courteous is to always say *"please"* and *"thank you."* These are two forms of common courtesy that I encourage you to practice.

I want to especially encourage you to be courteous at home with your family. I am trying to remember to always say *"please"* when I ask Dave to do something for me, and *"thank you"* when he has done it. It is very important that we don't take our loved ones for granted. Having good manners in public should be an overflow of what we normally do at home behind closed doors.

Love is not rude, according to 1 Corinthians 13:5. Rudeness usually results from selfishness, and one way to fight it is to use good manners at all times. Our society is filled with rudeness, harshness, and crudeness, but this does not display the character of God. Jesus said He is "not harsh, hard, sharp, or pressing" (Matt. 11:30), and we need to follow His example.

We certainly need to make a point of being thankful and expressing our gratitude. In several places, the Bible makes the point that we are to be thankful and say so. We may think we are thankful, grateful people, but what is in the heart does come out of our mouths (see Matt. 12:34). If we are indeed appreciative, expressing thanks should come naturally for us.

Trust in Him Do you say "*please*" and "*thank you*"? Don't overlook "common" courtesies as being trivial. Trust that showing kindness and respect to others is pleasing to God and reveals His character.

November 22

You Don't Have to Burn Out

And Jesus said to them, The Sabbath was made on account and for the sake of man... MARK 2:27

Are you excessively tired all the time, and even after sleeping, do you wake up feeling tired all over again? You may be experiencing some of the symptoms of exhaustion, or what is commonly called "burnout." Long periods of overexertion and stress can cause constant fatigue, headaches, sleeplessness, gastrointestinal problems, tenseness, a feeling of being tied in knots, and an inability to relax. Some other signals of "burnout" are crying, being easily angered, negativity, irritability, depression, cynicism (scornful, mocking of the virtues of others), and bitterness toward others' blessings and even their good health.

"Burnout" can cause us to not exercise self-control, and when this happens, we will no longer produce good fruit in our daily lives. "Burn-out" steals our joy, making peace impossible to find. When our bodies are not at peace, everything seems to be in turmoil.

God established the law of resting on the Sabbath to prevent "burn-out" in our lives. The law of the Sabbath simply says we can work six days, and rest one day. We need to rest and worship and play. Even God rested after six days of work. He, of course, never gets tired, but gave us this example so we would follow the pattern. In Exodus 23:10–12, we find that even the land had to rest after six years, and the Israelites were not to plant in it the seventh year. During this rest, everything recovered and prepared for future production.

Today in America, almost every business is open seven days a week. Some of them are even open twenty-four hours a day, seven days a week. When we make ourselves available at all times, we are in danger of "burnout." People today are quick to argue that they cannot afford to take a day off, but I say they cannot afford not to.

Trust in Him Some people feel guilty anytime they try to rest, but that guilty feeling is not from God. God wants us to live balanced lives, and if we don't, we open a door for the devil to bring some kind of destruction (see 1 Pet. 5:8). Trust God that your resting time is just as valuable as your working time.

November 23

Determining Your Priorities

For where your treasure is, there will your heart be also.
MATTHEW 6:21

The best way I have found to determine if God is first in my life is to slow down and ask myself some simple questions:

- What do I think about the most?
- What is the first thing on my mind in the morning and the last thing on my mind at night?
- What do I talk about the most? What do I do with my time?

If we spend only a few minutes a week praying and five or ten hours a week shopping, then shopping is a higher priority than God. If we spend thirty minutes reading the Bible every week, but spend fifteen hours a week watching sports shows, reality shows, and talk shows, then television is a higher priority than God. The truth is that we make time for what we really want to do. Make your time with God a priority and you will enjoy the rest of what you do much more.

What about your money? Is it easy for you to spend money on a new outfit, complete with new jewelry and shoes, or something for your house or car, but difficult to obey God at offering time? Do you find it easier to spend money on eating out than on Christian teachings and music that feed your spirit?

Money in itself is not evil—it's "the love of money [that] is the root of all evil" (1 Tim. 6:10 KJV). If you love God more than money, you can do with your money what God tells you to and be at peace. However, if you love your money more than God, you are probably going to get upset or act like you didn't hear Him when He asks you to do something with it that you don't want to do.

I challenge you to regularly stop, and take a good look at your life. Ask the Holy Spirit to show you where your priorities are out of line. Then, allow His conviction to motivate you to seek a deeper relationship with Him.

Trust in Him If you need to adjust your priorities, trust God and make whatever changes you need to make in order to keep God first in your life.

November 24

Burn On, Not Out

Look carefully then how you walk! Live purposefully and worthily and accurately, not as the unwise and witless, but as wise (sensible, intelligent people). EPHESIANS 5:15

One of the reasons I previously found myself stressed-out, burned-out, and sick was from not knowing how to say "*no.*" I wanted to take every ministry opportunity that came my way, but it just was not possible. We must all learn to let God's Spirit, and not other people's desires (or our own), lead us.

Frequently people tell me that God has shown them that I am supposed to come to their churches or conferences and be their speaker. There was a time when that would pressure me because I thought, *If I say no, then I am, in reality, saying they didn't hear from God.*

But other people cannot hear from God for us. We are individuals and have the right to hear from God ourselves. I started realizing that no matter what others thought they had heard, I could not do the engagement with peace if I had not heard from God about it myself.

Are you saying "*yes*" with your mouth while your heart is screaming "*no*"? If so, you will eventually be stressed-out, burned-out, and possibly sick. We just cannot go on like that forever without ultimately breaking down under the strain.

No matter how many people you please, there will always be someone who will not be pleased. Learn that you can enjoy your life even if everyone does not think you are wonderful. Don't be addicted to approval from people; if God approves, that is all that really matters.

Being committed is very good, but being overcommitted is very dangerous. Know your limits and don't hesitate to say "*no*" if you know that you need to. God has assigned a life span to each of us, and although we don't know exactly how long we have on earth, we should certainly desire to live out the fullness of our years. We want to burn on, not burn out. We should live with passion and zeal, not with exhaustion; we should be good examples to others.

Trust in Him Are you committed, or overcommitted? No one else will stand before God and give an account of your life; only you will do that. Be prepared to be able to say to Him, *"I trusted You and followed my heart to the best of my ability."*

November 25

You Can Live in an Atmosphere of Peace

He Himself withdrew [in retirement] to the wilderness (desert) and prayed. LUKE 5:16

We live in a noisy society. Some people have to have some noise in their atmospheres all the time. They always have music or the television on or the radio playing. They want someone with them all the time so they can talk. Each of these things done in balance is good, but we also need complete quiet and what I call "alone time."

In order to enjoy a peaceful atmosphere, we must create one. Outer peace develops inner peace. Find a place where you can go that is quiet, a place where you will not be interrupted, and learn to enjoy simply being quiet for periods of time.

I have a certain chair in my living room where I sit and recover. The chair is a white recliner that faces a window to our yard, which is filled with trees. In the spring and summer, I can watch the birds, rabbits, and squirrels. There was a time when I would have considered that boring, but not now—now I love it. When I return from a conference, I go home, take a hot bath, and then sit in that chair.

Sometimes I sit there for several hours. I may read a little, pray, or just look out the patio door window, but the point is I am *sitting still and enjoying the quiet.* I have discovered that quiet helps me recover.

Being still has a soothing effect on us. If we find peaceful places and remain in them for a while, we will begin to feel calmness engulf our souls. Waiting on God quietly does more to restore our bodies, minds, and emotions than anything else.

We regularly need quiet time to wait on God. Insist on having it; don't let anyone take it from you. Jesus made sure He had seasons of peace and alone time. He ministered to the people, but He slipped away regularly from the crowds to be alone and pray (see Luke 5:15–16). Surely if Jesus needed this type of lifestyle, we do also.

Trust in Him Where is your quiet place? Take my suggestion and try regular doses of "alone time." Rest in God's presence by trusting in Him and being quiet, and you will take His peace with you when you go back to normal activity.

November 26

Follow God's Plan for Your Life

A man's mind plans his way, but the Lord directs his steps and makes them sure. PROVERBS 16:9

I was pondering just this morning the future of our ministry. We have been in ministry since 1976, and many things have changed during those years. I realize that things will not be the same ten years from now, but I don't know exactly how they will be. Dave and I are getting a bit older, and we realize that we will not always be able to maintain the heavy travel schedule that we have now.

When I try to look into the future with my thoughts, I must admit I don't really see anything definite. I intend to keep doing what I am doing and prayerfully helping more and more people. And I believe whatever God does with our ministry, it will be good.

I believe it is important for many of our readers to realize that even ministers and authors, like myself, don't always have exact direction from the Lord; we walk by faith just like everyone else.

Having faith means that we don't see or have any natural proof of what tomorrow may hold. We believe for good things, we expect good things, and we wait on God. We may be disappointed occasionally, but in Christ we can shake off the disappointment or discouragement and move on with what God is doing—not with what we wish He did.

I trust that God will always take care of us, that He will always do the right thing. God does not make mistakes—people do. Often we make ours from excessive personal planning that becomes so important to us we miss what God wants to do.

God's plan is always better than ours, so we should be careful about making too many of our own. I always say, *"Make a plan and follow your plan, but be ready to let it go quickly if God shows you something else."* God should always have the right-of-way and the right to interfere with our plans at any time.

Trust in Him How much mental time do you spend planning what you will do tomorrow, or even the rest of your life? Try spending more time trusting the Lord's will, and asking Him to make His plans come to pass for you, then reap the benefits of your faith.

November 27

Trust Is Better Than Knowledge

In Him all the treasures of [divine] wisdom (comprehensive insight into the ways and purposes of God) and [all the riches of spiritual] knowledge and enlightenment are stored up and lie hidden.

COLOSSIANS 2:3

Sometimes we think we would like to know the future; yet in many cases if we did know all the future holds, we would be miserable and even afraid to go forward. Trusting God enables us to handle life one day at a time. God gives us what we need. We do not have everything we need right now for our future, because that time is not here yet, so if we did know the future—without having the tools we need to succeed—we would all feel overwhelmed.

I have discovered that I can lose a lot of peace by too much knowledge. Knowing is not all it is cracked up to be. Some things are better left alone. For example, I don't want to know if someone doesn't like me and has been talking unkindly about me; all that knowledge does is make me unhappy. Sometimes we are quite peaceful and then we receive some information, and suddenly we lose our peace over what we just learned.

I would love to know all the wonderful, exciting things that are going to happen in my future, but I don't want to know the difficult or disappointing ones. However, I realize both will be in my future. Just like everyone else, I will have good and bad times. I really believe I can handle whatever comes if I take it one day at a time, but knowing it all now would be too much. This is why God withholds information from us and tells us simply to trust Him.

Trust really is better than knowledge. Trust ministers peace, and that is very important. I suppose we can ask ourselves this question: *"Do I want peace or knowledge?"* I choose peace. How about you?

Trust in Him Do you want peace or knowledge? God has a reason for not giving you knowledge about your future. Trust God, and you can handle all of life's blessings and disappointments, one day at a time, in His peace.

November 28

Take Responsibility for Your Happiness

Don't point your finger at someone else and try to pass the blame!

HOSEA 4:4 NLT

We all have personal standards that we expect other people to meet, and we are disappointed when people fail to act the way we hoped. But is it really what they do that hurts us, or is it our own unrealistic expectations that set us up for the pain we feel when they don't perform to our standards?

For example, my joy is not my husband's responsibility—although I thought it was for many years. If he was not doing what made me happy, I became angry. I thought he should be more concerned about my happiness and do things differently. But it was *what I thought* that caused the problem, not what he did.

Dave and I have very few arguments now that I know my personal joy is my own responsibility, and not his. Dave should do some things for me that make me happy, just as I should try to please him, but there were many years in my life when it would have been practically impossible for anyone to keep me happy. My problems were in me; they were the result of abusive treatment in my childhood. Yet I was placing responsibility on Dave to make up for pain he had not caused.

Over time, I noticed that no matter had badly I acted, Dave remained happy. It irritated me, but also served as an example. I eventually became very hungry for the peace and joy I saw in his life, which were not dependent on any of his circumstances. In other words, he never made me responsible for his joy. If he had been dependent on me to make him happy, he would have never enjoyed life, because much of the time I gave him no reason to rejoice.

Are you possibly trying to make someone else responsible for things that only you can do something about? Let us take responsibility and stop expecting people to do for us what we should, in reality, be doing for ourselves or trusting God to do.

Trust in Him Put your trust in God and take responsibility for your attitudes and actions, and stop blaming others. If you are not happy, I suggest you look inward before you look around you to find something or someone to blame.

November 29

Be Self-Aware and Do Right

Therefore you have no excuse or defense or justification, O man, whoever you are who judges and condemns another. For in posing as judge and passing sentence on another, you condemn yourself, because you who judge are habitually practicing the very same things [that you censure and denounce]. ROMANS 2:1

Self-deception is one of the biggest problems we have as human beings. We easily and quickly see what is wrong with others but rarely, if ever, see what is wrong with us. We judge others, and the Lord tells us there is no justification for this.

Why would we judge someone else for the same thing we are doing? Because we look at others through a magnifying glass but see ourselves through rose-colored glasses, a tinted glass that makes everything look lovely whether it is or not. In our thinking, there is absolutely no justification for the wrong behavior of others, but for us there always is. We always seem to have some valid reason why we have behaved badly that excuses us from being responsible.

For example, someone might be short-tempered with us, and we feel it was inexcusable for him or her to treat us that way. We might have treated someone the same way on another day, but we justified it because we felt ill or had a bad day at work. In reality, we should honestly judge our own behavior rather than others because the Word tells us we will not be asked to give an account of their lives, but of our own (see Rom. 14:10).

When God admonishes me for my behavior in a relationship, it is particularly difficult for me if I feel the other person does the same thing that God is asking me to change. I have told God more than once, "*This is not fair. What about the other person?*" He always reminds me that *how* and *when* He corrects another is His business. Our responsibility is to follow God and obey Him, not to find fault with other people or how they are living their lives.

Trust in Him Let's be as forgiving of others as we are of ourselves. Don't worry about the faults of others, but trust God to correct their behavior in His own way and timing and listen when He chooses to correct yours.

November 30

God Meets You Where You Are

So whatever you believe about these things keep between yourself and God.
ROMANS 14:22 NIV

I try to eat reasonably healthy meals, and I have studied nutrition and its effects on the body. Consequently, I have strong opinions about how we should take care of ourselves. I do eat sweets, but only small amounts, and I am usually concerned when I see anyone regularly consuming large amounts of sweets and other foods that I know to be unhealthy.

I have tried to inform people when I see them eating poorly, and they have not received my advice well, to say the least. I even had one person say, *"If we are going to spend time together, I don't want you telling me what to eat all the time and making me feel guilty when I eat something you don't approve of."*

The person went on to say, *"I know I don't eat right, but I am just not at the place yet in my life where I am ready to do anything about it. I have lots of things wrong with me that I feel are more urgent than my appetite. So I am concentrating on what I feel God is dealing with me about, and I have no time to also pay attention to what you are dealing with me about."*

We all tend to put our convictions on others; we think if they are priorities for us, they must be priorities for everyone.

Romans 14 shares examples of how people were in a quandary about whether or not they should eat meat that had been offered to idols. Some thought it would be a sin, and others said the idols were nothing anyway and therefore could not harm the meat. Some could not eat because of their weak faith, and others ate because of their strong faith. Paul told them to each be convinced in their own hearts, and not try to force their personal convictions on others.

God seems to meet each of us right where we are in our faith. He begins with us at that point and helps us grow gradually and continually. Be led by the Holy Spirit yourself, and let others do the same thing.

Trust in Him Accept where you are right now, just as God does. Trust God to take you to a new level of living that is right for you and not for someone else.

December 1

What Causes Content?

May the God of your hope so fill you with all joy and peace in believing [through the experience of your faith] that by the power of the Holy Spirit you may abound and be overflowing (bubbling over) with hope. ROMANS 15:13

In my search for content I have discovered four things we must eliminate from our lives in order to be content.

The number one problem that leads to feelings of discontent is *greed*. Have you ever known someone who just could not be content no matter how much they had? I was once like this myself. Of course, I didn't think of it at the time as being greedy; I just always wanted more than I had. We must learn to enjoy where we are in each area of life, while we are on the way to where we are going. This means we can find our satisfaction in Him while we are on our way to the fulfillment of our hopes and dreams. I also believe *fear* causes many of us to be unhappy and discontent. We are afraid we will not get what we desire, and this causes us to be impatient.

Over time, I have learned that I could do the things God wanted me to do, and I could trust in and wait on His perfect timing to bring to me those things that He knew were best for me. Once we learn to trust God and step out even though we're afraid, God will provide the courage and boldness we need to overcome our fear.

Lack of trust in God is another cause of discontent, but simply trusting in God brings us into a place of rest, joy, and peace. *Looking for contentment in all the wrong places* is my fourth reason for discontent. Don't make the mistake of looking for contentment in things. If you do, the result will be that you will never find it. You will never be truly satisfied.

The answer to our frustration comes when we receive revelation that our satisfaction must be in Jesus and in His will and timing for our lives. When we are in a hurry to find contentment, it doesn't make God hurry. He has a plan, and only trusting Him will allow us to enjoy it.

Trust in Him Are you content? Trust God and find satisfaction in Him, and you will be content and have peace.

December 2

Please Don't Make Me Wait!

I wait for the Lord, I expectantly wait, and in His word do I hope.

PSALM 130:5

Waiting! It's a big part of our everyday lives, and most of us don't particularly enjoy it... or have time for it. Especially busy people who usually have way more to do in a day than they can possibly accomplish! But I can tell you from experience that our attitude about waiting can make all the difference in the world.

Like the Israelites who spent forty years making an eleven-day trip, I was stuck in a modern-day wilderness of my own. I had many wrong attitudes that contributed to the prevention of my progress, but one of the major roadblocks for me was an impatient attitude that made me want to scream: *"Please don't make me wait for anything. I deserve everything immediately!"* I had a long and interesting journey before I learned that waiting is part of our walk with God. We will wait—that is a given—but it is *how* we wait that determines how difficult the wait will be.

When you arrive for an appointment with your doctor or dentist, you have to wait your turn. The first thing the receptionist tells you is, *"Please have a seat while you're waiting."* Being seated indicates that a person is resting, and that's exactly what we should do, both in the doctor's office and in the wilderness experiences of our lives. While we're waiting for God to do the things that we asked for Him to do, we should rest in Him.

Another attitude that prevented me from making progress was *"I will do it my way or not at all."* This stubborn attitude is one that many people have to deal with. If it is not dealt with, the Promised-Land living becomes a blurry image and never a reality—something we see off in the future but never experience.

But it doesn't have to be that way. When we are serious about making some changes in our attitudes and allow the Holy Spirit to help us, we can take a shortcut through the wilderness instead of going the long way around!

Trust in Him Having a good attitude in a trying situation is at least 90 percent of the battle. There will always be trials in life, but as we trust God and continue to do what He is showing us to do, we will always come out victorious.

December 3

Don't Leave God Out of the Loop

I will say of the Lord, He is my Refuge and my Fortress, my God; on Him I lean and rely, and in Him I [confidently] trust!

PSALM 91:2

When we are frustrated, it is often because we are trying to do something in our own strength, instead of putting our faith in God and receiving His grace and help. Let us learn to pray for what we would like to be changed, and then cast our care on God. If He leads you to take some kind of action, then do it; but if He doesn't, then wait with peace.

I had to practice trusting God for a lot of things, but particularly finances. At one point in the beginning of my ministry, God asked me to trust Him to provide for my family financially without my working outside the home. I knew that I needed time to prepare for the ministry He had called me to. And working full-time in addition to being a wife and mother to three small children didn't leave much time to prepare to be an international Bible teacher.

As an act of faith, and with my husband's consent, I quit my job and began learning to trust God to provide for us. Dave had a good job, but his salary was forty dollars a month less than our bills. This meant we had to have a miracle from God every month.

I remember what a struggle it was to not go back to work—after all, I was a responsible woman and wanted to do my part. But I knew that God was asking me to keep preparing for the ministry He was calling me to and to trust Him for provision. Each month, He provided for our financial needs, and seeing His faithfulness was exciting, but I was accustomed to taking care of myself—all this "walking by faith" was crucifying my flesh big time.

Trusting God for the forty dollars a month we needed to pay our bills and for anything extra we needed was often difficult, but it helped us gain a strong foundation of faith that has helped us throughout our lives. I strongly encourage you to obey God and trust Him in every area of life. Each victory you have will increase your faith for the next challenge you face.

Trust in Him Little faith can become great faith when we see the faithfulness of God as He meets our needs. You can become a person who enjoys great peace by trusting God.

December 4

The Beauty of Submission

Be subject to one another out of reverence for Christ...
EPHESIANS 5:21

My husband, Dave, is anointed to be the head of our family, but if I have a negative and rebellious attitude toward Him, I will miss God's best for my life. However, if I stay under Dave's covering, pray for him, and respect his authority, God will be able to bless our entire family. God's Word says that where there is unity, there is blessing (see Ps. 133).

Let's learn to pray for those who have authority over us, rather than being angry and rebellious. James 5:16 says, "The earnest (heartfelt, continued) prayer of a righteous man makes tremendous power available [dynamic in its working]..." Just think of it—tremendous power is made available when we pray! Imagine the peace and content we would enjoy in our lives if we were to consistently pray for those in positions of leadership.

In the workplace, picture what could happen if we prayed for the boss instead of murmuring, faultfinding, and complaining about him or her, the way the company is run, or how underpaid we think we are! What if our prayers resulted in the boss being so blessed that he or she became a happier, more content person...and all that happiness and content filtered down to us. What glorious, joy-filled lives we could have if we were to live as Jesus instructed.

I believe there is beauty in godly submission. Even when we disagree with someone, we can learn to disagree, agreeably. We can show respect for them and their position of authority even when they do something that we think we would do differently. I believe a rebellious attitude is a very dangerous one, and I urge everyone to submit first to God and then to the authority He has placed you under.

Trust in Him Pray for the authority figures in your life—whether it be your parents, spouse, boss, or pastor—and trust God to bless you through them.

December 5

The Spirit of Grace

As God's fellow workers we urge you not to receive God's grace in vain. 2 CORINTHIANS 6:1 NIV 1984

One of the spiritual laws of the kingdom of God is, "Use it or lose it." God expects us to use what He gives us. When we use the grace offered to us, then more and more grace is available.

In Galatians 2:21 Paul stated, "I do not frustrate the grace of God..." (KJV). What did he mean by that? To find out, let's look at what he said in the preceding verse in The Amplified Bible: "...It is no longer I who live, but Christ (the Messiah) lives in me; and the life I now live in the body I live by faith in (by adherence to and reliance on and complete trust in) the Son of God, Who loved me and gave Himself up for me." Then he followed with his statement about not frustrating the grace of God. You see, it would have frustrated the grace of God if Paul had tried to live his life on his own, but he had learned to live by the power of Christ residing in him, which we know is the Holy Spirit.

I am sure most of us know how frustrating it is to try to help someone who keeps pushing us away. Imagine a drowning person who frantically fights and resists the lifeguard who is trying to save him. The best thing that person can possibly do is totally relax and allow the lifeguard to bring him to safety; otherwise, he may drown. You and I are often like the drowning swimmer. The Holy Spirit is in us. As the Spirit of Grace, He tries to aid us in living our lives with much greater ease, but we frantically fight to save ourselves and keep our independence.

Let us be wise enough to take full advantage of all that is offered to us. Let us welcome the Holy Spirit into our lives daily. By doing so, we will be letting Him know that we need Him and that we are very, very glad He has chosen us as His home.

Trust in Him Don't act like a drowning person, fighting the One trying to save you. Instead, trust God with your life and let Him bring you to safety.

December 6

The Spirit of Love

No man has at any time [yet] seen God. But if we love one another, God abides (lives and remains) in us and His love (that love which is essentially His) is brought to completion (to its full maturity, runs its full course, is perfected) in us! 1 JOHN 4:12

First John 4:12 is one of my favorite Scriptures. I love to read it and just take time to think about it: God's love is brought to completion in us! This Scripture helps me understand why I felt as if I had been filled with liquid love at the time of my baptism in the Holy Spirit. At that time, an extra measure of God's love was poured into my heart (see Rom. 5:5). I had to receive that love for myself, then I could begin returning it to God, and then, finally, I could start letting it flow out of me toward others.

We cannot give away what we don't have. It is useless to try to love someone else if we have never received God's love for ourselves. We should love ourselves in a balanced way, not a selfish, self-centered way. I teach that we should love ourselves but not be "in love" with ourselves. In other words, believe in the love that God has for you; know that it is everlasting and unconditional. Let His love affirm you and make you feel secure, but don't begin to think more highly of yourself than you ought to (see Rom. 12:3 KJV). I believe loving ourselves in a balanced way is what prepares us to let love flow to others around us.

Walking in love is the ultimate goal of Christianity. That should be the primary thing we all strive for. Jesus gave the command for us to love one another as He loves us. When I think of what I can do for myself or how I can get others to bless me, I am filled with *me*. When I think of other people and how I can bless them, I find myself filled with the Holy Spirit, Who is the Spirit of Love.

Trust in Him When the Holy Spirit comes to live in you, love comes to live in you. Trusting God's love for you will enable you to love yourself in a healthy way and let love flow through you to others.

December 7

Be a Person of Excellence

If you belonged to the world, the world would treat you with affection and would love you as its own. But because you are not of the world [no longer one with it], but I have chosen (selected) you out of the world, the world hates (detests) you. JOHN 15:19

Many places in the Bible say that though we are *in* the world, we do not have to be *of* the world. As believers, we don't belong to this world, but we are to be a light in it. Our standards as Christians should be much higher than the world's.

Ask yourself some of these questions:

- Would you rob a bank?
- Would you speak ugly gossip about a brother or sister in the Lord?
- Would you lie to your children or to your friends?
- Do you ever sign up to work in the church nursery and not show up?
- Do you exaggerate to make a story sound better?

Did you answer "yes" to any of these inquiries? Granted, most of us wouldn't even think of robbing a bank. But how many of us do compromise on things that we consider to be of lesser or minimal importance—things that Jesus, our standard of integrity, wouldn't do? We must not drift toward the ways of the world.

Integrity is being committed to a life of excellence. Our God is excellent. We must be committed to excellence if we are to represent Him to the world. Matthew 5:41 says to go the extra mile—don't just do what you have to do. I believe the Lord has caused me to know that real excellence is to do the more excellent thing even when nobody is looking—even when nobody is around to reward us, notice us, or recognize us as exceptional people.

Be a person of excellence. Make integrity a habit. Proverb 20:7 says, "The righteous man (or woman) walks in his integrity; blessed (happy, fortunate, enviable) are his children after him."

Trust in Him God created you for excellence. Trust Him enough to always go the extra mile and do everything the best way that you possibly can.

December 8

There Is Potential for Greatness in You

Therefore let us go on and get past the elementary stage in the teachings and doctrine of Christ (the Messiah), advancing steadily toward the completeness and perfection that belong to spiritual maturity.

HEBREWS 6:1

I am convinced that most people have potential for greatness, but just having potential is not enough unless you are willing to take a risk, step out, and let God go to work in your life. The word *potential* is defined as "existing in possibility but not in actuality; powerful but not in use."

Having potential doesn't necessarily mean that it is absolutely going to happen. It just means that it can happen if we add the other right "ingredients" along with it. For instance, if I have a cake mix on the shelf in my kitchen, then I have the potential of having a cake. But just because that cake mix is on my shelf doesn't guarantee that I am going to have cake. There are some things I must do to get it from a mix on the shelf to a cake on the table.

It's the same with us. Many people today are wasting their potential because they are not developing what God has placed in them. Instead of developing what they have, they worry about what they don't have, and their potential is wasted. They could have done something great, but they let the opportunity pass them by. You can make a difference in the world if you will develop what you have. But it takes time, determination, and hard work to develop potential into action or a result.

We are never fulfilled until we become all we can be. Each of us has a destiny, and unless we are pressing toward fulfilling it, we will be frustrated in life. Moving up to the next level requires a decision to press on, to let go of what lies behind, and refuse to be mediocre. I believe God wants to do more with your life than you ever imagined.

I also believe God is looking for people to promote. You can be one of them. There is potential for greatness in you!

Trust in Him Are you living up to your potential? God made you with potential—potential for greatness! If you do what you can do, and trust Him to do what you can't, you will grow into the person He gave you the potential to be!

December 9

Stand Up on the Inside

The Wicked flee when no man pursues them, but the [uncompromisingly] righteous are bold as a lion.

PROVERBS 28:1

I once heard the story of a little boy attending church with his mother, and he kept standing up at the wrong times. His mother repeatedly told him to sit down, and finally she got pretty harsh with him about it, telling him emphatically, *"Sit down now, or you will be in trouble when we get home!"* The little boy looked at her and said, *"I'll sit down, but I'm still going to be standing up on the inside."*

Have you ever noticed that there is always someone in life trying to get us to sit down? Through the years, many people tried to hold me back from the call on my life. There were those who did not understand what I was doing or why I was doing it, so they judged me falsely. At times their criticism and judgment made me want to "sit down" and forget about my vision from God. There were others who were embarrassed by having a "lady preacher" for a friend or relative; they wanted me to "sit down" so their reputations would not be adversely affected.

Many rejected me, and the pain of their rejection tempted me to "sit down." But God was standing tall inside of me, and "sitting down" wasn't an option for me. He caused me to stand up on the inside and be determined to go forward no matter what others thought, said, or did. It was not always easy, but I learned from my experience that being frustrated and unfulfilled due to being out of the will of God is much more difficult than pressing through all the opposition of other people.

Standing up on the inside doesn't mean being rebellious or having an angry attitude toward those who don't understand us. It means having a quiet, inner confidence that takes us through to the finish line. Confidence means knowing that despite what is happening outside, everything is going to be all right because God is with you, and when He is present nothing is impossible.

Trust in Him You can succeed at accomplishing all that God has for you to do. By trusting Him, you can keep standing up on the inside.

December 10

The Key to Your Future Is Hope

The Lord is good to those who wait hopefully and expectantly for Him, to those who seek Him [inquire of and for Him and require Him by right of necessity and on the authority of God's word].

LAMENTATIONS 3:25

Do you realize how important hope is to your mental, emotional, spiritual, and physical health? People without hope in their lives are destined to be miserable and depressed, feeling as if they are locked in the prison of their past. To get out of that prison and be free to move ahead into a more promising future, they need a key—and that key is hope.

Many years ago, I had an extremely negative attitude about my life because of the devastating abuse that had taken place in my past. The result was that I *expected* people to hurt me...and so they did. I *expected* people to be dishonest...and so they were. I was afraid to believe anything good might happen in my life. I had given up hope. I actually thought I was protecting myself from being hurt by not expecting anything good to happen.

When I really began to study the Bible and trust God to restore me, I realized my negative attitudes had to go. I needed to let go of my past and move into the future with hope, faith, and trust in God. I had to get rid of the heaviness of despair and discouragement.

And I did. Once I dug into the truth of what the Bible says about me and about my attitudes toward life, I began to turn my negative thoughts and words into positive ones!

We can practice being positive in every situation that arises. Even if what is taking place in our lives at the moment seems negative, expect God to bring good out of it, just as He has promised in His Word. You must understand that before your life can change, your attitude must change.

No matter how hopeless your situation seems to be or how long it has been that way, I know that you can change—because I did. It took time and a strong commitment to maintaining a healthy, positive attitude, but it was worth it. And it will be worth it to you, too.

Trust in Him Are you waiting hopefully and expectantly for all God has in store for your life? Whatever happens, trust in the Lord—He wants to be good to you!

December 11

Take Off the Mask and Behold His Glory

Rather, let our lives lovingly express truth [in all things, speaking truly, dealing truly, living truly]. Enfolded in love, let us grow up in every way and in all things into Him Who is the Head...

EPHESIANS 4:15

It seems that many people struggle to be real. We act one way on the outside, when really, on the inside, we are someone else. Because we have weaknesses, faults, or fears—things about ourselves that we think make us less likable or desirable—we'd rather hide from other people.

The danger of wearing these masks, of course, is that it misrepresents us. What other people see is a lie. It's not who we are...who we were born to be. By the time we reach adulthood, we've spent so many years hiding we've forgotten those things about ourselves that make us different and special.

What a shame! What a waste! Each of us—you, me, and every person—is uniquely created by a loving Father who rejoices in our individuality. In fact, it is those distinctive things about us, not our "sameness," that make us special to Him. The little girl with freckles, the young lady with the dimples, the beloved gray-headed grandmother with the sweet smile—they all stand out...they're special! And you're special, too!

Sure, we all have flaws. We're all less than perfect and wish we were better. But you need to know that God loves you just the way you are right now, and His love for you will never diminish.

God desires that we walk in truth, because only the truth will set us free (see John 8:32). He will help us to let down the defenses we've had up for so long. God knows how badly we want to fit in and be accepted. Trust Him to give you favor with people, instead of feeling that you must hide the real you. Learn to live truly by being genuine and real.

Trust in Him God loves *you*, and He wants you to trust Him enough to be fully who you are!

December 12

You Can Depend on God

Casting the whole of your care [all your anxieties, all your worries, all your concerns, once and for all] on Him, for He cares for you affectionately and cares about you watchfully. 1 PETER 5:7

God is always present in our lives—waiting to take over the heavy burdens we have if we will release them to Him. Like any loving father, He wants to help us handle our affairs just because He loves and cares for us. If we want to experience the peace that God desires for each of us, we must learn to cast ourselves and our cares completely into His hands...*permanently.*

Instead of giving our cares and burdens over to God completely and letting them remain with Him, many of us go to God in prayer just to get some temporary relief. After a while, we wander away and soon find ourselves struggling under the weight of the same old familiar burdens and cares—trying all the while to be more independent. The only way to really get rid of these burdens is to overcome the temptation to be independent people, placing ourselves totally in God's hands.

We must not allow ourselves to reach back and re-grab those things that we've already given over to Him. It's not our job to give guidance, counsel, or direction to God. Our job is to simply trust God with what is going on in our lives, having faith that He will let us know what is best for us.

God is God—and we aren't. As easy as that is to understand, it's hard for people who have been independent to walk it out in their daily lives. If we will yield ourselves and our burdens to Him and give up trying to be so independent, He will teach us His ways and care for us much better than we could ever care for ourselves.

Trust in Him You don't have to go through life independently. Trust yourself to God's care every day, and have faith that He will let you know what is best for you.

December 13

God Likes Playing Hide-and-Seek... So Keep Seeking!

"Ask, and it will be given to you; seek, and you will find; knock, and it will be opened to you. For everyone who asks receives, and he who seeks finds, and to him who knocks it will be opened."

MATTHEW 7:7–8 NKJV

Many people have asked me, *"Why can't I sense God's presence in my life?"* At times I have asked myself that same question. Some people may wonder if they've done something that caused God to leave them, but that is not the case.

In Hebrews 13:5, God Himself said, "I will not in any way fail you nor give you up nor leave you without support... [I will] not in any degree leave you helpless nor forsake nor let [you] down..." This verse makes it pretty clear that God does not abandon us. He is committed to sticking with us and helping us work through our problems.

While it is true that God never leaves us, He does sometimes "hide" for a while. I like to say that sometimes He plays hide-and-seek with His children. Sometimes He hides from us until eventually, when we miss Him enough, we begin to seek Him.

As children are growing up, their parents are happy to take care of them. But as the children grow and mature, the parents want their children to love them because of who they are, not because of what they can do for them. If our grown children only came to see us when they wanted something, it would hurt us. We want our children to visit us because they enjoy being in our presence.

It's the same with God; He wants to bless us with all good things, but when we only seek Him for the wrong reason—with the motive of just getting something from Him—it grieves Him. When this happens, He may hide from us for a time. If this happens to you, it's a good time to analyze your motives. Do you only seek God when you need something from Him? Or do you have a longing and desire to truly know Him intimately...all the time?

Trust in Him If you're tired of playing hide-and-seek with God, let Him know you trust Him and desire to have His presence in your life. As you seek Him regularly, with right motives, He will come out of hiding.

December 14

God Has Given You the Ability

As for you, be calm and cool and steady, accept and suffer unflinchingly every hardship, do the work of an evangelist, fully perform all the duties of your ministry. 2 TIMOTHY 4:5

I think a lot of people have *ability* because God has given them gifts, but they don't have *stability*, and so God cannot use their gifts publicly in ministry or business. They would end up hurting the cause of Christ because of their unpredictable behavior. I believe stability releases ability.

We can't be stable only when we're getting our way. We have to also be stable when we're having trouble and trials, when people are coming against us, or criticizing us. In the Scripture above, Paul knew a lack of stability would hurt Timothy's witness and anointing. Instability would prevent Timothy from hearing from God, so Paul instructed him to be calm and steady. We don't enjoy life unless we develop an ability to remain stable in the storm.

When we're upset, we are usually not listening. People don't hear because they don't get quiet enough to hear what God is saying. God isn't going to yell at you. He usually speaks in a still, small voice, and to hear Him, we must maintain an inner calmness. Actually, peace itself is a guideline for what God is approving and disapproving in your life. We must all learn to follow peace if we intend to follow God.

You have to choose purposely to stay calm, to put your confidence and trust in God, and to be a ready listener for His voice. Then you have to be willing to make whatever adjustments are necessary to have peace in your life.

Some people might say, *"Well, it's not fair for me to always be the one who's changing and adjusting to keep harmony with everyone else."* It might not seem fair, but God will bring justice in your life if you do what He's asking you to do, and your reward will be worth the effort you made.

Trust in Him Are you able to be stable through the storms of life? Choose to stay calm, keep your trust in God, and lead a peaceful and blessed life.

December 15

Trust God's Perfect Timing

But these things I plan won't happen right away. Slowly, steadily, surely, the time approaches when the vision will be fulfilled. If it seems slow, do not despair, for these things will surely come to pass. Just be patient! They will not be overdue a single day!

HABAKKUK 2:3 TLB

I'm sure that you are like most people—you want good things to happen in your life, but too often you want them now... not later. All of us tend to feel that way, but when the good things we desire don't happen in what we consider to be a timely manner, we are tempted to ask, *"When, God, when?"*

Most of us need to grow in the area of trusting God and shrink our focus that is on the "when" question. If your mind feels worn out all the time from reasoning, you are not trusting Him.

I spent a large part of my life feeling impatient, frustrated, and disappointed because there were things I didn't know. God had to teach me to leave things in His hands. I finally learned to trust the One Who knows all things, and I began to accept that some questions may never be answered. We prove our trust in God when we refuse to worry.

Trusting God often requires not knowing *how* God is going to accomplish what needs to be done and not knowing *when* He will do it. We often say, "*God is never late,*" but generally He isn't early, either. He uses times of waiting to stretch our faith in Him, and to bring about change and growth in our lives. We learn to trust God by going through many experiences that require trust. By seeing God's faithfulness over and over, we gradually let go of trusting ourselves and place our trust in Him.

Looking at it this way, it is easy to see how timing plays an important part in learning to trust God. If He did everything we asked for immediately, we would never grow and develop into the people He wants us to be. If you are waiting on something right now and you feel frustrated, learn to be happy "not knowing."

Trust in Him If you want peace, you need to trust God with *when* and *how* He will move in your life.

December 16

Make Allowances for One Another

I therefore, the prisoner for the Lord, appeal to and beg you to walk (lead a life) worthy of the [divine] calling to which you have been called [with behavior that is a credit to the summons to God's service, Living as becomes you] with complete lowliness of mind (humility) and meekness (unselfishness, gentleness, mildness), with patience, bearing with one another and making allowances because you love one another. EPHESIANS 4:1–2

If we truly love one another, we will bear with one another and make allowances for one another. Making allowances doesn't mean making excuses for people's wrong behavior—if it is wrong, then it is wrong, and pretending or ignoring it does not help. But making allowances for one another means we allow each other to be less than perfect. We send messages with our words and attitude that say, *"I won't reject you because you did that; I won't give up on you. I will work through this with you and believe in you."*

I have told my children that even though I might not always agree with everything they do, I will always try to understand and will never stop loving them. I want them to know they can count on me to be a constant in their lives. God knows all about our faults, and He still chooses us. He knows the mistakes we will make before we make them, and His posture toward us is, *"I will love you in your imperfection."*

When people do something that you just don't understand, instead of trying to figure them out, tell yourself, *"They are human."* Perhaps you don't understand them simply because they are different from you.

Jesus knew the nature of human beings, and therefore He was not shocked when they did things He wished they wouldn't have done. He still loved Peter even though Peter denied knowing Him. He still loved His other disciples even though they were unable to stay awake and pray with Him in His hour of agony and suffering.

What people do will not stop us from loving them, if we realize ahead of time they are not going to be perfect and prepare to make allowance for that human tendency that we all have.

Trust in Him Do you trust God to love you no matter how many mistakes you make? He will and He does. Are you willing to do the same for the people in your life?

December 17

Love Keeps No Record of Wrongs

Blessed and happy and to be envied is the person of whose sin the Lord will take no account nor reckon it against him.

ROMANS 4:8

The Bible says, "Blessed is the man whose sin the Lord will never count against him" (Rom. 4:8 NIV). That does not mean that God does not see the sin. It means that because of love, He does not hold it against the sinner.

Love can acknowledge that a wrong has been done and erase it before it becomes lodged in the heart. Love does not register or record the wrong; this way resentment does not have a chance to grow. Why not get out all the past-due accounts you have ever kept on people and mark them, "Paid in full"?

Some of us worry about our memory, but to be truthful we probably need to get better at forgetting some things. I think we often forget what we should remember and remember what we should forget. Perhaps one of the most godlike things we can ever do in life is to forgive and forget.

Some people say, *"I will forgive them, but I will never forget it."* The reality of that statement is that if we cling to the memory, we are not truly forgiving. You might ask how we can forget things that have hurt us. The answer is that we must *choose* not to think about them. When those things come to mind, we must cast down the thoughts and choose to think about things that will benefit us.

Clearing all your records will produce good results. It will relieve pressure and improve the quality of your life. Intimacy between you and God will be restored, and your joy and peace will increase. Your health may even improve, because a calm and undisturbed mind and heart are the life and health of the body (see Prov. 14:30).

Trust in Him If you are keeping records of others' offenses against you, make the choice to mark them "Paid in full." You can trust God not to charge you for your sins. If He is willing to forgive yours, you should be willing to forgive others.

December 18

Love Is Patient

Love endures long and is patient and kind...
1 CORINTHIANS 13:4

The first quality of love listed in Paul's discourse in 1 Corinthians 13 in the Bible is patience. Paul writes that love endures long and is patient. Love is long-suffering. It remains steady and consistent when things are not going the way you wish they would.

I have been practicing being patient with clerks who are slow, who can't find prices for items, who run out of register tape, or who linger on the phone trying to calm down an irate customer when I am standing right there, waiting to be helped. I have had several store clerks actually thank me for being patient. I am sure they take a lot of abuse from frustrated, impatient, unloving customers, and I have decided I don't want to add to the problem; I want to be part of the answer.

Sure, we are all in a hurry and want to get waited on right away, but since love is not self-seeking we must learn to put how the clerk feels ahead of how we feel. Recently a store clerk apologized for being so slow, and I told her that nothing I was doing was so important that I could not wait. I saw her visibly relax, and I realized that I had just shown her love.

We are encouraged in the Bible to be very patient with everybody, always keeping our tempers in check (see 1 Thess. 5:14). That is not only good for our witness to other people, but it's also good for us. The more patient we are, the less stress we have! Peter said the Lord is extraordinarily patient with us because it is His desire that none of us perish (see 2 Pet. 3:9). That is the same reason we should be patient with one another—especially with those in the world who are looking for God.

I urge you to pray regularly that you will be able to endure whatever comes with a good temper and patience. Trust me, things will come that have the ability to upset you, but if you are prepared ahead of time, you will be able to remain calm as you face those things.

Trust in Him God is extraordinarily patient with us. Trust Him to help you be extraordinarily patient with others.

December 19

Hold Your Peace

The Lord will fight for you, and you shall hold your peace and remain at rest. EXODUS 14:14

A few weeks ago, I preached on patience and being thankful no matter what your circumstances. I had done three major conferences in six weeks in addition to fulfilling several other commitments, and that Saturday-morning session was the last of that string of commitments. I was really looking forward to getting home early that day, eating a good meal, having Dave take me shopping for a while, taking a hot bath at home, eating ice cream, and watching a good movie. You can see I was prepared to reward myself for my hard work. I had a good plan for myself!

We got on the plane to return home, and the flight was scheduled to be only thirty-five minutes. I was so thrilled...and then something went wrong. The airplane door wouldn't shut properly, so we sat for almost an hour and a half while airline maintenance worked on the door. There was talk of not being able to fly out that day and perhaps renting cars and driving home.

I cannot tell you how hard it was for me to be patient. Just keeping my mouth shut was a huge accomplishment. I had preached on patience, and now I was being tested.

I realize we may not always feel patient, but we can still discipline ourselves to react patiently. I can't do anything about how I feel sometimes, but I can control how I behave, and so can you. I can assure you that I did not feel patient sitting on that runway, but I kept praying silently, *Oh, God, please help me stay calm so I am not a poor witness after what I just finished preaching.*

God helped me; and while things don't always turn out the way I want them to in those situations, in that case we ended up getting home in plenty of time for me to still do all the things I had planned.

Trust in Him When you find yourself in difficult or inconvenient situations, make an effort to hold your peace and trust God to help you act with godly character.

December 20

Love with Your Thoughts

Search me [thoroughly], O God, and know my heart! Try me and know my thoughts! PSALM 139:23

I believe thoughts work in the spiritual realm. That means that although they cannot be seen with the naked eye, our thoughts can be felt by other people. We think countless thoughts about other people, but we should do so responsibly.

What we think about people not only affects them, it also affects the way we treat them when we are around them. For example, one day I was shopping with my daughter, who was a teenager at the time. She had lots of pimples on her face that day and her hair was a mess. I remember thinking each time I looked at her, *"You sure don't look very good today."* I noticed as the day wore on that she seemed to be depressed, so I asked her what was wrong. She replied, *"I just feel really ugly today."*

God taught me a lesson that day about the power of thoughts. We can help people with good, loving, and positive thoughts, but we can hurt them with evil, unloving, negative thoughts.

I encourage you to take a person a day as a prayer project and practice thinking good things about them on purpose. Throughout the day, have some think-sessions where you meditate on the strengths of the person—every good quality you can think of that they have, every favor they have ever done you, and any complimentary thing you can think of about their appearance. The next day, practice on another person, and keep rotating the important people in your life until you have formed a habit of thinking good things.

Trust in Him Are you loving people with your thoughts? Trust God to show you anytime that you are not thinking with love, and be willing to change immediately.

December 21

Love with Your Possessions

Now the company of believers was of one heart and soul, and not one of them claimed that anything which he possessed was [exclusively] his own, but everything they had was in common and for the use of all. ACTS 4:32

Everything we have came from God, and in reality it all belongs to Him. We are merely stewards of His property, not owners.

Too often we grasp onto things too tightly. We should hold them loosely, so if God needs them, they are not difficult for us to let go of.

Paul told the Corinthians that their gifts to the poor would go on and endure forever throughout eternity (see 2 Cor. 9:9). Let's keep reminding ourselves that possessions have no eternal value. What lasts is what we do for others.

God wants us to enjoy our possessions, but He does not want our possessions to possess us. Perhaps a good question to ask ourselves regularly is: *"Do I possess my possessions or do my possessions possess me?"*

Sometimes I go on what I call a *"giving rampage."* I have a desire to be a blessing and want to use my possessions as a tangible way to show love, so I go through my house, my drawers, my closet, and my jewelry chest to find things I can give away. I never fail to find things. But it amazes me how I am tempted to hang on to them even though I may not have used an item for two or three years. We just like to own stuff! But how much better is it to use our possessions to be a blessing for someone else and make them feel loved and valuable?

If you are having difficulty seeing what you have to give, ask God to help you, and you will quickly find that you have a wealth of things that can be used to show love to hurting people.

Trust in Him Are you able to use what you have to bless people, or do you find it difficult to let go of things . . . even things you are not using? Show yourself to be a good steward of God's possessions and trust Him to bring into your life gifts for your own use and things you can share with others.

December 22

The Key to Happiness

External religious worship [religion as it is expressed in outward acts] that is pure and unblemished in the sight of God the Father is this: to visit and help and care for the orphans and widows in their affliction and need, and to keep oneself unspotted and uncontaminated from the world. JAMES 1:27

I went to church for thirty years without ever hearing one sermon on my biblical responsibility to care for orphans, widows, the poor, and the oppressed. I was shocked when I finally realized how much of the Bible is about helping other people. I spent most of my Christian life thinking the Bible was about how God could help me. It's no wonder I was unhappy.

The key to happiness isn't only in being loved; it is also in having someone to love. If you really want to be happy, find somebody to love. If you want to put a smile on God's face, then find a person who is hurting and help them.

Be determined to help someone. Be creative! Lead a revolt against living in a religious rut where you go to church and go home and go back to church, but you're not really helping anybody. Don't just sit in church pews and sing hymns. Get involved in helping people who are hurting.

Remember the words of Jesus:

> " 'I was hungry and you gave Me no food; I was thirsty and you gave Me no drink; I was a stranger and you did not take Me in, naked and you did not clothe Me, sick and in prison and you did not visit Me.'
>
> "Then they also will answer Him, saying, 'Lord, when did we see You hungry or thirsty or a stranger or naked or sick or in prison, and did not minister to You?'
>
> "Then He will answer them, saying, 'Assuredly, I say to you, inasmuch as you did not do it to one of the least of these, you did not do it to Me.' " (Matt 25:42–45 NKJV)

Trust in Him Are you ministering to Jesus? Jesus said ministering to others ministers to Him. Trust His life on earth to be an example of how you should live your life—going about doing good for others in need.

December 23

You Can Always Have Peace

The Lord will fight for you, and you shall hold your peace and remain at rest. EXODUS 14:14

Satan relentlessly attempts to steal everything God has provided for His children through Jesus Christ. Peace is one of the biggies; it is one of the things he works extra hard to prevent us from enjoying.

Remember, we have peace—Jesus provided it—but we must *appropriate* it. That means to take it and use it for our own use. Satan does everything he can to keep us from doing so, beginning with deception; he wants us to think that peace is not possible, that it is not even an option.

When we have a challenging situation, Satan says, *"What are you going to do? What are you going to do?"* We frequently don't know what to do; nevertheless, Satan pressures us for answers that we don't have. He tries to make us believe it is our responsibility to solve our problems when the Word of God clearly states that our job as believers is to believe—not solve our problems. We believe, and God works on our behalves to bring answers that meet our needs.

A good example appears in Exodus 14. The Egyptians were pursuing the Israelites; all the horses and chariots of Pharaoh, his horsemen, and army were in pursuit of God's people. When the Israelites found themselves stuck between the Red Sea and the Egyptian army, it seemed hopeless. They could see no way out, so naturally, they became fearful and upset. They began to complain and make accusations against their leader, Moses.

"Moses told the people, Fear not; stand still (firm, confident, undismayed) and see the salvation of the Lord which He will work for you today. For the Egyptians you have seen today you shall never see again. The Lord will fight for you, and you shall hold your peace and remain at rest" (Exod. 14:13–14).

It may have sounded foolish to the Israelites to stand still, hold their peace, and remain at rest, but that was God's instruction to them—it was their way to deliverance. When we remain peaceful in tumultuous circumstances, it clearly shows that we are trusting God.

Trust in Him Don't say, *"God, I trust You,"* if your actions show otherwise. Trust God with your words and actions; rest in His peace, and He will deliver you.

December 24

Recognize What Steals Your Peace

. . . Be joyful. Grow to maturity. Encourage each other. Live in harmony and peace. Then the God of love and peace will be with you.

2 CORINTHIANS 13:11 NLT

To enjoy a life of peace, you will need to examine your own life to learn what is stealing your peace. Satan uses some of the same things on everyone, but we also have things that are specific to each one of us. We are all different, and we must learn to know ourselves.

I can endure things better when I am not tired, and the devil knows this, so he waits to attack until I am worn out. I learned by pursuing peace what Satan already knew about me, and now I try to not get overly tired, because I know I am opening a door for Satan when I do.

Keep a list of each time you get upset. Ask yourself what caused the problem, and write it down. Be honest with yourself, or you will never break free. You may have things on your list like this:

- I didn't get my way.
- I had to hurry.
- I became impatient and got angry.
- Financial pressure upset me.
- I was too tired to deal with anything.
- I had to deal with a certain person who always frustrates me.
- A friend embarrassed me.
- I had to wait on a very slow clerk.
- A friend disappointed me.

You will have a lot of different things on your list, but it will help you to realize what bothers you. Remember, we cannot do anything about things we don't recognize.

Trust in Him I strongly encourage you to ask the Holy Spirit to reveal the truth to you about you, and it will be the beginning of enjoying a life of peace. Take responsibility for your reactions, trust God, and pursue peace!

December 25

Celebrate the Uniqueness of God's Children

... Encourage the timid and fainthearted, help and give your support to the weak souls [and] be very patient with everybody [always keeping your temper]. 1 THESSALONIANS 5:14

We seem to look at the way we do things as the standard for everyone. Instead, we should see that God created us all differently, but equally. We are not alike, and we all have the right to be who we are.

I talk a lot; Dave is quiet. I make decisions really fast, and he wants to think about things for a while. Dave loves all kinds of sports, and I don't really like any of them—at least not enough to put much time into them. Dave wants each item in a room to stand out, and I want everything to blend. I am sure you could tell similar stories about personal differences you have in your relationships with others.

Why does God make us all different and then put us together and tell us to get along? I am convinced that it is through the struggle of life that we grow spiritually. God purposely does not make everything easy for us. He wants us to exercise our "*faith muscles*" and release the fruit of the Spirit, including love, patience, peace, and self-control.

If everyone pleased us all the time, if our faith was never stretched and our fruit never squeezed, we would not grow spiritually. We would remain the same, which is a frightful thought. There are two kinds of pains in life: the pain of change, and the pain of remaining the way we are. I am more fearful of remaining the same than I am of changing.

Instead of rejecting others for their differences, see these unique qualities for what they are—gifts from God. Tell people the good qualities you recognize in them; don't point out what you think they need to improve. Compliment; don't fault-find. Accept; don't reject. Be positive, not negative. Be encouraging, not discouraging. You and I will never lack for friends if we will practice giving people the freedom to be themselves.

Trust in Him What good qualities do you recognize in the people around you? Trust God's design and purpose. Celebrate the uniqueness of His children—yourself included!

December 26

Be Happy for People

Rejoice with those who rejoice [sharing others' joy], and weep with those who weep [sharing others' grief]. ROMANS 12:15

I love to be around people who are really happy for me when I am blessed or have something wonderful happen in my life. But not everyone is like that.

I received a very special gift a while back, and it was interesting to see how differently people responded. Some said, "*Joyce, I am so happy for you. It really blesses me to see you blessed.*" I knew they were sincere, and it increased my joy. It also made me want to pray that God would do something awesome for them, too.

Another friend said, "*I wish someone would do something like that for me.*" Actually, this particular person almost always responds in a similar fashion when I receive nice things. Even when my husband does lovely things for me, this individual will say, "*My husband just doesn't seem to know how to do things like that.*"

These responses indicate a spirit of jealousy or some deep-seated feeling that she believes she is not getting what she deserves in life. It prevents me from wanting to share what God is doing in my life because I know she cannot be truly happy for me. I also believe it prevents her from being blessed.

At one time I was like that: I pretended happiness for people when God blessed them in some special way, but inside I didn't really feel it. At that time in my life, I compared myself to others and always competed with them, because the only way I could feel good about myself was if I was ahead of or at least equal to others in possessions, talents, opportunities, and literally anything else you can think of.

I am grateful that God has worked in my life, and now I can be genuinely happy for others when He blesses them. I am not responding perfectly yet, but at least I have made progress.

Trust in Him Are you able to be truly happy when someone else is blessed? Ask God to help you be happy for others, and trust Him to also bring blessings into your life.

December 27

God Wants You to Show Mercy to Others

If you forgive those who sin against you, your heavenly Father will forgive you. But if you refuse to forgive others, your Father will not forgive your sins. MATTHEW 6:14–15 NLT

Why is it so hard to completely ignore offenses? Even when we do overlook offenses, we want to mention the fact that we overlooked them so the people who offend us do not think they can treat us improperly and get away with it—it is a type of self-protection. But God wants us to trust Him to protect us as well as to heal us from *every* hurt and emotional wound, *every day*.

I wonder how weary we would be at the end of each day if God mentioned every tiny thing we did wrong. He does deal with us, but I am quite sure He also overlooks a lot of things. If people are corrected too much, it can discourage them and break their spirits. We should form a habit of dealing only with what God Himself prompts us to address, not just everything we feel like confronting or every little thing that bothers us.

I am the type of person who is not inclined to let anybody get away with anything. I don't like feeling someone is taking advantage of me, partially because I was abused in my childhood and partially because I am human, and none of us embrace disrespect. In the past, I was quick to tell everyone his or her faults, but I have learned that is not pleasing to God. Just as we want others to give us mercy, we must give it to them. We reap what we sow—nothing more or less. God may even withhold His mercy from us if we are unwilling to give mercy to others.

Jesus said He gives us power even to "trample upon serpents and scorpions, and [physical and mental strength and ability] over all the power that the enemy [possesses]" (Luke 10:19). He promised that nothing will harm us in any way. If we have power over the enemy, surely we can overlook the offenses of others.

Trust in Him Are you able to overlook offenses—painful or simply obnoxious ones—completely? God has given you the ability to forgive and show mercy to everyone who offends you, and He wants you to trust Him to heal you from every hurt, every day.

December 28

The Bible Says to "Shake It Off"

And whoever will not receive and accept and welcome you nor listen to your message, as you leave that house or town, shake the dust [of it] from your feet. MATTHEW 10:14

I often share a teaching that I call *"Shake It Off,"* which is based on the time Paul was on the island of Malta (see Acts 28). He was helping some people build a fire, when a poisonous serpent crawled out and attached itself to his hand. At first, when the people saw it they thought he must be wicked to have such an evil thing happen to him. They watched, waiting for him to fall over dead.

But the Bible says Paul simply *"shook it off."* We can learn so much from that. When somebody offends or rejects us, we need to see it as a bite from Satan, and just shake it off.

In another instance in the Bible, Jesus told the disciples that if they entered towns that didn't receive them, they should just go to the next town. He told them to shake the dust off of their feet and move on. He didn't want the disciples to dwell on the rejection they had experienced; He wanted them to stay focused on sharing their testimony of His works in their lives. Likewise, as we follow the Spirit, we can shake off offenses and hold on to our peace. When others see that we are able to remain calm even when "the serpent" bites us, they will want to know where that peace is coming from in our lives.

When we are in a state of upset, we cannot hear from God clearly. The Bible promises us that God will lead us and walk us out of our troubles, but we cannot be led by the Spirit if we are offended and in turmoil. We can't get away from the storms of life, or the temptation to be irritated by someone; but we can respond to offenses by saying, *"God, You are merciful, and You are good. And I am going to put my confidence in You until this storm passes over."*

Trust in Him Has someone offended or rejected you and you need to *"shake it off"*? Trust God to give you the grace to act godly even in an ungodly situation, and to help you shake it off in order to be a witness to others.

December 29

Blessed Are the Peacemakers

Blessed (enjoying enviable happiness, spiritually prosperous—with life-joy and satisfaction in God's favor and salvation, regardless of their outward conditions) are the makers and maintainers of peace, for they shall be called the sons of God! MATTHEW 5:9

Pursuing peace means making an effort. We cannot maintain peace simply by our own fleshly efforts; we need God's help and we need grace, which is His power assisting us and enabling us to do what needs to be done.

The efforts we make must be *in Christ.* Too often we just try to do what is right without asking for God's help, and that type of fleshly effort never produces good fruit. The Bible calls this a "work of the flesh." It is man's effort trying to do God's job.

What I am saying is, be sure you lean on God and ask for His help. When you succeed, give Him the credit, the honor, and the glory because success is impossible without Him.

Jesus said, "Apart from Me [cut off from vital union with Me] you can do nothing" (John 15:5). It takes most of us a long time to believe this Scripture enough to stop trying to do things on our own, without leaning on God. We try and fail, try and fail; it happens over and over until we finally wear ourselves out and realize that God Himself is our strength, our success, and our victory. He doesn't just give us strength—He is our strength. He does not just give us the victory—He is our victory. Yes, we make efforts to keep peace, but we dare not make efforts without depending on God's power to flow through us; failure is certain if we do.

The Lord blesses peacemakers, those who work for and make peace. Peacemakers are committed to peace—they crave peace, pursue peace, and go after it. They don't just hope or wish for it, they don't just pray for it. They aggressively pursue it in the power of God. Make a commitment to pursue peace from this day forward.

Trust in Him Call yourself a peacemaker, one who works for and pursues peace with God, self, and others. It is easy to live in peace if you are trusting God.

December 30

Nothing Satisfies Like God

Little children, keep yourselves from idols (false gods)—[from anything and everything that would occupy the place in your heart due to God, from any sort of substitute for Him that would take first place in your life]. 1 JOHN 5:21

Adam and Eve believed Satan's lie that there was something outside of God's provision that would satisfy them (see Gen. 3:1–7). We each make this same mistake until we learn that *nothing* can deeply satisfy us except the presence of Almighty God.

For years, I wanted my ministry to grow. When it didn't, I became frustrated and dissatisfied. I fasted, prayed, and tried everything I knew to get more people to come to my meetings. I remember complaining when God would not give me the increase I wanted. I would go to a meeting, and everybody would be late, nobody would be excited, and sometimes the attendance would be half of what it was the time before.

Then I would leave the meeting questioning, *What am I doing wrong, God? Why aren't You blessing me? I'm fasting. I'm praying. I'm giving and believing. God, look at all my good works, and You're not moving on my behalf.*

I was so frustrated. I even asked, *"God! Why are You doing this to me?"*

He said, *"Joyce, I am teaching you that man does not live by bread alone."*

I knew God had spoken to me from the Bible, but at that time I wasn't familiar enough with it to know where that Scripture could be found. So I searched the Scriptures for more explanation, but I didn't like what I found. Deuteronomy 8:2–3 showed me that God was humbling me and wanted my desires to be purely for more of Him—not for more attendants.

The Lord said to me, *"Anything that you need besides Me to be satisfied is something the devil can use against you."* It's not that we shouldn't want things; God just doesn't want us to put them before our desire for Him.

> *Trust in Him* If you feel like you're doing all the right things but still aren't experiencing your breakthrough, examine your priorities and motives. God wants to bless you, so trust Him completely and make Him first in your life and you will be satisfied.

December 31

Trusting God Through Emotional Trials

> *"Father, if You are willing, remove this cup from Me; yet not My will, but [always] Yours be done."* LUKE 22:42

Growing into a mature Christian who follows the Holy Spirit is not something that happens overnight—it is a learning process that takes time. Little by little, one experience after another, God tries and tests our emotions, giving us opportunities to grow.

God allows us to go through difficult situations that stir up our emotions. In this way, you and I are able to see for ourselves how emotionally unstable we can become and how desperately we need His help.

Jesus exemplified this for us. The night before He died for our sins, He was in great emotional turmoil; He didn't want to die, but moved past His emotions and prayed to God, *"Not My will, but Yours be done."* Things certainly didn't get better immediately, but in the end Jesus emerged victorious through the greatest trial possible.

You can make it through your emotional trials. Jesus wasn't led by His feelings, and you don't have to be, either. When God lets things affect you emotionally, seize the moment and view it as an opportunity to step into a place of absolute trust in God.

Trust in Him If you'll trust in God as you encounter emotional trials, you'll have the peace and confidence you need to make it through. Remember the example of Jesus and say, *"Not my will, but Yours be done,"* and you can rest knowing He loves you and has your best interests in mind even when it doesn't make sense.

About the Author

Joyce Meyer is one of the world's leading practical Bible teachers. A #1 *New York Times* bestselling author, she has written nearly 100 inspirational books, including *Change Your Words, Change Your Life*, *Making Good Habits, Breaking Bad Habits*, the entire Battlefield of the Mind family of books, and two novels, *The Penny* and *Any Minute*, as well as many others. She has also released thousands of audio teachings, as well as a complete video library. Joyce's *Enjoying Everyday Life®* radio and television programs are broadcast around the world, and she travels extensively conducting conferences. Joyce and her husband, Dave, are the parents of four grown children and make their home in St. Louis, Missouri.

Other Books by Joyce Meyer

*Battlefield of the Mind** (over three million copies sold)

*Making Good Habits, Breaking Bad Habits**

*Do Yourself a Favor... Forgive**

*Power Thoughts**

*Living Beyond Your Feelings**

*Eat the Cookie... Buy the Shoes**

Never Give Up!

I Dare you

The Penny

The Power of Simple Prayer

*The Confident Woman**

Look Great, Feel Great

*Approval Addiction**

*The Love Revolution**

Any Minute

Start Your New Life Today

21 Ways to Finding Peace and Happiness

A New Way of Living

Woman to Woman